POPES, LAWYERS, AND INFIDELS

The Church and the Non-Christian World 1250-1550

THE MIDDLE AGES
a series edited by

EDWARD PETERS
Henry C. Lea Associate Professor of Medieval History
University of Pennsylvania

POPES,
LAWYERS,
and
INFIDELS

JAMES MULDOON

UNIVERSITY OF PENNSYLVANIA PRESS | 1979

Copyright © 1979 by James Muldoon
All rights reserved
Printed in the United States of America

Library of Congress Cataloging in Publication Data

Muldoon, James, 1935-
  Popes, lawyers, and infidels.

  (The Middle Ages)
  Bibliography: p. 197
  Includes index.
  1. Persons (Canon law) I. Title. II. Title: The
church and the non-Christian world, 1250-1550.
III. Series: Middle Ages.
Law   262.9'32   79-5049
ISBN 0-8122-7770-8

Designed by Adrianne Onderdonk Dudden

CONTENTS

INTRODUCTION

CRITICISM of the way in which Europeans have treated the inhabitants of the non-European world in the course of European expansion has a long history. Three centuries before Christopher Columbus encountered the American Indians, European intellectuals and clergymen had criticized the treatment of the peoples whom the crusaders and other Europeans encountered as they moved outward from the heartland of European civilization. These criticisms sound familiar to anyone acquainted with the sixteenth-century critics of the Spanish conquest of the Americas. Yet comparatively little attention has been paid to the relationship of sixteenth-century critics of European expansion to their medieval predecessors.

The concentration upon post-Columban expansion and its effects is associated with the popular tendency to distinguish sharply between the medieval world and the modern. No one today would flatly deny the existence of some continuity between medieval culture and institutions on the one hand and their modern counterparts on the other. Few, if any, contemporary historians would accept the late nineteenth-century view that the Renaissance, the Reformation, the scientific revolution, and the discovery of the Americas marked a sharp break with the medieval past. Current scholarship has placed much stronger emphasis upon the continuities between the medieval and the modern eras. The problem is, of course, one of emphasis and degree, not of absolutes.

For the medieval historian, the continuity between the medieval and the modern worlds is obvious, so much so that in recent decades medievalists have devoted much time and effort to demonstrating the medieval origins of numerous ideas and institutions generally labeled modern. Medievalists have placed the Italian Renaissance in a medieval perspective and have shown the medieval origins of

Martin Luther's theology, as well as pointing out the origins of the scientific method in thirteenth-century England.[1] Other historians have discussed the expansion of Europe not since 1492, but since 1415, using the Portuguese capture of Ceuta in North Africa to mark the beginning of European overseas expansion.[2] Even earlier dates could, however, be advanced. By the middle of the fourteenth century, European seamen had encountered the Canary Islands, which were to play a vital role in later expansion into the Atlantic. It is even possible to date European expansion from the announcement of the First Crusade in 1095.[3] From that point onward, constant pressure was applied to the border regions of Europe, leading to the extension of European culture, values, institutions, and, above all, religion into new lands. Expansion would seem to be an essential characteristic of European culture. To a great extent, it is connected with European religious values: Christianity is a missionary religion seeking to bring into the fold all mankind. Other factors, such as the well-known desire of Europeans for spices, also encouraged European interest in the world beyond Europe. When Vasco da Gama responded to an Indian official who asked why he had come by saying we "have come to seek Christians and spices," he was summing up the motivation for several hundred years of European expansion.[4]

Just as there was an underlying continuity between the successors of Columbus and his predecessors, so too there were critics of expansion before Columbus as there were after him. The links between the first generation of post-Columban critics, the Spanish writers Francis Vitoria and Bartholomew de Las Casas, and medieval critics of the behavior of Europeans toward non-Europeans have become obvious in recent years.[5] Their criticism was rooted in medieval arguments about the rights of infidels in the face of a European invasion. What has led to an increased awareness of the role of medieval arguments about the rights of non-Europeans has been an increased interest in medieval canon law. It was this legal tradition that underlay many of the arguments that Vitoria, Las Casas, and other critics of Spanish imperial policy presented. At the same time, those who defended and supported the Spanish conquest of the Americas also relied upon the medieval legal tradition. When friars read the *Requerimiento,* a statement of Spanish intentions, to uncomprehending American Indians, they too were acting as they believed the medieval legal tradition demanded. As a result, the conquest of the Americas generated a debate about the rights of the conquered that was shaped by almost three hundred years of legal argument. Until comparatively recently, canon law was viewed as an exotic aspect of medieval life, not worthy of the intensive study that had been given to the development of English common law.[6] Canon law, as the law of the universal Church during the Middle Ages, played a much more important role in medieval life and intellectual development than has often been recognized. In countries not affected by the Protestant Reformation—Spain, for example—medieval canon law continued to shape intellectual life into the modern era. Even in those countries where the Reformation succeeded, the canon law tradition continued to influence policy and institutions. One need look no further than the list of references to canon law appended to a modern edition of John Calvin's *Institutes of the Christian Religion* to appreciate the use of canon law in the Reformation itself.[7]

Only because of the recent work in medieval canon law can scholars now come to deal effectively with Garrett Mattingly's statement some years ago about the relationship between Vitoria and Las Casas and their medieval predecessors: "the conclusions at which the Spanish school arrived are obviously implicit in twelfth-century canonists with explicit elaborations in the fourteenth and fifteenth centuries."[8] Mattingly, and those who adhered to his opinion, presented little evidence to demonstrate the dependence of the sixteenth-century writers upon the medieval canonists, and the evidence given was often based on a failure to understand the work of the medieval canonists correctly and on conclusions drawn by scholars who were enthusiastic about what they saw as the Spanish contribution to the formation of modern international law. More often, in spite of Mattingly's specific reference to medieval canon law as the source of sixteenth-century thinking about the rights of non-Europeans, scholars sought the origins of such thought in the medieval tradition of scholastic philosophy.[9] While Vitoria was a formally trained scholastic philosopher, he was more eclectic than that phrase would imply. He also drew upon the canon law tradition when he considered the plight of the Indians of South America.

The present study is the result of a dozen years of studying the canonists' writings from the thirteenth to the sixteenth century. The purpose has been to test the accuracy of Mattingly's statement about the debt of the sixteenth-century Spanish critics of the conquest to the medieval legal tradition. At the outset, it should be made quite clear that Mattingly set the starting point of any such research too early. While it is true that canon law emerged as a fully developed branch of legal science in the mid-twelfth century with the appearance of Gratian's *Decretum,* nevertheless interest in the rights of non-Christians became a significant aspect of canonistic thought only in the mid-thirteenth century. The starting point of this study is the pontificate of Pope Innocent IV (1243–54). Before he ascended the papal throne, he had been, as Sinibaldo Fieschi, a noted canon lawyer, the man F. W. Maitland described as "the greatest lawyer that ever sat upon the chair of St. Peter."[10] As a canonist, Innocent IV brought together several strands of legal thought relating to infidels in the first attempt to consider the relations that could exist between Christians and infidels. As pope, Innocent IV initiated the Mongol mission, the first attempt to deal with the Mongol threat to eastern Europe on a diplomatic level, as well as to convert the Mongols to Christianity. The result was the blending of legal theory and papal practice in a single career. It was the union of these two traditions that formed the intellectual background of Vitoria and Las Casas. Innocent IV remains the crucial figure in this development, however, because although many of his successors as pope were also legally trained, none showed both the legal imagination and the personal interest in the problem of the infidels to bring the analysis of the rights of infidels to a more sophisticated level. For three centuries following Innocent IV's death, his thinking influenced the thought of those who wrestled with the problems created when Europeans moved out from Europe itself and encountered people of various levels of culture and civilization.

In writing any scholarly book, an author incurs debts of appreciation to colleagues who have assisted him in various ways. While it is dangerous to cite specific individuals for fear that some others will be omitted, justice demands that several people be thanked. In the first place, I owe a great deal to Professor Brian Tierney of Cornell University, who introduced me to medieval canon law. Anyone who works in the field of canon law also owes an enormous debt to Professor Stephan Kuttner of the University of California at Berkeley. In my case the debt is quite personal because of his very kind assistance to me on the first day I worked in the Vatican Library. For the past dozen years, Professor Edward M. Peters of the University of Pennsylvania has been not only a good and kind friend, but a great source of encouragement. When I first began this project, Professor Edward J. Pfeifer, then chairman of the St. Michael's College (Vermont) History Department, provided various kinds of help and assistance that encouraged me to begin work in an area with which I was unfamiliar. Any medievalist today must also thank the organizers of those scholarly conferences that offer the opportunity to present ideas to fellow medievalists without exposing oneself permanently in print. The sponsors of the Conference on Medieval Studies at Western Michigan University have enabled me to present some of this material in early form and to benefit from the comments of a number of colleagues. The American Philosophical Society provided a travel grant that enabled me to examine materials in the Vatican Archives and the Vatican Library. Rutgers University granted me two semesters of leave, which provided the time to visit archives and to write, as well as a grant to underwrite typing costs.

Finally, I owe a great deal to my wife, Teresa, to whom this book is dedicated, and to our children, Margaret and Robert. My wife worked strenuously to turn my prose into English. Our children's contribution was to insure that their father did not take himself too seriously.

POPES, LAWYERS, AND INFIDELS

1 § CHRISTIAN RELATIONS WITH INFIDELS: THE THEORY

ANON lawyers approached the question of the rights enjoyed by infidels by drawing upon several distinct lines of analysis relating to this issue within the canonistic tradition. In the first place, lawyers had long considered the status of Christian schismatics and heretics. Such persons had placed themselves outside of the Church, though not beyond the Church's jurisdiction. The lawyers had also devoted some thought to the status of Jews who dwelled within Christian Europe, considering, for example, to what extent Jews should be allowed to practice their religion and to participate in the public life of a Christian society. Finally, the canonists dealt with the status of Moslems, or Saracens, as they usually termed them. The Moslems presented two kinds of problems for the canonists to consider. There were some Moslems living within Europe, and so their position could be considered analogous to that of the Jews. Then there were the Moslems who lived along the borders of Europe from the Near East to Spain. Although the popular image of Christian-Moslem relations during the Middle Ages is that of constant warfare, the crusades against the Moslems were punctuated with long periods of peace during which a great deal of trade went on between Christians and Moslems. As a result, the canonists had to consider the possibility of peaceful relations with the Moslems as well as hostile ones. The canonists tended to lump together the various kinds of people who were not members of the Church, so that legal principles and practices developed for dealing with one class of people defined as *extra ecclesiam* were applied to another class. Thus, when the canonists came to consider the situation of non-Christians who lived beyond the bounds of Christendom, they began by extending previous discussions of non-Christians living within Europe to fit the new peoples whom they encountered.

Initially, canonistic treatment of those who were not members of the Church centered on study of the *Decretum*, the collection of canons that Gratian published around 1140. His major interest was in the status of heretics and schismatics, and he gave only slight attention to the Jews and even less to infidels. For example, one of the canons encouraged debates between Christians and infidels so that nonbelievers might be led to the true faith by the force of rational argument.[1] Another canon discouraged marriages between Christians and Jews because of the potential harm to the Christian partner.[2] In all of these cases, the non-Christian was assumed to be an inhabitant of Christian Europe and subject to Christian rulers.

The view of Christian-infidel relations found in the *Decretum* reflected the state of the Christian world in the mid-twelfth century, when the volume was compiled. For the most part, the Church had little contact with societies beyond the frontiers of Christendom. There was, of course, contact with the schismatic Eastern Church, but the crusades, one of the major points of contact between Christians and infidels, had barely begun.

By the time that Pope Gregory IX (1227–41) published the second volume of canon law, the *Decretales*, in 1234, Jews and infidels had come to play a somewhat larger role in the papal view of the world. Because non-Christians had only a small place in the *Decretum* and because of the manner in which that book had been constructed, material dealing with non-Christians could be uncovered only with some difficulty. The *Decretales*, however, was compiled in such a way as to facilitate the identification of material concerning such persons. In the fifth book of the *Decretales*, three titles, or chapters, were devoted to non-Christians, heretics, schismatics, Jews, and Saracens.[3] Although the amount of space devoted to these topics was small, the fact that these categories of non-Christians were clearly identified made it possible for canonists to begin the study of such people in a coherent fashion. Furthermore, the presence of a title of canon law devoted to Jews and Saracens reflected the increasing impact such people were having on Christian Europe.

The decretals that concerned Jews and infidels generally considered their status within Christian Europe; for example, they forbade the keeping of Christian slaves by Jews and the building of new synagogues by Jewish communities living in Europe.[4] These prohibitions were not new in the thirteenth century; they restated old policies that had not been stressed for some time. The decretals that dealt with the infidels, however, recognized that the crusades had changed the relations between Christians and their neighbors. Christians who traded arms and other materials of war with the enemies of Christendom were excommunicated.[5] Another decretal restricted this prohibition to wartime, indicating that peaceful relations could exist between Moslems and Christians.[6]

As a contemporary student of the crusades has observed, the lack of any legal treatise devoted exclusively to the status of the crusader was a curious omission since the crusade involved a number of legal issues.[7] Because of this omission, the canonists considered only some aspects of the crusade, such as the right of Christians to wage war on the Moslems, and these they examined in the general context of the just war.[8] As far as the general history of Christian-infidel relations is concerned, the absence of a canonistic treatment of the crusades is significant because Christian-Moslem relations formed the great bulk of Christian relations with non-Christians during the Middle Ages. An extended discussion of the crusades might have led the canonists to a general consideration of the relations that could exist between Christian and non-Christian societies, leading, perhaps, to a theory of international relations. As it was, the theory of international relations was developed only in the sixteenth and seventeenth centuries, when a line of scholars culminating in Hugo Grotius broke out of the limited framework provided by their medieval predecessors.[9] The canonists' failure to develop a theory of international relations was probably due to their professional interest in the right ordering of Christian society. Their interest in those outside the Church, with the exception of heretics and schismatics, was limited to the effect such people might have on Christians.

From the point of view of the canonists, there was no reason to develop a theory of relations between Christians and those infidels who lived outside of Christian Europe because the Church, as opposed to individual Christian states, had no reason to enter into relations with infidel states. In the mid-thirteenth century, however, a leading canonist, Sinibaldo Fieschi, better known as Pope Innocent IV (1243–54), developed a legal basis for a theory of papal relations with non-Christian societies.[10] While it is not clear why Innocent IV initiated canonistic thinking in this area, it is worth noting that he was also the initiator of the Mongol mission, the attempt to come to an understanding with the Mongols of Central Asia who were

threatening the eastern borders of Christendom in the mid-thirteenth century.[11]

The starting point for Innocent IV's discussion of papal-infidel
relations was his commentary on a decretal of Pope Innocent III
(1198–1216). The decretal, *Quod super his,* was located not in the
title devoted to Jews and Saracens, but in the seemingly irrelevant
title headed "Concerning the vow and the fulfillment of a vow by
some other means."[12] This particular decretal concerned the fulfillment of vows to go on crusade to the Holy Land and the circumstances under which the performance of the promised journey could
be delayed or commuted. In commenting on this decretal, Innocent
IV raised the obvious question: "is it licit to invade the lands that
infidels possess, and if it is licit, why is it licit?"[13] By raising the
question in such general terms, not restricting the discussion to the
specific case of the crusades in the Near East, Innocent IV set the
stage for a wide ranging discussion of papal relations with infidel
societies. Furthermore, the very form of the question indicated that
peaceful relations between Christians and infidels were possible, if
not probable.

Innocent IV began his discussion of the issue by commenting on
the words "for the defense" that appeared in *Quod super his.* Innocent III's decretal had referred to those "who vowed to go on
pilgrimage for the defense of the Holy Land." This choice of starting points might have permitted the commentator to restrict the
discussion to the just war of defense, an issue that the canonists had
previously considered at some length. Instead, Innocent IV began
by asserting that the pope did have the right to order a Christian
invasion of the Holy Land and to authorize indulgences for those
who went there to fight. The justification for invading the Holy
Land and seeking to restore Christian control there was that the
Saracens had seized it in an unjust war from its Christian inhabitants.
The pope was only seeking to defend the rights of the Christians to
whom the Holy Land rightfully belonged. In addition, the Holy
Land was rightfully Christian because Christ's life and death there
had consecrated the land. His followers, not those of Mohammed,
should therefore dwell there.[14]

If these arguments did not convince the skeptic that the crusades
were a lawful exercise of papal power, Innocent had two more
arguments in his armory. In the first place, he reminded his readers
that the pope was the heir of the Roman emperors by the terms of

the Donation of Constantine.[15] This famous eighth-century forgery purported to record the emperor Constantine's grant of the western lands of the Roman Empire to Pope Silvester I (314–35) and specifically mentioned Judea as one of the regions included in the grant.[16] As a result, the pope as the lawful heir to the Holy Land was completely within his rights when he called upon Christian warriors to assist him in regaining that which was rightfully his. Innocent recognized that the authenticity of the Donation was questioned in the thirteenth century; indeed, doubts about its authenticity had surfaced as early as the eleventh century. Furthermore, there were also doubts about the validity of such a donation even if the document was authentic.[17] Gratian had not included it in the original version of the *Decretum*, perhaps because of doubts about its authenticity or its validity, although the text of the Donation was included in the *Decretum* by Gratian's successor in the work of compilation. Later canonists did not place much emphasis on the text and usually gave it only brief attention when they commented on the *Decretum*. As a result, Innocent presented a second argument justifying the crusades in terms of a defensive war. Even if the argument from the Donation was rejected, the pope could still call upon Christians to defend the Holy Land because the Holy Roman Emperor, in his capacity as king of Jerusalem, was the rightful possessor of the Holy Land.[18] This claim to Christian ownership of the Holy Land differed from the claim based on the Donation, in that this title was derived from a treaty between the Emperor Frederick II (1194–1250) and the sultan of Egypt, al-Kamil, signed at Jaffa in 1229. The Treaty of Jaffa confirmed Frederick's claim to the title king of Jerusalem, which he had first obtained through his marriage to Isabel of Brienne, heiress to the Brienne family's claims to the throne of the crusader kingdom of Jerusalem. Conveniently overlooking the origins of the imperial claim to the kingdom of Jerusalem and the strong papal objections to the treaty with the sultan, Innocent pointed out that the pope could legitimately assist the king of Jerusalem in protecting his kingdom from the Saracens.[19]

Innocent was not, however, primarily interested in justifying the crusades; the general theory of the just war did that.[20] What interested him was the problem of whether or not Christians could legitimately seize lands, other than the Holy Land, that the Moslems occupied.[21] Did, in fact, Christians have a general right to dispossess infidels everywhere? His response to this question was an interesting amalgam of citations drawn from the Bible and from Roman law.

As might be exepected, Innocent began his discussion of Christian-infidel rights with a line from the Bible: "the earth and its fullness are the Lord's." Citing Genesis, he argued that in the beginning all property was held in common.[22] Because of conflicts among the descendants of Adam, the need for private ownership of property became apparent, and so groups of men took specified tracts of land for themselves and their families. Under such circumstances, it was proper to take unoccupied land but wrong to seize the land of another. To illustrate this process, Innocent pointed to the division of land between Abraham and Lot as typical of the process by which men gradually came to distinguish between mine and thine.[23] In this way, a fundamental cause of human conflict would be avoided because every man would know clearly what belonged to him. Innocent went on to observe that in this early stage of human development, all men were free and there were no slaves. This conclusion was supported by reference to the Roman law's definition of natural law and its effects.[24] In the contemporary world, however, the law of nations that allowed private property, slavery, and war had replaced natural law as the basis upon which men dealt with one another.

Having dealt with the origins of private property, Innocent turned to the origins of government. He began by defining lawful authorities as those men who possess the power to do justice and impose discipline on those who do not abide by the laws governing the relationship of men with their neighbors. Lawful authority, like all created things, originated with God. The first person to exercise this authority was the father of a family, but as society developed and became more complex, the powers of the patriarchs were gradually reduced until in the contemporary world they were almost nonexistent.[25] As the patriarchal figure declined, the prince emerged as the bearer of lawful authority in society. Here again, the experience of the Israelites illuminated the course of this transformation. The election of Saul as king over the Israelites was the beginning of political society, as distinct from patriarchal rule.[26] For some reason, Innocent omitted the period of the judges, who had ruled the people of Israel between the patriarchs and the selection of King Saul.

Saul's election as king was, in Innocent's opinion, evidence that all "rational creatures" had the right to select their own rulers. This right did not rest on any special divine grant of authority, nor was it restricted to the ancient Israelites. By the laws that were common to all men, private property and self-government were the right of all men.[27] Even in the contemporary world, infidels continued to enjoy these rights without interference because these rights were as common to all men as the sunshine that warmed all men, Christian and infidel alike. As a consequence, it was not licit for the pope or anyone else to wage a campaign to deprive infidels of their property or their lordship simply because they were infidels.[28] Innocent thereby effectively demolished the possible claim that the responsibility of the Church for the souls of all men authorized any war that Christians chose to wage against infidels.

If Innocent had ended his discussion of the rights of infidels at this point, there would have been no basis on which to develop a theory of papal-infidel relations, except in terms of the just war of defense. His commentary continued, however, in order that he might explain how the pope's responsibility for the souls of all men, Christian and non-Christian alike, justified papal intervention in the functioning of infidel societies. Innocent's argument paralleled the one earlier canonists had used to assert the autonomy of the secular power within Christendom and, at the same time, to assert an overriding papal right to intervene in the secular sphere under certain conditions.

The canonists who discussed the nature of legitimate authority within Christian society fall into two categories, dualists and hierocrats.[29] Both agreed that all power ultimately came from God. They divided on the issue of whether all legitimate authority in Christian society must come through the mediation of the Church. The dualists argued that secular power could exist lawfully without ecclesiastical intervention because the ruler received it from God through the people. The hierocrats denied the legitimacy of secular power that was not obtained from God through the Church. In the hierocratic view, the pope was the undisputed ultimate authority in all matters within Christian society. The dualist position recognized the secular power as an autonomous sphere of jurisdiction not under the regular and direct control of the Church. In the dualist view, the pope possessed an indirect power over secular rulers, however, because as members of the Church they were subject to ecclesiastical jurisdiction. In the final analysis, the difference between the hierocrats and the dualists revolved around whether the pope could intervene directly or indirectly in secular affairs.

In developing a basis for considering Christian relations with in-

fidels, Innocent IV followed the dualist line of argument. He asserted that although infidels, like all other rational creatures, could
freely select their own rulers, the pope was responsible for their
souls before God. In the first place, Christ, as God, had power over
all men by virtue of creation, and Christ's vicars on earth, Peter and
his successors, shared in this responsibility. Christ as pastor had
instructed Peter to "feed my sheep," an injunction binding on
Peter's successors. This command did not differentiate between
Christians and non-Christians. The flock of Christ comprised all
men, and so the gospel must be preached to all men. Developing
this notion, Innocent stated that Christians and infidels alike were
"sheep of Christ by virtue of creation although they are not both
of the flock of the Church."[30] As a result, the pope's pastoral
responsibilities consisted of jurisdiction over two distinct flocks, one
consisting of Christians and one comprising everyone else. Innocent
added that the pope "has jurisdiction and power over infidels *de iure*
but not *de facto*."[31]

Once Innocent had asserted the existence of papal jurisdiction
over infidels, he went on to qualify his statement lest it be taken to
mean that the pope could legitimately deprive infidels of their lands
and property without specific just cause. Returning to the general
canonistic discussion of the pope's right to judge those who lived
within the bounds of Christendom, he began by stating the obvious
fact that no one denied the pope's right to judge Christians when
they violated the laws of God as found in the Bible.[32] Furthermore
the pope could judge Jews when they violated the law found in the
Old Testament if their own leaders did not enforce the law. The
pope was even responsible for the orthodoxy of Jewish religious
doctrine. Innocent observed that both he and his predecessor Gregory IX had ordered the public burning of the Talmud because
"those volumes . . . contained many heresies." Here again, the
failure of those normally responsible for safeguarding the purity of
doctrine to fulfill their responsibilities justified extraordinary papal
intervention. In the ordinary course of events, the Jewish community was self-governing with regard to religious matters, just as
the secular authority in Christendom was normally autonomous.[33]

Moving logically from the idea of papal responsibility for all men,
the existence of a natural law known to all men, and the right of the
pope to judge the Jews according to the Mosaic law, Innocent
argued that the pope could judge infidels in cases where they vio-

lated the natural law if their own rulers failed to punish them first. Infidel rulers who failed to insure their subjects' conformity to the norms of natural law failed to do what rulers were established to do: that is, to make justice. Innocent did not spell out the details of the natural law, but he did suggest that sexual perversion would constitute a violation of it. He did not define what perversions he meant, except to say that the right of the pope to intervene in infidel societies was modeled upon God's destruction of Sodom and Gomorrah. The only other violation of natural law he mentioned was the worship of idols; this was forbidden because it was known to all men that there was only one creator, whom men ought to worship. This creator was not to be identified with the various man-made idols worshiped by deluded people.[34]

Although the sins of the infidels could call forth Christian armies blessed by the pope, such forces could not be employed to impose baptism on the infidels because conversion to Christianity was a voluntary act and could not be coerced.[35] Presumably, once Christian armies had ended those practices deemed in violation of natural law, they would withdraw from the infidel society, just as Innocent IV and Gregory IX did not interfere in Jewish society after burning copies of the Talmud.

In addition to forcing the infidels' adherence to natural law, the pope's responsibility for their spiritual welfare authorized him to send missionaries into their lands to instruct the nonbelievers in the proper way of worshiping God. Should an infidel ruler block the entry of peaceful Christian missionaries, the pope could order him to admit them or face an invasion by Christian armies. Should the ruler continue to block the missionaries in spite of this warning from the pope, the pope was then entitled to call upon the Christian rulers of Europe to provide the troops required to insure the missionaries' safety while they preached. In addition, should the pope learn of a kingdom whose infidel ruler was engaged in persecuting the Christians among his subjects, he could order the king to desist from the persecution or face an invasion by Christian forces. An infidel ruler who failed to heed such a papal warning could be removed from office by invading Christian troops acting on the pope's behalf, or his Christian subjects could be withdrawn from his jurisdiction, again with the support of papally sponsored forces.[36] Innocent was careful not to advise the Christian subjects of an infidel ruler to rebel against their lord. He recommended instead patience and forbearance lest infidel rulers conclude that their Christian subjects were potential rebels and so begin a persecution to forestall a revolt.[37]

In this discussion of the occasions on which the pope could intervene in the affairs of infidel societies, Innocent was careful to stress that the pope alone could authorize an attack on an infidel society in order to enforce adherence to the natural law. Individual Christian rulers had no such right.[38] In this way, the desire of Christian rulers to aggrandize themselves at the expense of infidels would be subordinated to the papal view of the right order of society and the most effective way of achieving the salvation of the infidels. Here, Innocent was extending to Christian-infidel relations the kind of control over warfare that canonists and popes had sought to impose on wars between Christians within Europe, without much success, it might be added.

Finally, in an interesting turnabout, Innocent raised the issue of whether infidels could employ his own arguments against Christians. He posed two ironic questions. The first was: could the infidels who lived along the borders of Christian Europe legitimately seek to regain control of Europe because it had once been ruled by infidels?[39] The second concerned whether Christian rulers had to admit peaceful infidel missionaries into their kingdoms.[40]

The first question was the easier to answer. Innocent argued that no infidel could use the argument that previous infidel possession of Europe justified attempts to conquer Europe because the Christianization of Europe had not occurred by force, as had the Islamization of the Holy Land. The rulers of Europe voluntarily became Christians, and their people freely followed.[41] As a result, the demise of infidel religions in Europe was the result of voluntary action on the part of the Europeans. Presumably, if the Holy Land had come into Moslem hands as the result of voluntary conversion, the pope could not authorize crusades to restore it to Christian control.

Innocent's discussion of the concurrent conversion of Europe's rulers and people led him to consider whether a people converted to Christianity should continue to remain subject to a ruler who was still an infidel. In his opinion, the ruler still commanded the obedience of his subjects because his *dominium* did not depend upon his being in the state of grace. As long as the ruler did not interfere in his subjects' religious practices, they had no cause to depose him. Should he begin to persecute them or should he in any way become a threat to their spiritual well-being, his subjects would then have the right to remove him from office.[42] Here again, Innocent IV was not anxious to encourage subjects to rebel against their legitimate rulers. He suggested that in the event that a people became Christians while their ruler remained an infidel, he should voluntarily resign his office in return for being compensated for his loss of property and lordship.[43] This line of argument seems to have been designed to protect Europeans from the charge that they had illegally ousted their infidel rulers. Thus, Innocent eliminated the possibility that his argument about the right of Christians to regain the Holy Land would be turned against the Christians' possession of Europe.

In spite of having developed this defense against the inversion of his argument, however, Innocent seems to have remained concerned about its logical consistency with his position on *dominium* in infidel hands. In effect, he had to reconcile the spiritual well-being of a Christian population with the right of its infidel ruler to retain his office. To effect this reconciliation of interests, he drew upon Roman law, citing laws granting freedom to slaves who performed certain deeds judged of significant value to the common good. These acts included turning in military deserters and informing on coiners of false money. In such cases the value of the actions for the common good exceeded the value of the slave's labor to his master. As a result, the slave's manumission was a suitable reward even though his master was actually punished by it through no fault of his own.[44]

This careful arrangement of rights suggests the similar use of a hierarchy of rights in marriage law, the so-called Pauline Privilege. By the terms of that privilege, if one of the partners in a marriage converts to Christianity while the other remains an infidel, the marriage ought to remain binding. If, however, the infidel partner interferes with the religious practice of the Christian, the Christian partner can leave the infidel spouse and legitimately remarry, even though the first marriage was a valid one in the eyes of the Church. In both cases, the spiritual welfare of the Christian is superior to the natural-law rights of a ruler or spouse.[45]

Innocent noted another objection that an infidel acquainted with canon law might raise in regard to Christian possession of Europe. "How could the Roman Church and all the other [Christian] Churches and all the individual Christians [in Europe] licitly hold

property and lordship since the Roman Emperors took all of their
lands and lordships by force of arms, thus holding them illicitly?"[46]
Innocent's response was that if Christians had simply taken from the
Romans lands that had been unjustly taken from their lawful possessors, then indeed Christians would not hold their lands in Europe
licitly, any more than a receiver of stolen goods truly possessed
such goods. Contemporary Christians, however, could not possibly
know whether or not the Romans had seized their empire illegally.
In the absence of evidence proving that the Roman Empire was
illegally won, those Christians who had subsequently carved out
principalities for themselves could accept the benefit of the doubt
in the matter. Furthermore, even if some of the lands had been
unjustly taken and the original possessor was not known, Christians
could continue to occupy the territory in question because in such
cases the legal title to the land reverted to the Church and to the
pope who represented all men.[47] By this twist of argumentation,
Innocent returned the entire argument to its starting point, that all
right to lordship and property derived from God the creator. The
pope, as God's representative on earth, could step in to insure that
property rights were recognized and conflicts rooted in disputes
over land were prevented.[48]

The final question in this series dealt with the right of infidels to
send peaceful missionaries into Christian lands. This question con-
jured up the vision of Pope Innocent IV, in his capacity as secular
ruler of Rome, facing a Moslem preacher quoting the canonist
Sinibaldo Fieschi on the right of free entry for missionaries. As one
would expect, the response here was a resounding no. The reason
was simple. The Moslem faith could not be treated as the equal of
the Christian faith, and so its missionaries could not be treated as
Christian missionaries ought to be, "because they are in error and
we are on the righteous path."[49]

Innocent's discussion of the relationship between the Christians
and infidels continued a process of extending papal power beyond
the narrow confines of the Church proper. The process had begun
during the eleventh century with the Investiture controversy in
which supporters of the pope sought to oust laymen from the administration of the Church. Gradually, they asserted the superiority
of the spiritual power over the temporal. The climax of this process
came when Bernard of Clairvaux, a strong supporter of the superiority of the spiritual power, asserted that the two swords mentioned

in the gospel as being in Peter's possession referred to the spiritual and the temporal powers. Previously, the two swords were held to mean the two kinds of disciplinary power the Church possessed and could exercise against its members, the spiritual ones, such as excommunication, and physical or material ones, such as deprivation of office. Bernard argued that Peter and his successors possessed both swords, but that they delegated the material sword representing legitimate secular authority to the secular rulers of Christian society. In this way, the pope became the ultimate source of all authority in Christian society, not simply the source of spiritual authority. The exercise of papal power in ecclesiastical matters was, of course, a direct use of power, while in secular affairs, the pope could act only indirectly, as in cases where the secular ruler failed to fulfill his responsibilities.[50] In normal circumstances the secular sphere was autonomous. When Innocent IV described infidels as belonging to Christ's flock, though not to the Church, he was continuing the practice of extending papal jurisdiction. Furthermore, he recognized that this papal jurisdiction over infidels was *de iure,* not *de facto,* a phrase that would also describe papal claims to indirect jurisdiction over Christian secular rulers to a great extent.

It goes without saying that the development of theological and legal theories about the powers of the pope in the twelfth and thirteenth centuries paralleled the expansion of the real power that the papacy exercised. The activity of the papal court sitting in a judicial capacity expanded greatly during the thirteenth century. The peak of papal power was probably reached in the first half of the thirteenth century, the period that began with the accession of Innocent III to the papal throne and ended with the death of Innocent IV. The latter's crushing victory over Frederick II marked the high point of papal power in the Middle Ages. It is probably not a coincidence that Innocent IV, the victor in the final clash with Frederick II, was the pope who asserted the right of the pope to intervene in the affairs of infidel societies in order to insure the spiritual well-being of all men, Christians and infidels alike.[51]

A further extension of the line of argument that Bernard and Innocent IV developed appeared in the work of a major canonist not long after the appearance of Innocent's commentary on the *Decretales.* A student of Innocent IV, Henry of Segusio, generally known as Hostiensis, denied that infidels possessed the right to lordship and property. What made his rejection of Innocent's views on the subject so interesting was that throughout his commentary on the *Decretales*, Hostiensis referred flatteringly to the opinions of "*dominus noster*," that is, Innocent IV.[52]

Hostiensis' commentary on *Quod super his* became the standard response to Innocent's views on the rights of infidels. In keeping with the common practice of the canonists, Hostiensis began his commentary on *Quod super his* by repeating that of Innocent IV. Here and there he added another illustration or citation to his master's argument, but otherwise repeated the previous commentary verbatim. Hostiensis then bluntly denied the validity of the argument he had just presented.

> It seems to me that with the coming of Christ every office and all governmental authority and all lordship and jurisdiction was taken from every infidel lawfully and with just cause and granted to the faithful through Him who has the supreme power and who cannot err.[53]

This argument was not one that Hostiensis himself had invented. About the beginning of the thirteenth century, an English canonist, Alanus Anglicus, had first stated this opinion.[54] This argument was an extension of the ancient Donatist heresy, which had asserted that priests who were not in the state of grace could not exercise sacramental authority within the Church.[55] Though such priests might perform the proper ritual actions, these actions would have no effect because God did not work through sinful priests. This theological opinion was rejected by the Church as heretical, in part, at least, because the Donatist teaching involved the definition of the Church's nature: if the efficacy of a sacrament depended upon the personal qualities of the minister, the Church as an institution would dissolve into a series of sects led by those believed to be sinless. The orthodox position was that a validly ordained priest who administered the sacraments according to the prescribed ritual was a legitimate minister of the sacrament even if he himself was in the state of sin. In applying this Donatist notion to political office, Alanus, and Hostiensis after him, was continuing the process of extending ideas about the nature of the Church to the political sphere, as Bernard of Clairvaux, for example, had done earlier.

Hostiensis began his discussion of the rights of infidels by observing that in the Book of Ecclesiasticus it was said that "lordship passes from one people to another because of injustices and wickedness and outrages and other kinds of evil."[56] Christ, like Melchisidek both king and priest, possessed ultimate jurisdiction over both spiritual and temporal affairs.[57] He could, therefore, deprive sinners of their property and lordship and give them to others. Infidels, by the very fact of not being Christians, were sinners, so that when Christ became incarnate, infidels automatically lost their right to hold property and lordship legitimately. As Peter and his successors were the vicars of Christ, they too had the power to deprive infidels of office and lands.[58] The result was the assertion that the pope had the right to intervene directly in the affairs of infidel societies because infidel rulers had usurped lands and power that now rightfully belonged to Christians. "*De iure*, infidels ought to be subject to Christian rulers," not the reverse, as was too often the case in his opinion.[59]

Having stated that infidels were usurpers, Hostiensis might have proceeded to encourage widespread crusading activity. Instead, he turned to qualifying the implications of his position. Infidel rulers who recognized the suzerainty of Christians should be tolerated and allowed to retain their lands and offices, since to dispossess infidels willing to accept Christians overlords would be to force them to convert simply in order to retain their goods.[60] This violated the general principle that no one should be forced to accept baptism. Furthermore, he went on to argue that although the infidels were usurpers, Christians should not use their claim to universal domination as the initial basis for dealings with infidel societies. Peaceful missionaries should be the first stage of Christian entry into infidel lands, not armed crusaders.[61]

The opinions of Innocent IV and Hostiensis provided the canonists with the framework for debating the rights of infidels. The debate paralleled the better-known debates among the canonists about the respective roles of the spiritual and the temporal powers within Christian society. Furthermore, as the conquest of Spain advanced, the problem of Christian-infidel relations within Europe came to play an ever larger role in legal thinking. The difference between the opinion of Innocent IV and that of Hostiensis was a small but crucial one: whether the pope's power with regard to infidels was direct or indirect. Both Innocent and his student took similar approaches to the actual exercise of the power that they claimed for the pope. Innocent's opinion would require the pope to demonstrate either that infidels who were the objects of a Christian invasion

occupied previously Christian territories or that they clearly violated
the terms of the natural law. Hostiensis' argument would not require such a demonstration because the infidels by definition were
usurpers, not lawful possessors. Finally, even though Hostiensis'
argument would seem to authorize any Christian ruler to launch an
invasion of any infidel territory he desired, Hostiensis, like Innocent,
insisted that the pope alone could authorize such wars.[62] The overriding concern of both writers was for the spiritual mission of the
Church, something that the anarchic loosing of crusading armies on
the infidels would slow, if not block entirely. While Hostiensis'
opinion in this matter might appear paradoxical, it in fact is quite
consistent not only with the lawyers' general opinion that the purpose of the law was to assist in the achievement of the Church's
pastoral work, but also with Hostiensis' strong support of papal
power.[63] Here again, the secular power could act in matters concerning the Church's pastoral mission only at the direction of the
pope. Hostiensis was as much opposed to the possibility of unchecked wars against the infidels as he was to the unchecked wars
among Christians that were constantly occuring within Europe,
because both kinds of war interfered with the pastoral work of
the Church.[64]

The opinions of Innocent IV and Hostiensis on the rights of infidels were given wide circulation because they were both presented
in one of the most important later commentaries on the *Decretales*,
that of Joannes Andreae (1270–1348). This commentary was a
compilation of canonistic opinions so extensive that it was often
mined by later canonists. Joannes repeated both basic opinions on
the rights of the infidels contained in the commentaries on *Quod
super his* without drawing any conclusion of his own.[65]

From the fourteenth century onward, discussion of the rights of
infidels began to appear in treatises and in collections of legal opinions, *consilia*, as well as in the traditional form of commentaries on
the *Decretales*. These newer forms of legal literature enabled the
canonists to approach the question of the rights of infidels more
directly than the use of the commentary had allowed.[66] Now the
canonists could begin a discussion of the rights of infidels by describing a situation involving non-Christians and then presenting
the legal arguments relating to the issue.

One of the first lawyers to deal with the rights of infidels in his
consilia was Oldratus de Ponte (d. 1335), who devoted all or part of

several *consilia* to problems connected with infidels. Like many of the canonists of the fourteenth and fifteenth centuries, Oldratus concentrated his attention on the status of infidels who were living in Europe, not on those beyond the frontiers; during these centuries the contacts with the non-European world that inspired Innocent IV to begin discussion of relations with infidel societies beyond Europe were not as significant as they once were. Because of the rapid advance of the reconquest during the thirteenth century, Oldratus focused on the problem of the infidels who lived in Spain.[67]

Oldratus admitted that his contemporaries generally followed Innocent IV, but he did not.[68] Along with Hostiensis, Oldratus saw the birth of Christ as ending the right of infidels to possess lands and lordships according to natural law. He reasoned that because all men were created to worship the one true God, those who did not do so deserved to lose their possessions to Christians, so that they might be led to the worship of the true God.[69] As a logical consequence, Oldratus argued that infidels ought to be subject to Christians. Turning to the Bible for support, he cited Psalm 8, which declared that God made man and "has given him dominion over the works of thy hands; thou has put all things under his feet, all sheep and oxen, and also the beasts of the field. . . ." He identified the sheep with Christians but the oxen and wild animals with the Moslems, a variation on Innocent IV's use of the flock as a symbol of papal jurisdiction. The sheep are clearly subject to Peter and his successors. As for the Moslems, they are not simply members of another flock subject to the pope; they are wild animals who should be forcibly subjected to Christian control.[70] By contrasting the domesticated sheep with the untamed animals of the field, Oldratus may have been suggesting that infidels are by nature uncivilized and therefore deserve conquest, not only on religious grounds but also because of their barbarous way of life.

Turning to specific cases, Oldratus offered the situation in Spain. He observed, citing Innocent IV, that infidels who wished to live at peace with Christians ought to be tolerated, but his discussion of the apparently barbarous nature of infidels would seem to indicate that such a situation was not very likely to occur.[71] In reality, he argued, the Moslems have a long history of attacks on Christians, so that Christians must be constantly on their guard. Therefore, Christians are within their rights when they wage war against their Moslem neighbors.[72] In an interesting piece of argument, Oldratus pointed out that the origins of the conflict with the Moslems stemmed from the fact that they were the descendants of Ishmael, the son of Abraham by a slave woman, while the Christians were descended from Abraham's son by his lawful wife, Sara. Ishmael and his descendants formed the peoples of the desert, who were always at war with the settled peoples inhabiting the agricultural lands that bordered the desert. Against these desert nomads the hands of all men were turned because Ishmael was "a wild ass of a man" (Gen. 16:12) who deserved to be subjected to the bridle of civilization, presumably by Christians.[73]

As for Spain, Oldratus pointed out that Christians were clearly within their rights when they fought with the Moslems to restore that once-Christian land to Christian control. Before the Moslem invasion, Spain was the home of numerous Christians who had erected various monuments to the Christian faith in the form of churches and monasteries. The Moslem invasion had been God's warning to the Christians that they were sinners and deserved punishment.[74] By the thirteenth century, however, the Spanish Christians had presumably been purged of their sinfulness and so could legitimately regain control of Spain from the Moslems, who had now served their purpose in the divine plan.

Like Hostiensis, Oldratus did not conclude that once the infidels came under Christian rulers they should be forced to convert or be expelled from their property. In another *consilium*, changing his tone from that of the belligerent defender of Christian rights to that of the pastor concerned for the spiritual well-being of infidels, Oldratus declared that for a Christian ruler "to expel non-Christians from his lands without reason violates the precepts of charity." In the first place, a Christian would not wish to be dispossessed by infidels if the situation were reversed, and so he should not want to eject peaceful infidels living in his domains.[75] Furthermore, Christians should love all men, Jews and Saracens included, because they shared the same physical nature with Christians. Hopefully, non-Christians would share the same spiritual nature as the Christians as well. As long as the infidels lived in peace with their Christian neighbors and posed no military or spiritual threat to them, the Christians should not molest them. The Christians should, of course, endeavor to bring these lost sheep into the flock of Christ's Church.[76]

Turning to the disciplining of non-Christians living either within or outside of Christendom, Oldratus observed that such people were rightfully members of Christ's flock and therefore subject to the pope's pastoral embrace. Following Innocent IV's line of argument, Oldratus argued that when non-Christians living among Christians were not properly punished for their crimes by their own leaders, Christian princes might intervene to punish them. If the crimes of the infidels warranted it, the Christian prince might exile them from his domains as a punishment.[77] In an apparent break with Innocent and Hostiensis, Oldratus appears to have believed that a Christian ruler could act against non-Christians without seeking papal approval, at least when they were inhabitants of his lands.

A striking aspect of Oldratus' views about Christian relations with infidels was his belief in the natural ferocity of the desert peoples. Not only did this ferocity justify defensive wars with the infidels; it also seemed to justify offensive wars designed to subdue them permanently. He seems to suggest that the natural violence of the descendants of Ishmael led to an uncivilized way of life that in turn caused them to violate constantly the precepts of natural law. Under such circumstances, Christians could be thought of as having a responsibility for pacifying the infidels so that they might then be led to the baptismal font and a civilized way of life.

Toward the middle of the fourteenth century, Joannes de Legnano (d. 1383) placed the canonists' discussion of infidels' rights in the broader context of the just war. His *Treatise Concerning War, Reprisal and the Duel* was the first formal treatise devoted to the problem of the just war.[78] Its title indicates something of its rudimentary nature, acts of war and the problems associated with acts of private violence forming a single subject for his analysis. The text was a mixture of Roman and canon law, theological, philosophical, and even astrological thought. The wide spectrum of material that Joannes drew upon indicated the intellectual lengths to which a fourteenth-century scholar had to go in order to compile a treatise on the issue; no single discipline contained sufficient material to provide a basis for a general theory of the just war.

In a chapter devoted to the problem of who had the right to declare war, Joannes raised the question of whether the Church had the right to invade infidel lands and grant indulgences for crusaders. His argument followed the lines of Innocent IV's: he recognized the right of infidels to possess lands and lordships without interference, presumably according to the terms of natural law.[79] At the same time, however, he did not repeat Innocent's arguments verbatim. His version of the answer to the question rested more heavily upon the prohibition against forcing infidels to accept baptism than upon the natural right of the infidels to possess land and office.[80] He also stressed that should the Christian subjects of an infidel ruler require the assistance of their fellow Christians for protection against their ruler, European Christian armies could assist them. Christians could invade the country to prevent the infidel ruler from interfering with his Christian subjects.[81]

Joannes also raised the question of whether the pope or the emperor had jurisdiction over the infidels. Roman law had described the emperor as the *dominus mundi*, a title that would seem to conflict with the pope's claim to be the *de iure* superior of all men. Joannes concluded that there was but one lord of the universe, God, and that His representative on earth was the pope.[82] Indeed, according to this argument, if Christ had not entrusted the infidels to Peter and his successors, He would have shown a lack of interest in a large part of His creation. Such papal jurisdiction over infidels was, of course, *de iure*. It became *de facto* only if infidels violated the natural law.[83] Although his argument was brief, Joannes clearly accepted Innocent IV's argument that the pope could discipline infidels and Jews according to the laws that were applicable to them.

In Joannes' opinion, the crusades to regain the Holy Land were also a legitimate exercise of papal authority. He argued that "the pope as a true prince" could legitimately declare war against the Moslems who occupied the Holy Land as the result of an unjust war of aggression.[84] Presumably, the pope's princely right to the Holy Land stemmed from the Donation of Constantine. In another of his writings, however, Joannes argued that the Donation only confirmed papal jurisdiction over these lands. God had originally granted the pope jurisdiction over the entire world in both spiritual and temporal affairs.[85]

Finally, Joannes denied that either the pope or the emperor had any general right to intervene in the affairs of infidel societies. The pope could intervene in specific situations—for example, to protect Christian subjects of infidel rulers—but not otherwise. The same was presumably true of the emperor, who could assist the pope in cases where intervention in the internal operations of an infidel society was justified. Inasmuch as Joannes was presenting current views of the nature of Christian-infidel relations, it is curious that he did not present those of Hostiensis, if only to refute them. It may have been a tribute to the dominance of Innocent IV's arguments on the subject that Hostiensis' opinion was not even mentioned.

Another approach to the problem of Christian-infidel relations emerged in the work of Peter de Ancharano (1330–1416). In contrast to Joannes de Legnano, who began with general propositions about the just war, Petrus used a small incident in an Italian city as the basis for a *concilium* concerning the problem. The *concilium* posed the question of whether secular or church courts had jurisdiction over a Jew who hurled mud at a crucifix being carried in procession through the town.[86]

The first argument Peter presented was that the case was a matter for the secular courts because the Jew was by definition not a member of the Church.[87] On the other hand, Church courts did have jurisdiction in matters involving sacrilege, and hurling mud at a crucifix was clearly a sacrilegious action. At this point, Peter observed that it was incorrect to exclude absolutely infidels and Jews from the jurisdiction of church courts. He agreed that when Jews or infidels failed to observe the laws governing them, especially natural law, they could be tried in Church courts because, as Innocent IV had argued, even those who were not members of the Church were subject to ecclesiastical jurisdiction under certain circumstances.[88]

Peter's resolution of the problem involved determining which jurisdiction had priority. In the case given, a Jew would normally be subject to secular jurisdiction, as would any other layman, and he cited several passages from Roman law to defend this position. Should the secular power fail to act, then the ecclesiastical power could intervene in order to insure that justice, the purpose of all government, was done.[89] His reason for giving priority to the secular jurisdiction in this case was that spiritual courts could only impose spiritual punishments, which would have no effect on nonbelievers.[90]

In another *consilium*, Peter considered the degree of toleration that Christian rulers should grant non-Christians who dwelled within their domains. The discussion centered on a practical problem created by the toleration of Jews in Christian societies. If Jews were tolerated and allowed to live according to their own laws within Christian society, could they be allowed to loan money at interest, a practice forbidden to Christians? His answer was to note that Roman law allowed the loaning of money at interest, as did Jewish law, so that the practice was not against the *ius gentium*. Furthermore, the public good could benefit from the practice: charity might even be advanced if money was available to assist the needy.[91] Peter made it clear that he himself did not really approve of usury. He pointed out, perhaps ironically, that like usury, theft and homicide were sometimes allowed by human law, suggesting that at best the practice is to be tolerated because of the fallen nature of man.[92]

Finally, Peter dealt with the issue of allowing non-Christians, specifically Jews, to hold public office in Christian societies. In the course of the discussion he observed that it is usually said that only those who are "faithful and devoted to the holy Roman Church" should hold office in Christian societies. Citing Innocent IV, Petrus observed that a Jew or other non-Christian could be loyal to the Church as a terrestrial institution, though not a member of the Church as a spiritual community, and, therefore, infidels could possibly hold office within Christian societies.[93]

The arguments of Peter de Ancharano effectively reduced the power of the Church to intervene directly in secular affairs, both within and beyond the borders of Christendom. Furthermore, he stressed the primary role of the secular power in dealing with infidels. He also suggested that secular rulers could act against infidels on their own initiative without papal permission. If these arguments, designed to resolve questions concerning infidels within Europe, were applied to infidels beyond the borders of Europe, they would authorize secular rulers to intervene in the affairs of infidel rulers without first requesting papal permission. This would in effect increase the power of secular rulers and reduce that of the pope. Perhaps the most important point that he made concerned the status of Jews as ordinary laymen, subject to the same laws as other laymen, at least in cases involving normal criminal and civil jurisdiction. They were not considered a special class subject to ecclesiastical jurisdiction.

During the fifteenth century the canonists either accepted the views of Innocent IV on the rights of infidels or presented both sides of the argument without taking a stand of their own. They seem to have become wary of supporting the Hostiensian position without feeling obliged to support explicitly Innocent IV's position. Niccolo de Teudeschis, better known as Panormitanus (1386–1453), a leading canonist of the first half of the fifteenth century, offered a commentary on *Quod super his* that summed up the problem as fifteenth-century canonists saw it. He began his response to the question of whether it was licit for Christians to invade the lands of infidels by remarking that Innocent IV had discussed the issue "elegantly" in his commentary.[94] Panormitanus then repeated Innocent's conclusion that infidels did legitimately possess lordship and property, as did all rational creatures. As a result, Christians had no general right to seize the lands of infidels.[95] Turning to the opposing argument, Panormitanus presented Hostiensis' position without making any comments upon its quality or soundness.

Panormitanus raised another issue concerning the right of Christians to invade infidel societies. Like Joannes de Legnano, he asked whether the emperor as the *dominus mundi* had universal jurisdiction that would allow him to order the invasion of infidel territories.[96] Taking the position that the good order of the world required the close cooperation of pope and emperor, Panormitanus defined the role that each should play with regard to infidels. Extending logically the generally recognized papal power over heretics and Jews, he argued that the pope could judge infidels when they committed "ecclesiastical crimes" such as violations of the laws of marriage.[97] While he did not spell out what he meant by such crimes, he may have had in mind polygamous marriages, a practice that the canonists argued was typical of infidel societies and that was forbidden to all men. On the other hand, where infidels were guilty of violating civil law, the imperial courts took precedence.[98]

Because contacts between Christians and the infidel world beyond Europe declined toward the end of the thirteenth century, not to become significant again until the middle of the fifteenth, early fifteenth-century canonists showed more interest in the status of infidels within Europe than in the status of those outside. As Oldratus had recognized much earlier, the status of Jews and infidels living in the reconquered areas of Spain was of much more immediate interest to Christian thinkers than potential relations with various infidel societies far away. As a result, the canonists of the early and mid-fifteenth century tended to discuss the specific kinds of crimes that could bring infidels before ecclesiastical courts, developing further the line of discussion that Panormitanus had mentioned but not developed.

Alexander Tartagni (1427–77), for example, dealt with the problem of whether loaning money at interest was a crime that could be punished by ecclesiastical courts. In a *concilium* he posed the question of whether the will of a known Jewish usurer could be accepted as valid if it did not contain a clause providing for compensating his borrowers for the usurious interest he had charged. The decretal *Quanquam* that Gregory X issued at the Second Council of Lyons (1274) required that wills make such provision.[99] The decretal was obviously aimed at Christians who engaged in the loaning of money. Alexander noted, however, that in some places bishops had applied it to Jews.[100] What made such applications questionable was the fact that the only punishments mentioned in the decretal were spiritual ones, such as the denial of burial in consecrated ground. Such penalties could have no effect on nonbelievers. Alexander recognized the inapplicability of the stated punishments, but he also pointed out that elsewhere in canon law there was provision for requiring Jewish moneylenders to repay interest charged to Christians. In such cases, the secular ruler was called upon to enforce the decision of an ecclesiastical court.[101]

Moving to the general problem of the status of Jews within Christian Europe, Alexander described both pope and emperor as having responsibility for insuring that Jews obey the Mosaic law. Inasmuch as the law of Moses was the special law for the Jews, it took precedence over both natural and common law where they were concerned. He compared the relationship of the Jews to their special law with the unique relationship of Christians to the law of Christ. In both cases, the special laws applicable to these people were more restrictive than the natural or the common law. Where cases involving Christians and Jews were being decided, the Christian law took precedence.[102]

As for infidels, Alexander argued that infidels living within Christian Europe were subject to the normal secular courts, not to ecclesiastical courts, because they were not subject to canon law. Should secular judges fail to act in cases where infidels were involved, the Church could, of course, intervene in order to see that justice was done. Although Alexander claimed to be simply following the arguments of Innocent IV in this matter, he seems in fact to have granted a great deal more scope to the secular courts than Innocent had.[103]

In another *concilium*, Alexander dealt at greater length with the nature of papal and imperial jurisdiction over infidels. Within Europe, the Church could assert direct jurisdiction over nonbelievers only where ecclesiastical officials held both spiritual and temporal power.[104] The Papal State was the only major area where this would be the case. Elsewhere, Jews and infidels, like other laymen, were responsible to secular judges. Lest his words be taken as encouraging secular rulers to take undue interest in the activities of their non-Christian subjects, Alexander also argued that nonbelievers should not be harassed by Christian rulers without just cause. They were to be tolerated and loved as fellow human beings.

By the late fifteenth century, the canonists had concluded that Christians had no blanket right to dispossess nonbelievers or invade their lands. Perhaps the ideas of Alanus and Hostiensis would have influenced more canonists if the condemnation of John Wyclif had not riveted attention on the Donatist implications of the notion that infidels lost their right to lands and office when Christ was born.[105] It is more likely, however, that the Donatist overtones would have become apparent eventually. The Hostiensian argument was in the long run too extreme for the canonists to accept. As in the case of the relation between the spiritual and the temporal powers within Christian society, papal power over infidels could only be indirect. Thus, Innocent IV's claim to an indirect power over infidels based on spiritual considerations was in keeping with the mainstream of canonistic thinking on the relationship between the spiritual and the temporal powers within Europe. The papal power to intervene in situations involving the European Jewish population provided the lawyers with a model of the way in which papal power could be extended to all kinds of nonbelievers.

At the same time, the later canonists did not follow Innocent's arguments without some qualifications. The most important of these qualifications concerned the universal role that Roman lawyers claimed for the emperor. Paralleling the canonistic argument that the pope's experience with the Jews within Europe indicated the way in which infidels everywhere should be treated by him, the Roman lawyers argued that the Roman law's discussion of the relationship between the Christian emperors and the Jews indicated that the emperor also had a special relationship with infidels. If fully developed, these arguments could have culminated in an assertion of imperial jurisdiction over the entire world beyond Europe. Under such circumstances, papal jurisdiction over infidels would have been restricted to clearly ecclesiastical matters. All other cases would be subject to imperial court jurisdiction, unless the imperial judges failed to act. In those situations, the papacy could act in lieu of imperial action.

In seeking to devise a role for the emperor in the jurisdiction that
Christians claimed over infidels, the lawyers were following in the
footsteps of those proponents of secular power who were continually battling against the extreme jurisdictional claims being asserted by some proponents of papal power. When these lawyers
asserted that infidels were subject to imperial courts, as any other
layman would be, they were proposing to authorize the emperor
to act against infidels guilty of crimes covered by secular law without first seeking papal authorization. Like other opponents of papal
power, they sought to restrict papal jurisdiction to clearly ecclesiastical matters and to the imposition of spiritual penalties. Those
who presented the imperial case were, of course, primarily interested
in restricting power within the empire. The German states had little
interest in the infidels beyond Europe. The discussion of the rights
of infidels, however, provided a convenient opportunity to insist
upon limiting papal power within Europe.

The discussion of the rights of infidels might even have faded
away in the works of the late fifteenth-century canonists if Europeans had not recommenced extensive contacts with the world
beyond Europe in those years. The gradual Portuguese expansion
into the Atlantic Ocean, leading to encounters with the inhabitants
of the Atlantic islands and then with the peoples of sub-Saharan
Africa, meant that the problem of Christian-infidel relations was
about to take on new importance although the lawyers were un-
aware of it.

2 § INNOCENT IV: THE THEORIST AS PRACTITIONER

Just as Innocent IV as a canon lawyer was the most important theorist of Christian-infidel relations during the Middle Ages, so too as pope he played an important role in implementing policies for dealing with infidels. The interplay in Innocent's career between the role of theoretician and that of practitioner was highly unusual though not unique. In his personal copy of the *Decretales* he included several decretals which he had issued as pope and which he then commented upon as canonist. As a result, Innocent's work in both roles provides an unusual insight into the relationship between legal theory and papal practice in the development of Christian-infidel relations.[1]

Innocent's dealings with infidels can be categorized in several ways. In the first place, there were three general groups of infidels that concerned him: the Saracens or Moslems; the Prussians, Lithuanians, and other infidels of northeastern Europe; and the Tartars or Mongols. Looked at from a different perspective, however, these groups of infidels may be divided into those who lived within Christian Europe, those who were recent converts to Christianity, and those who lived beyond the bounds of Christendom. The last category included both groups who posed a direct military threat to Christendom, such as the Tartars, and those that did not, like the Moslem societies of North Africa. Thus, while some of the infidel societies could be seen as the objects of just wars of defense, others could be seen as having the potential for peaceful relations with Europeans. Finally, the infidels could be divided into those who seemed open to conversion to Christianity and those whose conversion did not appear likely.

The wide variety of actual and potential relations between Christians and non-Christians appears clearly in the letters found in Innocent IV's register. The letters indicate that in his administrative practice, as in his legal theory, Innocent was not a radically novel thinker. To a large extent he developed relationships that had begun before he became pope. Even the most striking diplomatic gesture of his pontificate, the sending of an embassy to the Tartar khan in 1245, was in keeping with an old papal practice of seeking to negotiate with infidel rulers who showed a willingness to reach agreements with the Christians on matters of mutual interest.

In general, Innocent saw Christendom as surrounded by fierce and unrelenting enemies. The Tartar nation, for example, was "the enemy of God and the friend of the devil."[2] Similar terms were used to describe the Saracens and Lithuanians.[3] The letters in the register used traditional papal rhetoric to describe the various enemies of the Christian world. Other letters, however, contained evidence of a more objective appraisal of the infidel peoples who bordered Europe, indicative of Innocent's interest in reaching an accommodation with infidels where possible.

The Status of Nonbelievers in Europe

Christian relations with the Jews provided the model for relations between Christians and infidels within Europe. In commenting upon *Quod super his*, Innocent IV had referred to one of his own papal letters ordering the burning of copies of the Talmud because it contained material the pope defined as heretical. According to him, the leaders of the Jewish community should have destroyed the Talmud. In the absence of action in this matter by responsible Jewish authorities, the pope was empowered to insure the purity of Jewish doctrine and its conformity to the teachings of the Old Testament. The letter to which he referred was the bull *Impia iudaeorum*, issued in May 1244. The picture of the Jews it contained was not a pleasant one, a picture of a wicked people, blind to the truths that Christ brought to them. In spite of this, Christians were willing to live at peace with them, ungrateful though they may be to Christ and to His followers who had patiently sought to convert them. Their ingratitude was shown in two ways: they rejected the beliefs of their ancestors, and they also accepted beliefs that were insulting to Christianity. They followed the Talmud, a book filled, the pope heatedly declared, with blasphemous teachings about God, Christ, and His mother, the Virgin Mary. In addition, the Talmud contained a number of "confusing tales, wicked errors, and unheard-of bits of foolishness." Gregory IX had previously ordered copies of the Talmud burned, but the stiff-necked Jews had obviously persevered in their wicked ways, and so Innocent ordered Louis IX of France to search out surviving copies of the Talmud in his kingdom and to destroy them.[4]

In addition to ordering the burning of the Talmud, Innocent repeated the older papal bans on the use of Christian nurses and servants in Jewish families. In explaining the need for this ban, the pope again employed the story of Sara and Agar, this time to demonstrate that the child of a free-born mother should not serve the child of a slave-born mother. In this case, the Jews were still enslaved by sin while the Christians had been freed by the redemptive sacrifice of Christ. Thus, it would be improper to allow Christians to serve Jews.[5]

In making these points, Innocent was keeping well within the tradition of papal limitations on relations between Christians and Jews. The Jews were to be tolerated within Christian society—but just barely. They were not to be forced to convert, but they were not to be allowed to develop their religious beliefs and practices beyond what the Christians believed to be the Old Testament version of Judaism. The pope, not the leaders of the Jewish community, was the ultimate judge of what constituted correct Jewish doctrine. The Jewish communities were scattered throughout Europe and had been in existence for centuries in many cases. They were what might be termed a normal part of Christian Europe. Furthermore, the attitude of the Church toward the Jews was based on the realization that Christianity had sprung from Judaism. The Christians were the new Chosen People, the offspring of Abraham and Sara in the new dispensation. The relationship between the two peoples was therefore a long-standing one and one that did not necessarily assume innate hostility between them.

During the thirteenth century, however, a new group of non-Christians began to provide a more complicated set of problems for the Christian Church. The reconquest of the Spanish peninsula brought large numbers of Moslems under Christian domination.[6] The successful campaigns of James I (1213–76) of Aragon highlighted the kinds of problems that both secular rulers and ecclesias-

tical officials faced when presented with large communities of infidels within Christian kingdoms.[7] Kings and popes had conflicting
interests where infidel communities were involved. On the one
hand, ecclesiastical restrictions on the activities of non-Christians
dwelling within Christian kingdoms were designed to protect
Christians from the evil influences that the presence of untruth
would engender. On the other hand, the rulers of the various Christian kingdoms in Spain found both Jews and Moslems valuable
servants in a number of ways. Jews often served as diplomats,
financiers, and physicians at Christian courts; Moslems formed a
large part of the agricultural work force in the reconquered areas.
As a result, ecclesiastical prohibitions against the use of non-Christian officials in Christian states were often ignored by Spanish rulers
anxious to retain the services of Jews and Moslems. Jews and Moslems who found the restrictions on their activities within a Christian
society too confining could and did migrate to Granada or to North
Africa, thus causing a brain and labor drain in Castile and Aragon.
Consequently, the rulers of these kingdoms were often anxious to
placate their non-Christian subjects in order to achieve their own
political and economic goals while rejecting ecclesiastical interests.[8]
Innocent IV met this situation directly. He repeated an earlier ban
issued by Gregory IX on the recruitment of Moslem settlers for
reconquered lands which had been abandoned by their previous
inhabitants and for which no Christian settlers could be found. He
feared the deleterious effect of the Moslems on the Christians who
would rule over and live among them.[9] The kingdom's need for
settlers, however, outweighed the Church's desire to protect its
members from unbelievers. The revolt of Moslems in Valencia in
1248 no doubt struck Innocent as a suitable reward for James I's
excessive toleration of the Moslems in his kingdom.[10]

At the opposite end of Europe, the conversion of the pagan Lithuanians provided another illustration of the conflicts that could erupt
because of the differing views of secular and ecclesiastical officials
concerning infidels. In this case, the infidels were on the verge of
becoming Christians, at least as the papacy saw matters. The greed
for land shown by the Christians who lived on the border of Lithuania interfered with the missionary efforts. In 1250 the king of the
Lithuanians, Mindowe, became a Christian. Mindowe's conversion,
along with the conversion of his subjects that was expected to follow, eventually would lead to the pacification of the border be-

tween the Teutonic Knights and the kingdom of Poland on the one hand and the pagan Slavs on the other. Innocent pointed out to the bishop of the Cumans, under whose jurisdiction the converted Lithuanians would come, that the new Christians should be treated gently lest they be turned away from the Church by the harshness of their bishops and clergy.[11] Although he did not mention any specific problems, earlier critics of the manner in which converts were made in this area pointed to the greed and rapaciousness of the Christians, both laymen and clerics, who moved among the converts.[12] Innocent's warning to the bishop reflected a general awareness of the difficulties involved in the early stages of mass conversions.

Innocent instructed the bishop that in converting to Christianity the Lithuanians were passing from the law of nature to the superior law and precepts of the Church. As a result, they might find various aspects of the Christian life difficult at first because they lacked familiarity with its terms. In particular, they might find the payment of the tithe, a matter of controversy even in established Christian communities, a strange and heavy burden. Priests assigned to the newly created parishes within the Lithuanian kingdom should use great care in imposing the tithe and other ecclesiastical burdens on the converts until they became accustomed to the Church's yoke. The pope also advised secular rulers to use similar care in dealing with converts from paganism who dwelled within the borders of their kingdoms.[13]

The conversion of Mindowe did not lead to the immediate acceptance of the Lithuanians by their Christian neighbors. The Teutonic Knights and the Poles continued to move against Lithuania, and their desire to acquire the lands occupied by the Lithuanians was not dampened by the waters of baptism or by papal demands for gentle treatment of the converts.[14] Unlike the situation in Spain, where the need for labor was so great as to require the toleration of infidels in spite of papal objections, the desire for land in the East led the expanding Poles and Teutonic Knights to clear the lands they conquered of the native population, even when the natives were Christians and under the protection of the Church. Here again, the papacy proved unable to convince secular rulers or the leader of a religious order that the Church's approach to the problem of infidels, this time converts, should be followed. The territorial aims of the Christian neighbors of the Lithuanians overrode the Church's goals.

Defensive Wars with the Infidels

The major source of contact between European Christians and the non-Christian world during the pontificate of Innocent IV remained, of course, the constant frontier wars along the edges of Christendom. As the presence of infidels within Europe posed a spiritual threat to European Christians, so too the presence of infidels on the borders posed a military threat. Even if this was not a serious threat to the heartlands of Christendom, it was a real and present danger to the border kingdoms. Innocent's letters concerning the border kingdoms reflected the papacy's fears about the encroachments of infidel armies along the edges of the Christian world.[15] As leader of the Christian world and shepherd of Christ's flock, the pope was responsible for the physical welfare of Christians as well as their spiritual welfare.

The Moslem threat along the Mediterranean border of Europe was of long standing. Innocent's letters contained the usual calls for crusaders to free the Holy Land from the infidel and restore Christian control of the area.[16] In addition, his letters contained support for the efforts of the Spanish kings, such as James I of Aragon, to reconquer the Iberian peninsula. The capture of Valencia by James I in 1245 elicited enthusiastic praise from the pope.[17] Elsewhere Innocent authorized crusading indulgences for those who would continue the work of reconquest in Spain.[18]

The pope was also concerned by reports that Christian merchants were selling arms and war materials to the Moslems. The prohibition against such trade was an old one in canon law and had been the subject of earlier papal letters.[19] Innocent was repeating traditional papal policy, not breaking new ground. At the same time, it should be noted that the prohibition concerned only war materials and weapons in time of war.[20] In times of peace, trade was not forbidden; indeed, the threat to ban trade with Moslem countries was occasionally used as a form of economic warfare, suggesting that the papacy was well aware of the role that trade with Europe played in the economic life of the North African states.[21]

In the eastern part of Christendom there were two threats to peace, the traditional one from the Slavs and the more recent one from the Tartars. Early in his pontificate, Innocent called for yet another crusade against the Prussians and the Lithuanians, and he authorized the Dominicans to preach a crusade in Germany.[22] The crusading army would be spearheaded by the Teutonic Knights, who played the leading role in the conquest of the Baltic lands during the thirteenth century. The stated goals of the proposed crusade were the extension of the Christian Church into new territory and the protection of the Christian settlers who already lived along the borders with the infidels. In addition to the usual difficulties of raising adequate numbers of crusaders and settlers to occupy the lands taken from the Slavs, Innocent later noted that Christian merchants were selling arms to the infidels as well, making the conquest even more difficult.[23]

The Lithuanians, Prussians, and other peoples who were indigenous to northeastern Europe were not a major threat to Christendom. This area provided a fertile area for expansion by the Teutonic Knights and the kingdom of Poland. There was, however, no threat of a Slavic invasion of the rest of Europe. The Tartars posed a great, though undefined, threat to all of Europe, or at least so many people believed. Ever since the Tartars had appeared in Russia at the beginning of the thirteenth century, they had been the subject of terrifying stories about their origins and their aims.[24] It was not clear whether they planned to sweep over all of Europe or whether they would stop at the eastern borders. The major obstacle to a Tartar sweep across Europe was the kingdom of Hungary. As a result, a number of Innocent's letters dealt with assisting the Hungarians in their struggle with the invaders. The crusaders would bear the banner of Christ against "the devil's envoys," that is, against the Tartars.[25] Innocent was not, however, very successful in providing assistance for the besieged kingdom of Hungary. In 1245 he was forced to release King Bela IV of Hungary from an oath of fealty he had given to Emperor Frederick II some years earlier because the emperor had failed to provide the military assistance he had promised as a condition of the oath. The pope was reduced to writing words of encouragement to the Hungarians in lieu of more substantial help and advising them where they might go to save themselves from the infidel onslaught.[26]

Tartar attacks on Russia also attracted Innocent's attention. Prince Daniel of Galicia, whom the pope described as the king of Russia, sought papal assistance in his attempt to defend his principality against the onrushing Tartars. The Teutonic Knights were ordered to assist Daniel and another Russian ruler whose principality was also being threatened by the Tartars.[27] These orders were of little avail, however, because no concerted European Christian campaign could be made against the Tartars. The internal divisions of the European states and the bitter struggle between Innocent IV and Frederick II that was to come to its dramatic end with Frederick's death in 1250 prevented the kind of cooperation that was necessary if the eastern flanks of Christendom were to be protected.[28] The long history of squabbling among the leaders of crusades going to the defense of the Holy Land should have warned the pope that he would not be more successful than his predecessors had been when faced with a strong military threat from infidel armies.

Innocent IV—Peaceful Relations with Infidel Societies

In spite of the great attention paid to relations between Christians and infidels in terms of the just war of defense or recuperation, peaceful relations were also believed possible in the thirteenth century. As in the case of tolerating non-Christians within Christian society, coexistence was not the highest goal the popes and the canon lawyers could envisage, but it was an acceptable situation. Two aspects of Innocent IV's policies demonstrated the belief that peaceful relations could exist between Christians and non-Christians. The first was his development of a statement of powers to be granted to missionaries working among infidels, as well as among heretics and schismatics. The second was his attempt to open relations with the Tartar khans of Central Asia.

The need for a basic statement of the goals of missionary work and the responsibilities of missionaries sprang logically from the general conception of the pope's responsibility for the souls of all men. The bull *Cum hora undecima*, first issued by Gregory IX in 1235, contained the basic statement of the church's missionary function.[29] It was continually reissued throughout the thirteenth, fourteenth, and fifteenth centuries. The later versions of the bull were virtually identical with the version Innocent IV issued in 1245.

The opening lines of *Cum hora undecima* reflected the apocalyptic tradition that was strong among the members of the Franciscan order in its early years.[30] Gregory IX and his successors who reissued the bull began by reminding the missionaries that "since the eleventh hour has come in the day given to mankind . . . it is necessary that spiritual men [possessing] purity of life and the gift of intelligence should go forth with John [the Baptist] again to all men and all peoples of every tongue and in every kingdom to prophesy because, according to the prophet Isaias, the salvation of the remnant of Israel will not occur until, as St. Paul says, the *plenitudo gentium* enters first" into the kingdom of heaven.[31]

The task of the missionaries was to fulfill Christ's injunction to preach the gospel to all men so that the process of salvation might be completed. They were to strengthen those Christians whose faith was weak, to correct the false doctrines of heretics, and to bring the non-believers into the fold. In order to facilitate the missionaries' work, Gregory IX granted them a number of special privileges, including the right to hear confessions anywhere, to absolve ex-communicates, to dispense converts from various kinds of irregularities, probably referring to minor impediments involving marriage, and generally to ease the way into the fold of those outside of it.[32]

When Innocent IV reissued *Cum hora undecima* ten years after Gregory IX had issued it, he gave it the form it was to retain, except for minor modifications, in later reissues. The difference between Gregory's version of the bull and Innocent's lay in the amount of specific detail Innocent added. The later version listed eighteen peoples, besides the Saracens and pagans, to whom the missionaries were being sent. The list included the various Christian schismatics in the East, Greeks, Bulgarians, Georgians, and Armenians. Reflecting perhaps Innocent's personal interest in the Asian mission, the letter also listed the Nestorians, Alans, and the people of India, probably a reference to the Nestorians of the Malabar coast. Finally, the expanded salutation referred to friars working in Africa among the Ethiopians and the Nubians.[33]

The body of Innocent's version of the bull moved on to define more precisely the nature and extent of the powers possessed by the missionaries. Where the earlier letter simply referred to "irregularities" from which the friars could dispense converts, the new version specified certain irregularities connected with the ordination of schismatic clerics that might impede their reconciliation with Rome, and also some connected with the marriage laws of schismatic and infidel societies.[34] For example, those outside the Church often contracted marriage within the degrees of consanguinity and affinity forbidden by canon law but not by natural law. The pope's goal was to encourage the reconciliation of schismatics and the conversion of infidels with a minimum of difficulty by not insisting on imposing the canonical laws of marriage as a condition for baptism. If this had been done, the work of the missionaries would have been even more difficult than it was, because many non-Christians were accustomed to marrying within the first four degrees, while the Latin Church required a dispensation to marry within the second, third, and fourth degrees. Here Innocent IV was drawing upon a decretal issued by Innocent III around 1200 in response to a request on behalf of potential converts from Mohammedanism in the Holy Land.[35] Innocent IV's position was that it was reasonable to apply the standards of natural law concerning marriage to infidels because that was the only law they knew before becoming Christians.

The bull seems to assume the willingness of infidel societies to admit peaceful missionaries, and there was concrete evidence for this assumption. Innocent IV's attempt at opening relations with the Tartars was not the first example of such activity, though it may have been the most dramatic. Ever since the eleventh century, the papacy had engaged in relations with various Moslem rulers in North Africa. The Mongol mission was rooted in the experience provided by these earlier contacts. Experience revealed to the papacy that under some conditions, Christians and infidels could find a basis for agreement, especially concerning the treatment of Christians living under Moslem rule.

Papal interest in dealing with the Moslem rulers of North Africa stemmed from the survival of Christian communities there. When the Moslems conquered North Africa, they overran one of the most heavily Christianized areas of the Roman world. The Christian communities of the area, the heirs of Saint Augustine and other outstanding figures in the history of the Christian Church, survived precariously under Moslem rule. From the late eleventh century on, there was a slight but steady stream of letters from the papacy to the rulers of the North African states. The letters suggest periods of strong interest in the situation of the Church under the Moslems, followed by long periods in which little attention was paid to the problem. A number of letters that survive from the pontificate of Gregory VII (1073–85) illustrate the kind of relations that could exist between the papacy and Moslem rulers. In 1076, when responding to a request from a Moslem ruler in North Africa to consecrate a new bishop for the Christian community in his domain, Gregory VII used the occasion to thank the ruler for his kindness toward his Christian subjects and to raise some additional points about the situation of the Christians there. In words that sound more like those of a contemporary ecumenical figure than those of a fiery exponent of ecclesiastical reform, the pope reminded the Moslem ruler that a special relationship existed between Christians and Moslems because "we who believe in and confess the one God, although we do so in different ways, daily praise and worship Him Who is the creator and ruler of this world."[36] Gregory apparently hoped that the conditions under which the Christians in North Africa were living might be improved if the papacy and the ruler could come to some sort of agreement. He also seems to have been anxious to emphasize that neither he nor the Christians living in North Africa posed a threat to the ruler's continued control of his principality.

During the first half of the thirteenth century, there was an increasing amount of papal activity involving the Christians of North Africa. Much of this was due to the founding of new religious orders that took a special interest in the Moslem world. Some were interested in the redemption of Christians who had been captured by Moslem slave traders and sold into slavery. Other orders, among whom the Franciscans played the most famous role, were interested in the conversion of the Moslems. Pope Innocent III was a strong supporter of both efforts.[37] In 1198 he wrote to the ruler of Morocco to introduce members of the Order of the Most Holy Trinity for the Redemption of Captives, who were anxious to purchase the freedom of Christian captives. The pope added the suggestion that the prince might also be interested in exchanging Moslems held by Europeans for Christians held captive in Morocco.[38]

During the pontificates of Honorius III (1216–27) and Gregory IX, the missionary zeal of the Franciscans and Dominicans led to further papal contact with the ruler of Morocco. In order to ease their way, Honorius authorized some modifications in the garb they wore so that they would not attract unnecessary attention.[39] Some years later, Gregory IX wrote to the ruler of Morocco inviting him to receive baptism at the hands of the friars working in his land, an invitation that was refused.[40] On the other hand, the ruler of Morocco was not uninterested in relations with the papacy. In 1235 he sent an embassy consisting of two Genoese merchants to the pope seeking to arrange a treaty with the papacy. The embassy, which is known from Gregory's response, led to the dispatching of a Franciscan friar to Morocco for discussions with the Moroccan ruler.[41] The use of a Franciscan as the papal envoy suggests that the main purpose of an agreement with the Moroccan ruler was the protection of the Christians living there and the friars who were being sent to minister to them. In addition, the friars were expected to preach to the Moslems.

The pontificate of Innocent IV saw a flurry of activity involving the North African states. In 1245 a Moslem ruler who was styled the king of Sale, a principality northeast of Rabat in modern Morocco, informed the master of the Spanish crusading Order of Saint James that he wished to become a Christian. As this figure appears to have been a local official momentarily asserting his independence of his overlord, the king of Morocco, the proposed conversion may have been linked with the hope of Christian support of his struggle for independence. Innocent pointed out to the master of the order the numerous advantages that would accrue to the Church as a result of the conversion of the land of Sale: not only would the inhabitants of that region be brought to the true faith, but the kingdom would also serve as a base from which missionaries and crusaders could operate, eventually bringing about the relief of the Holy Land.[42] Although the conversion of Sale was never accomplished, the case illustrated the optimism about the possibilities of converting the infidels that marked Innocent's reign. Even while there was little optimism about stopping infidel assaults on Europe militarily, there remained some hope of bringing peace through the conversion of the enemy.

In the fall and early winter of 1246, Innocent wrote several letters to North African rulers seeking to insure the safety of the Christians living there. Writing to the rulers of Tunis, Ceuta, and Bougie, he pointed out that each of their lands held a sizable Christian population. He was sending a bishop to their lands, accompanied by Franciscan friars, and hoped that these rulers would welcome them. Furthermore, Innocent reminded these rulers that in addition to their Christian subjects, there were other Christians who visited their lands from Europe.[43] Presumably, the pope was referring here to merchants, especially Italians, who traded extensively in North Africa, and who would require the services of priests while living there.[44] There was a hint here that if the friars were harassed, the pope might forbid Christian merchants to trade with these lands, thus affecting the local economies.

The possibility of a major Christian advance in North Africa appeared in a letter Innocent wrote to the king of Morocco, reminding him of the benefits that his predecessors had received from Christians in the past. He pointed specifically to the Christian mercenaries who served in the army of the king and his predecessors and who had enabled them to retain their throne. These rulers had traditionally shown favor to their Christian subjects in return for the services that the Christians provided. In Innocent's mind, the Christians were clearly good and loyal subjects. Once more, the pope also tried to win the soul of the king and bring him to the baptismal font, holding out the promise that if the ruler did become a Christian, he would be placed under the special protection of the papacy. Moving from hope to reality, Innocent concluded the letter with a request that Christians be permitted to establish their own communities apart from those of the Moslems. The pope was proposing armed towns located along the Mediterranean coast, apparently so that the Christians would be permanently secure from assault by mobs of Moslems who saw them as infidels.[45] Several years later, Innocent wrote again to the Moroccan ruler stating that the bishop of Morocco had informed him of the king's failure to take any steps to implement the pope's earlier request. As a result, when Christian soldiers in the ruler's army left their homes to serve the ruler in battle they could not rest assured about the safety of their families.[46] In order to bring pressure on the ruler to establish the kind of towns that his earlier letter had described, Innocent stated that he had instructed the Christians living there not to serve the king until the issue was resolved. He also instructed potential mercenaries living in Europe not to enter the Moroccan service.[47] This kind of pressure, though no doubt of little real effect, was the kind that Innocent's legal theorizing would authorize a pope to use. He did not state that he would lead a crusade against Morocco, nor did he propose encouraging the Christians there to rise up against their Moslem ruler. He was acting as a pastor should act, insuring that his flock could observe their religious practices without interference.

Against the background of papal relations with the Moslem rulers of North Africa, the mission that Innocent sent to the Tartar khan takes on a different character. It was not a unique move, but rather an application of an old practice to a new situation. Indeed, there were several analogies between the situation in North Africa and that in the steppes. Both the Moslems and the Tartars posed military threats to Christendom. Both societies also had significant Christian populations living in their midst. On the other hand, Moslem-Christian relations were probably locked into place because of the long history of wars and because of their conflicting religious positions. The Tartars were a new threat and, so far as the papacy knew, were not armed with a competing religion. At the same time, the papacy was aware that some Moslem states were willing to make treaties of a limited kind with the papacy and with other European kingdoms where the interests of Christians and Moslems coincided. This experience may have encouraged the pope to believe that it would be possible to find areas of mutual interest with the Tartars as well. In addition, there were widely repeated stories about the khan's interest in Christianity, which may also have inspired Innocent to seek out the leader of the Tartars.

From the papal perspective, dealings with the Tartars were virtually impossible because little was known about their goals and their way of life. During the first half-century of the Tartar advance in eastern Europe, numerous stories about their origins and aims had circulated throughout Europe. These stories tended to accentuate the fears of Europeans because they stressed the horrible nature of Tartar warfare and the barbaric nature of their lives. In March 1245, on the eve of the First Council of Lyons, which had as one of its major purposes the arranging of the defense of eastern Europe against the Tartars, Innocent dispatched two groups of friars to seek out the great khan of the Tartars. One mission, consisting of two Franciscans, Lawrence of Portugal, and John of Plano Carpini, was to travel by way of Russia. The other, consisting of the Dominicans Ascelinus and Andrew of Longjumeau, was to go by way of the Near East.[48]

The Franciscans, and presumably also the Dominicans, bore two letters that were to introduce them to the khan and to instruct him in Christian doctrine. The theme of both letters was that the universe functions along rational lines and that men, as rational creatures, are capable of knowing the God Who created this universe. In addition, each letter had its own special theme: one reproached the Tartars for their attacks on Christian Europe; the other was a statement of basic Christian beliefs.

In the first letter, Innocent argued that everything in the universe, including men, was part of the "world machine" that ought by rights to function harmoniously.[49] The invasion of the Tartars, however, was upsetting the peaceful order of the world. Innocent made it clear that the Tartars were the unprovoked aggressors. No one had attacked them; they simply attacked everyone at will. In his capacity as vicar of Christ, the King of Peace, the pope requested that the invaders lay down their arms and live at peace with their neighbors, especially the Christians. If the Tartars did not do this voluntarily, Innocent held out the threat that God Himself would punish them for their evil ways.

The statement of Christian belief sent to the Tartars reflected the theory held in some intellectual quarters, especially among the Dominicans, that infidels would be brought to accept the true faith through rationally presented arguments that could lead them to the brink of faith.[50] Innocent stressed that man's capacity for knowing ultimate truths was blocked by the consequences of sin. Christ, however, acted as mediator between God and man so that these consequences could be overcome. After His death, Christ left his vicar to care for all men in His name, and so as Christ's vicar and in obedience to the responsibility that he bore for the salvation of all men, Innocent was sending learned and holy friars to instruct the Tartars in the way of salvation. He asked the khan to welcome his representatives, listen to their words, and insure their safety while they traveled in the Tartar lands. The pope emphasized that this mission was primarily a religious one. He noted that if "ecclesiastical prelates or other powerful men would be more profitable and more acceptable to you we would have sent them."[51] That is, if the mission had been of a strictly political or diplomatic nature, such figures would have been more suitable; this being an essentially religious mission, however, learned and holy men were appropriate representatives because they, not powerful ecclesiastical diplomats, were more likely to win the souls of the Tartars.

The Dominican mission fared rather differently. After an unsuccessful attempt to obtain the assistance of the sultan in crossing over from the Moslem-held lands of the Near East into the Tartar lands, the two Dominicans reached the Tartars by different routes. One by-product of the Dominican contact with the sultan was a letter from him to Innocent IV concerning the possibility of a disputation between representatives of both faiths. The sultan pointed out that the Dominicans did not know Arabic and that there was no one among his subjects sufficiently learned in Christian teachings to debate the Dominicans effectively.[52] The sultan may have feared that the Dominicans were being sent to the East to arrange an alliance between the Christians and the Tartars that would have the Moslem world as the object of a jointly pursued war. In 1247, after various adventures, Friar Ascelinus reached the camp of Baiju, a Tartar commander in Armenia and Mesopotamia. After several weeks in the camp, during which the friar's arrogant demands that Baiju and his people immediately receive baptism almost led to his execution, Baiju sent him home to the West.[53]

Both the Franciscan and the Dominican missions brought back letters from the Tartars for the pope. Guyuk, the grandson of Ghengis Khan and now the great khan, responded vehemently to Innocent's request that he become a Christian. In a letter entrusted to John of Plano Carpini, Guyuk commanded the pope "at the head of all the princes [of Europe], come at once to serve and wait upon us! At that time I shall recognize your submission." To the pope's argument that he was God's representative on earth, the great khan replied the "eternal God has slain and annihilated these lands and peoples, because they neither adhered to Ghengis Khan, nor to the khagan [the supreme ruler], both of whom have been sent to make known God's command nor to the command of God."[54] Like the pope, the khan saw himself as God's agent on earth, and the success of the Tartar armies proved to him the correctness of his opinion. As a result, all men should pass under his sway, not that of the pope.

As for becoming a Christian, Guyuk was astounded by the pope's impudence in requesting that he become "a trembling Nestorian Christian," worship the Christian God, and become "an ascetic." As John of Plano Carpini and other papal envoys to the Tartars had noted, the Nestorians, who were numerous in the areas under Tartar domination and who provided administrative services in parts of the empire, were scorned by the Tartars. Furthermore, in a passage that suggested some skepticism on his part about his own assertion that he was God's agent, the khan asked how the pope could be so certain that he, and not the khan, was God's agent on earth. After all, could the Tartar conquests have occurred if such was "contrary to the command of God?"[55]

The Dominican envoys apparently brought back with them letters of similar import. In addition, however, they arrived back in Europe with representatives of Baiju. In 1248 Baiju's representatives returned to their home bearing a letter from the pope. In an attempt to pacify the Tartars, Innocent stressed in this new letter that the papal court had received the Tartar ambassadors kindly and treated

them as befitted their important mission.[56] Innocent may have been
anxious to prove that Guyuk was in error when he accused Christians of mistreating earlier Tartar representatives, who had been sent
to the Christian Kingdoms in eastern Europe. Innocent went on to
emphasize yet again that his interest in the Tartars was restricted
to the salvation of their souls and that he had no warlike intentions
toward them. He added he was now more upset about the condition
of their souls than previously because, having heard of the truths of
Christianity from the friars who had visited them, the Tartars could
no longer plead ignorance of the true faith when God called them
for judgment. Innocent also repeated his earlier opinion that God
was losing patience with the Tartars and was liable to inflict His
wrath upon them at any moment.

Conclusion

In general, Innocent IV's dealings with the infidels both inside
Europe and beyond its borders followed the pattern that he had set
out in his commentary on *Quod super his*. In the first place, although
he threatened the Moslems with economic boycott and the Tartars
with God's wrath, he never denied the right of their rulers to
govern their possessions. He recognized that they, in common with
all men, had the right to *dominium*. They need not convert to Christianity in order to retain the lands they held justly. He also recognized that men should not be forced to become Christians.

Having recognized the right of the infidels to *dominium*, Innocent went on to assert the responsibility he bore for the souls of all
men. The most obvious use of this power was his ordering the
burning of the Talmud in order to protect the Jews from false
teaching within their own tradition. At the same time, however, he
also exercised his responsibility for the Jews by insisting that Christian rulers not harass their subjects or force them to convert to
Christianity. On the other hand, his responsibility for Christians
meant that he could not allow non-Christians living in Europe to
endanger the souls of Christians who lived around them. He seems
to have seen the Moslems living in Europe as a greater threat to
Christians than the Jews, so that his strongest strictures were against
the toleration of Moslems in Spain.

When Innocent dealt with the problem of defending Europe

from infidel attacks he was clearly within the traditional theory of the just war that he himself had used in his commentary. His willingness to authorize indulgences for crusades to restore the Holy Land to Christian hands or to oust the Moslems from Spain was in accord with his argument that lands unjustly seized from Christians could be legitimately retaken from the Moslems.

Finally, when Innocent wrote to infidel rulers advising them on how they should treat their subjects, he was acting both according to papal practice for over two centuries and according to his legal theorizing. He based his demands for the protection of the Christian subjects of infidel rulers on his role as Christ's vicar who was responsible for the souls of Christians everywhere. Likewise, his call for infidel rulers to become Christians and to protect Christian missionaries working within their domains was rooted in his responsibility for the souls of infidels. Although the pope accepted the legitimacy of the power that the infidels exercised, he did not hesitate to threaten infidel rulers who failed to cooperate in the work of the missionaries with economic boycott or divine wrath. He was careful not to threaten them with conquest and forced conversion, not simply because it was impractical but, more importantly, because it violated the basic principle that baptism was a voluntary acceptance of Christianity and could not be imposed. The infidels could, of course, be reminded of the dangers they faced if they failed to heed the message of the missionaries who preached to them.

There are two puzzling aspects of Innocent's interest in Christian-infidel relations. One involves the chronological relationship between what he wrote as a lawyer about the rights of infidels and what he did as pope. The other concerns the effect of the increased knowledge of the infidel world that the friars brought back to Europe on the shaping of legal theory and papal practice.

Inasmuch as Innocent does not appear to have completed his commentary on the *Decretales* until 1250, it is reasonable to believe that his theoretical treatment of Christian-infidel relations was developed in conjunction with his experience as pope in dealing with infidel societies.[57] In practice, much of what he did as pope in this regard clearly owed a great deal to the efforts of his predecessors: even the Mongol mission was an application to the infidels of the East of practices long employed in dealing with the Moslem states of North Africa. To a large extent, Innocent's major contribution was in synthesizing existing papal practice toward various categories of infidels. His most significant personal contribution was the assertion that infidels possessed *dominium*. Innocent's unwillingness to deny *dominium* to infidels may be based on three intellectual currents. In the first place, as Aristotelian political thought was revived in thirteenth-century Europe, the notion that man has certain natural rights was becoming more acceptable intellectually.[58] Second, Innocent may have grasped before other lawyers the danger in denying to infidels the right to property and lordship because they were not Christians. He may well have realized that the same argument could be used against Christian rulers who were notorious sinners and also against the clergy—even popes. The risk of a Donatist revival may have been in his opinion too great a risk to run.

Finally, Innocent's interest in the question of property and *dominium* may have been linked to his involvement in the struggle over property that was dividing the Franciscan order. In 1245 he issued the bull *Ordinem vestrum*, designed to resolve the question of whether or not the order should own property.[59] The spiritual wing of the order argued that friars should own nothing and live by begging alone; the moderate wing was moving in the direction of possessing its own houses as the older orders did. Innocent's bull sought to avoid splitting the order by vesting the ownership of property given to the Franciscans in the Holy See and authorizing the Franciscans to use the property. While it would be too much to attribute to Innocent the foresight to perceive the great battle over property and poverty that was to divide the friars in the fourteenth century, it is not too much to suggest that his views on property in this situation were connected to his opinion about the right of infidels to *dominium*. In both cases, he worked from the assumption that the possession of property was a natural right of all men. While individuals or groups might voluntarily give up the exercise of that right in the pursuit of spiritual perfection, the right was still theirs. The right to property did not rest upon being in the state of grace, and, on the other hand, the perfection of the Christian life did not depend upon denial of the right to possess property. In both cases, Innocent IV was walking a narrow line between two radical views on property.

The other puzzling aspect of Innocent IV's dealings with the infidels is the lack of any serious discussion of the terms of the natural law according to which he claimed the right to judge infidels. In his commentary on *Quod super his* he alluded to sexual abuses and idolatry an areas in which he could act as judge of infidels and order their punishment. These vague statements were not developed in any detail in the letters that he wrote to infidel rulers. Descriptions of life among the Tartars provided by missionaries who had returned from the East must have suggested the need to spell out the details of natural law. For example, John of Plano Carpini observed that the Tartars were polygamous.[60] Did the practice of polygamy violate natural law? If so, what should the friars tell their converts—that they should retain only one wife? The Franciscan friar seems to have recognized that polygamy was a significant element of the Tartar social structure, not simply evidence of the lasciviousness of the infidels. The only answer that Innocent IV could give was that polygamous converts must give up all spouses except the first one. This answer was an old one, a solution ordered by Innocent III half a century earlier and not significantly modified later.[61]

The result is that in spite of Innocent IV's legal theorizing and practical experience, the problem of Christian-infidel relations proved too difficult to resolve completely. No pope was better equipped to deal with the task of dealing with infidels, and yet Innocent was unable to make the breakthoughs necessary to improve relations. A major difficulty was that there were conflicts among the various goals that Innocent sought to achieve. As universal pastor, he wanted the conversion of the infidel. As head of Christendom, he sought to protect eastern Europe from Tartar invasion and to return to Christian hands the Holy Land and other territories lost to Christians by the advance of the Moslems. Furthermore, as the situation in Lithuania demonstrated, he could not guarantee that infidel converts would be safe from Christian depredations. What advantages would accrue to converts if they were to win the salvation of their souls and suffer the loss of their lands?

For contemporaries, the death of Innocent IV did not mark the end of an era. There was good reason to assume that the last half of the thirteenth century would see the fulfillment of the policies that had guided popes since the days of Gregory VII. At the mid-century mark, the papacy was still riding the crest of the reform movement that had made it the moral arbiter of Europe. With the death of Frederick II in 1250 and the subsequent collapse of the Hohenstaufen family's pretensions to imperial grandeur, the papacy appeared unchallengeable in the political sphere. Beyond Europe, the Latin emperors still ruled at Constantinople, and the crusader states maintained their precarious existence in the Near East. If the contacts with the Tartars could be extended and if the conversion of the Lithuanians could be completed without further hindrance, the northern and eastern borders of Christendom would be secure.[1]

Of course, these optimistic dreams did not come true. The fifty years spanning the period from Innocent's death to that of Benedict XI (1304) saw the papacy's position within Europe erode dramatically. Instead of being the unchallenged moral leaders of Europe, the fourteenth-century popes came under strong criticism for being the chaplains of the French kings. The installation of Michael VIII Palaeologus as emperor at Constantinople in 1261 ended the Latin Empire.[2] The fall of Acre to the Moslems in 1291 ended the last vestiges of Latin Christian power in the Near East.[3] These events also meant the end of hopes for reuniting the Latin and the Greek churches. Elsewhere, the Tartar armies continued to advance, and attempts at negotiation with them failed. In the political realm, the events of those last decades of the thirteenth century formed for the papacy the reversal of fortune that is the essence of tragedy.

The Infidels within Europe

The last decades of the thirteenth century saw increased papal concern about the effects that contact with non-Christians had upon Christians. Both Jews and Moslems seemed to pose for the papacy a threat far out of proportion to their actual numbers in Europe. Each group posed a unique threat to Christians: according to papal letters, the Jews were making converts from among their Christian neighbors; as for the Moslems, because they lived in those parts of Spain taken during the reconquest, various popes saw them as potential allies for armies coming from the remaining Saracen kingdoms in Spain or armies that might come from Africa. Thus, Innocent IV's successors were constantly warning the faithful of the dangers that Jews and Moslems posed to both their spiritual and to their physical well-being.

Clement IV's bull *Turbato corde*, issued in 1268, summed up the papal view of the Jewish threat to Christian souls. Addressing the Franciscans and Dominicans of the Inquisition, the pope indicated his dismay about reports that some Jewish converts to Christianity had relapsed. Furthermore, "many Christians, turning their backs on the truth of the Christian faith, have, to the damnation of their souls, become Jews." He instructed the inquisitors to weed out and punish those who had apostasized. In addition, they were to punish Jews who were seeking to make converts among the Christian population.[4] Like Innocent IV, Clement IV (1265–68) did not believe that the obligation of non-Christian rulers to admit Christian preachers meant that Christian rulers were obliged to admit representatives of other religions to preach in their domains.

It is difficult to believe that any significant number of Christians converted to Judaism during the thirteenth century. The Church had exerted strong pressures against conversions even before Clement IV issued *Turbato corde*. In spite of this, Gregory X reissued the bull in 1274, as did Nicholas IV in 1288.[5] No doubt the real fear was that Jewish converts in Spain had not been truly converted and would lapse back into Judaism if the papacy did not exert continuous pressure to prevent it. Another problem arose from the appointment of Jews to important positions in the Spanish kingdoms. Clement IV had to instruct the king of Aragon not to allow Jews to hold public office lest they be in a position to harass Christians.[6]

Some years later, Nicholas IV wrote to the king of Portugal about that ruler's similar failure to maintain the traditional restrictions on the activities of Jews in his kingdom.[7]

Papal restrictions on Jews and Moslems to prevent harm to the bodies or souls of Christians were not sufficient. Papal policy actively supported converting them to Christianity and assisting them to adjust to their new way of life. Urban IV provided financial support for some converts who were being harassed by their former coreligionists.[8] If such activities were not checked, they would block the planned conversion of those outside the Church. Nicholas III took a special interest in expanding missionary efforts among the Jews. In 1278 he devoted a bull, *Vineam Sorec velut*, to the problem of converting them. He described the Jews as like the barren fig tree of which Christ spoke. They would bear fruit only when missionaries had properly cultivated them with the truth Christ had brought. Preachers should therefore be sent among them so that Christ's word would fructify the Synagogue. Should any Jews refuse to hear the preachers, the local secular ruler should force them to attend the sermons because it was in their own best interest to hear the word of God; although baptism could not be forced on anyone, enforced attendance at sermons designed to inspire nonbelievers to accept the faith was permissible.[9] The papal registers of this period also contain numerous letters emphasizing that Christians must not abuse Jews who live among them.[10] Conversion, not persecution, was the goal.

Finally, the successors of Innocent IV continued to stress their responsibility for insuring the purity of Jewish doctrine. In 1267 Clement IV ordered the king of Aragon to see to the collection of all Jewish books so that the archbishop of Tarragona might examine their content.[11] In doing so, Clement was following in the footsteps of Gregory IX and Innocent IV.

The Moslem population of Europe posed a more complex problem for the papacy because the Moslems were both a military and a spiritual threat to Christians. At the same time, the Moslem inhabitants of the lands recovered by the Christians during the reconquest of Spain provided the labor force required for working the land. Clement IV warned James I of Aragon of the danger his Moslem subjects posed to the spiritual well-being of his Christian subjects.[12] They also formed a potential fifth column, available to assist Moslem armies from Africa should they come again.[13] The pope's letters had little influence on the king, however, and so the Moslems continued to live in Aragon.[14]

The letter of 1266 in which Clement exhorted James I to protect his Christian subjects from his Moslem subjects also contained injunctions against appointing Jews to public office in Aragon.[15] In the pope's opinion, Jews and Moslems formed a joint threat to the Christian faith. Thus, it was possible to see the Jews not only as spiritual enemies, but as enemies in the temporal sphere as well, allies of the retreating Moslems. The late thirteenth century saw a blurring of the lines distinguishing Jews and Moslems. Christians saw them as joined by common opposition to the Christian faith and overlooked the religious and other differences between them. This blurring of distinctions between various non-Christians seems part of a general process of reducing the world to two classes of people, those within the Church and those outside of it. Innocent IV had employed three divisions to categorize mankind according to the kind of law to which each was subject; Clement's letter was moving in the direction of two categories, based not on laws but on relationship to the Church. This simpler categorization also appeared in the salutation of the missionary bull *Cum hora undecima*, where schismatics, heretics, Moslems, and infidels were listed indiscriminately.

Relations with Africa

Papal interest in the Spanish crusade naturally reinforced papal interest in North Africa. Although Innocent IV's successors did not make any new initiatives in Africa, they did strive to maintain the level of relations that their predecessors had reached. There was, however, ambivalence in papal interest in North Africa, the desire to bring the Spanish crusaders across the Strait of Gibraltar being counterbalanced by a desire to insure the safety of those Christians who lived there.

The nature of the papal dilemma regarding North Africa appeared in a letter of 1255 from Alexander IV to Bishop Wolf of Morocco, the papal legate for the region. Alexander informed the legate of Alfonso X of Castile's plans for a crusade in Africa.[16] The pope recognized that under the circumstances the legate's position was precarious, secure only as long as the local secular ruler tolerated his presence. The bishop could not even leave the diocese to visit the papal court without the sultan's permission. As the pope saw it, the bishop lived "in the midst of a perverse nation."[17] Great care was necessary in dealing with North Africa lest the Moslems begin to persecute the Christians who lived there. In spite of the delicate situation there, however, the Christian community continued to survive and even to rebuild decaying churches, as a letter in Boniface VIII's register indicates.[18]

The interest of the Aragonese and Castilian rulers in African conquests was, of course, directly linked to the reconquest of Spain. Recruits from Africa aided the Moslem kingdoms of Spain in their wars with the advancing Christians. Aragonese pressure against the Moslem kingdom of Murcia, for example, led to African troops reinforcing the Murcian army. Clement IV pointed out the danger these additional forces posed to the Christians of Spain by seeking to block the rightful Christian conquest. Furthermore, the Moslems were traditional enemies of Christendom. For both reasons, the Christians were justified in planning an invasion of Morocco and the neighboring regions.[19]

Clement was also interested in the status of Christians living in Egypt. A new sultan abrogated an agreement authorizing the public practice of the Christian religion, and a number of Christians died in the persecution that followed. This action reinforced the Christian picture of the Moslems as the inveterate enemies of Christianity, a people who could not be trusted to keep an agreement.[20]

For the remainder of the thirteenth century, papal policy toward Morocco and Egypt alternated between calls for new crusades and attempts to restore peaceful relations with the Moslems. On the one hand, Gregory X took steps to block North African support for their brethren in Spain. He repeated the traditional prohibition against selling arms and war materials to the Moslems and, in 1275, called for a crusade.[21] On the other hand, some peaceful contacts with the Moslems continued, chiefly through the work of ransoming their Christian captives. Nicholas III requested additional funds for furthering this work, an indication that peaceful relations were possible under certain circumstances.[22]

Nicholas IV's pontificate (1288–92) saw revived interest in Africa as well as in other infidel lands. He retained the ban on trade in war materials with the Moslems, but he also showed some flexibility on the broader issue of trade in other materials with them. One Christian community that had made a trade agreement with the sultan of Egypt was expressly exempted from the ban on trade with the Moslems; this community was even allowed to deal in war materials. In this case, the pope apparently believed that the survival of the community depended upon its ability to trade with the Moslems, with the result that he was willing to authorize the normally forbidden trade.[23]

Nicholas also renewed ties with Christians living elsewhere in North Africa. In 1290 he wrote to Christian mercenaries in the Moroccan and other North African armies. In his view, these soldiers were also missionaries, whose good example could lead their Moslem neighbors to the true faith. To emphasize his interest in the Christians there, he introduced to them a Franciscan, Brother Roderick, their new bishop and the pope's legate.[24] In another letter, Nicholas informed the Moroccan Christians that he intended to maintain the ties with them that his predecessors had created. He pointed particularly to Alexander IV's earlier appointment of a legate for Morocco.[25] Recognizing the precarious position of the North African Christians, Nicholas indicated an interest in acquiring the support of the area's Moslem rulers for the new legate's efforts.[26]

Furthermore, Nicholas made contact with the Christians of Ethiopia. Although the bull *Cum hora undecima* had mentioned Ethiopia and Nubia, there is no evidence that missionary efforts actually were made in those lands. In 1289, however, Nicholas wrote to the emperor of Ethiopia asking for an end to the schism separating the Ethiopian Church from Rome.[27] The Ethiopians belonged to the schismatic Jacobite Church and were subject to that church's patriarch at Alexandria.[28] The pope's reaching out to these separated Christians must be seen as part of the twofold papal policy of finding allies against the encroaching Tartars and Moslems and ending the divisions within the larger Christian world.

Papal interest in North Africa continued during the pontificate of Boniface VIII (1294–1303). In 1297 he reissued the ban on trade with the Moslems, observing that such a policy was in accord with the policy of Nicholas IV and his other predecessors.[29] Boniface's pontificate also saw a new direction in papal relations with Africa. In 1295 Roger Doria, admiral of Sicily, captured two small islands, Gerba and Kerkeni, off Tunis. Doria gave these islands to the papacy on the condition that Boniface then grant the islands to him and his heirs as a fief.[30] The capture of these islands was not in itself a significant aspect of the Christian wars against the Moslems. The willingness of the pope to act as Doria suggested was, however, an important precedent for papal dealings with lands taken from infidels. The pope stated that he had the right to accept these islands and then to grant them as a papal fief because they did not belong to any Christian ruler.

The granting of newly conquered lands as papal fiefs was not a new practice; popes had been receiving and granting lands in this fashion since the eleventh century. Furthermore, newly converted rulers of kingdoms along the borders of the Holy Roman Empire had often sought protection from German expansion by becoming papal vassals holding their kingdoms as fiefs.[31] What was new in Boniface's acceptance of Doria's conquest was that the lands involved were not part of the European mainland or islands lying immediately off the European coast. In accepting and legitimizing Doria's African conquests, Boniface was extending beyond Europe the traditional papal policy with regard to newly conquered or converted regions.

The basis upon which Boniface accepted Doria's conquests and made them a papal fief has been the subject of scholarly debate in recent years. Professor Luis Weckmann has argued that Boniface was acting according to the terms of the Donation of Constantine.[32] In his opinion, that famous eighth-century forgery granted lordship of all islands to the papacy. Weckmann has constructed his argument around a series of papal letters, stretching from the eleventh to the fifteenth century, involving jurisdiction over islands. The earliest examples of this power concerned the disposition of an island adjacent to Pisa and the Lipari Islands off Sicily in 1091, and the papal bulls involved specifically mentioned the Donation of Constantine as the basis upon which the pope was acting. The later bulls used by Weckmann to support his argument do not, however, explicitly mention the Donation. One of these, Adrian IV's *Laudabiliter*, authorizing the English invasion of Ireland in the twelfth century, justified the invasion on the grounds that the Irish had lapsed from the Christian faith, without mention of the Donation of Constantine.

Furthermore, the canon lawyers of the thirteenth century did not generally employ the Donation of Constantine when explaining papal authority over secular rulers. The Donation does appear in

Gratian's *Decretum*, but it was added after Gratian's death by a successor who completed the work. The canonists who commented on the *Decretum* made only a few glosses on the Donation.[33] They may well have found it embarrassing to derive papal authority from the gift of a secular ruler.

As a result, Boniface VIII, a lawyer as well as a pope, did not cite the Donation of Constantine when he granted the islands of Gerba and Kerkeni to Roger Doria. Like the other lawyers and popes of the thirteenth century, he found the Donation a weak basis for asserting papal authority. Instead, Boniface explained in his bull that he was granting these islands as a fief because the infidels who inhabited them threatened the security of Christendom. Doria had every right to seize the islands because no other Christian ruler possessed a legal claim to them. Doria's gift of the islands to the papacy and his subsequent acceptance of them as a fief legitimized his possession of them. The pope granted him and his heirs *merum et mixtum imperium*, full jurisdiction over the islands, as a consequence of the "apostolic plentitude of power." In turn, Doria was to hold the islands against the enemies of the faith and to work for the conversion of the native population to Christianity.[34] The terms of the award were similar to the terms by which the Teutonic Knights held their conquests. The principles of the just war as the popes and lawyers of the thirteenth century developed them, not the Donation of Constantine, governed papal policy toward land captured from infidels.[35]

The Teutonic Knights, Poland, and Lithuania

The conversion of King Mindowe of the Lithuanians did not have the results Innocent IV expected. Most important of all, Mindowe's conversion did not lead to the pacification of Christendom's northeastern border. Innocent assumed that his successors would complete the work begun by Mindowe's conversion with further efforts that would bring the Lithuanian population to the baptismal font. This did not, however, occur. Several factors impeded the expected missionary work, the most important of these being the conflicts between the Teutonic Knights and various groups of converts.

As a consequence of the crusades in northeastern Europe, the

Knights claimed possession of all lands occupied by infidels in that region. The papacy, however, was willing to exempt from the Knights' jurisdiction those areas whose inhabitants had voluntarily received baptism.[36] In 1256 Alexander IV informed the Polish bishops that infidels who had voluntarily accepted baptism were to receive from their Christian neighbors "protection and defense, notwithstanding any concessions previously granted by the Holy See to the Teutonic Knights in that area."[37] The pope limited the Knights' jurisdiction to those areas whose inhabitants had to be conquered by force of arms. In exempting voluntary converts from the Knights' power, Alexander was acting in accordance with Innocent IV's opinion that lands seized in the course of a just war could be retained by Christians. Infidels who signified their willingness to live at peace with Christians by accepting baptism secured their property and lordship from seizure by the Knights. The pope was not anxious to authorize the conquest of people who were no longer infidels even if, as the Knights appeared to think, they still posed a threat to Christendom.

Alexander's register contained several letters referring to the complexity of the situation in the northeast. Early in 1257 he wrote to the Dominicans and Franciscans working in Poland and the surrounding regions about the excommunication of the Knights by the papal legate because the Knights had seized lands in Prussia occupied by converts, an action that violated the agreements made when the infidels had become Christians.[38] In a letter to the Knights, Alexander reminded them of the terms governing their crusading efforts. He observed that the Culmans had become Christians through the efforts of Polish missionaries, and so the Knights could no longer claim jurisdiction over them.[39] This exchange of letters did not end the problem. The interests of all the parties involved, the papacy, the Knights, the Poles, and, of course, the converts, remained in conflict.

Mindowe's conversion also provided a new problem for the papacy regarding the possession of conquered territory. The Lithuanian king sought papal recognition of the conquests he had made in Russia, fearing that unless the papacy legitimized Lithuanian possession of the area, the Knights would claim those lands for themselves on the grounds that infidels dwelled there. Alexander did as Mindowe requested, observing that the Lithuanians had seized the lands in question from infidels who were the enemies of the Christian faith. Now that a Christian ruler claimed the area, the Knights had no right to it.[40]

Innocent IV's successors learned that the work of pacifying the northeastern border of Christendom raised problems similar to those found along its other borders. In 1262 Urban II complained about Christian merchants who were selling arms and war materials to the infidel Livonians in violation of a long-standing prohibition.[41] The condemnation was modeled on the ban on such trade with the Moslems.

Urban IV also faced the possibility that various groups living along the northeastern border might combine against Christendom. In a letter to the king of Bohemia he noted the threat of an alliance between the Lithuanians and the Tartars, which the schismatic Ruthenians might also join. Unless the Lithuanians remained in the fold, an unholy alliance of lapsed Catholics, schismatics, and infidels might overrun northeastern Europe. Poland would be the immediate object of such an assault, and so the pope hoped that Christian warriors would flock to that kingdom's defense. As an inducement for the king of Bohemia to join the work of defending Poland, Urban pointed out the advantages that would accrue to the victors. Lands taken from the Ruthenians and the Lithuanians by Bohemian armies could be retained by the king unless the Teutonic Knights or some other Christian ruler had a prior claim on the lands.[42] The pope added his prayer that the constant wars with the enemies of the faith on the borders of Poland and Bohemia would eventually end successfully. In another letter, the pope described the infidels of the region as "sheep without a shepherd," language reminiscent of Innocent IV.[43] Like his predecessor, Urban IV saw the solution to the military problems along the borders of Europe as depending upon the conversion of the infidels and their inclusion within Christ's flock under the headship of the pope.

The problems of northeastern Europe received little papal attention during the remaining years of the thirteenth century. Clement IV did encourage the Bohemians to keep up the fight against the infidels, and he confirmed earlier papal grants of captured infidel lands to them.[44] The conflict between Christians and infidels continued without reaching a permanent resolution because the infidels resisted both conquest and conversion. The conflicting interests of the various Christian parties in the area blocked the creation of a united Christian front against the common enemy. In 1299 Boniface

VIII found himself making peace between the Teutonic Knights and the archbishop of Riga after the Knights had seized lands belonging to the archbishop.[45]

The Tartars

During the last half of the thirteenth century, Christian contacts with the Tartars increased, and so did skepticism about their motives. At the same time, optimism about the possibility of converting them declined. Tartar khans continued to propose alliances with the Latins against the Moslems, but the papacy appears to have become increasingly wary of alliances with them.

The possibility of a Christian-Tartar alliance appeared as early as 1248, when a representative of the great khan visited Europe. Louis IX of France, Saint Louis, whose enthusiasm for crusading exceeded his success in battle, became interested in such an alliance.[46] The goal would be the reconquest of the Holy Land. He sent a party of friars to meet with the great khan and work out the details of an alliance. The result disappointed the king. What he had seen as an alliance between equals for specific common goals, the Tartars saw as the submission of the Europeans to Tartar domination.[47] Recalling their experience with the small Christian states of Asia, the Tartars assumed that the western ruler sought the vassal status the Armenians and Georgians had accepted. These small states, fearing Moslem domination, allied themselves with the Tartars only to be reduced to vassalage. The great khan no doubt believed that the same fear of Moslem domination would force the Latin Christians to make the same choice if they wished to survive. In the light of the numerous failures of Latin armies in the crusades, the Tartars had reason to assume that Louis IX would do as his Armenian and Georgian counterparts had done.

Some years later, the Tartars offered an alliance to Bela IV (1235–70) of Hungary. Situated as he was on the edge of the Tartar empire, he found it much harder to refuse the Tartar proposal. The Tartars suggested a marriage alliance, uniting one of Bela's children with a member of the khan's family. King Bela informed Pope Alexander IV of the offer and requested advice. The pope responded in a lengthy letter in which he admitted the precariousness of the Hungarian position and recognized that the

Hungarians had received little help from their brethren in the West; nevertheless, the king should not despair in spite of the pope's inability to send more than consoling words to assist him. The pope feared not only the marriage alliance but also the clause in the agreement requiring Bela to provide troops for the Tartar army. Such troops would join contingents from Armenia and Georgia in attacks upon their fellow Christians. In Alexander's view, such an alliance was only a ruse whereby the Tartars would enslave the Hungarians.[48]

Alexander's basic reason for counseling avoidance of alliances with the Tartars was that they could not be trusted. The oaths that both Tartars and Hungarians would take to seal an alliance would have no meaning because the infidel Tartars would not feel bound by oaths sworn on Christian relics: "Infidels, since they do not possess the true faith, certainly cannot be bound" by oaths whose sanction was the judgment of the Christian God.[49] In addition, the pope observed that the different conceptions of marriage in Tartar and Christian societies meant that a marriage alliance binding Tartars and Hungarians offered no guarantee of security for the Hungarians.[50] For the Hungarians, the proposed alliance could only be disastrous or, as Alexander phrased it, "an outrage to your Creator."[51] The pope's letter concluded on a more practical note, with the promise of aid for the beleaguered Hungarians.

Underlying Alexander's rejection of alliances with the Tartars was an increasing awareness of both the Tartars' intentions and the cultural differences dividing Tartar and Christian societies. Although papal letters of this period made few direct references to specific cases of Tartar deceit, the experience of the eastern Christian kingdoms in the face of Tartar expansion obviously warned the papacy to move carefully in establishing relations with the Tartars.[52] The experiences of the Georgians and Armenians, as well as Louis IX's negotiations, could only reinforce the fears about Tartar intentions that the khan's letter to Innocent IV must have generated. The Tartars were clearly bent on conquest, and they were as willing to conquer by deceit as by the sword. Furthermore, Alexander's objection to an alliance with the Tartars had echoes of Hostiensis' argument about *dominium* not existing outside of the Church. In Alexander's mind, true faith in an alliance could not exist on the part of an infidel signatory of a treaty with Christians. As for marriage, the Tartars corresponded to the canonistic cliché that all infidels were polygamous.[53] Furthermore, they married within the forbidden degrees. The defects of marriages among infidels symbolized the weakness of alliances with them: the strength of a diplomatic alliance between Christians and infidels was only as great as the strength of the marriage bond uniting representatives of the two societies.

The cumulative effect of experience with the Tartars during the thirteenth century may have contributed to the increasing emphasis upon reaching the infidels through missionaries rather than through diplomats. Once the Tartars, or any other infidel people, became Christians, then diplomatic alliances would be possible. Without baptism, however, the infidels could not be trusted to keep their engagements with Christians.

Thus, when Alexander IV did attempt to develop further contacts with the Tartars, he continued to use friars and emphasized that theirs was a religious mission. In 1260, for example, the Dominican David of Ashby went to visit the court of the il-khan, or lesser khan, of Persia, Hulagu (1256–65), whose success in fighting the Moslems had attracted the interest of the papacy.[54] Eventually the il-khan responded to Alexander's interest by dispatching an embassy to the West. Alexander had died by the time the embassy arrived, and so the envoys presented Hulagu's letter to the new pope, Urban IV. Although the proposed alliance was never consummated, this exchange of representatives marked the beginning of continuous contacts between the West and the il-khans lasting into the fourteenth century. In this case, a true alliance between equals seems to have been the Tartars' goal because the il-khan was expanding his power at the Moslems' expense. In order to win domestic support for his policy, the il-khan had allied himself with the Christian inhabitants of his domains. He had opposition in this policy from the khan of the Kipchaks, who favored the Moslems and persecuted the Christians in his domains. For Hulagu, an alliance with the eastern Christians that would counterbalance the Kipchak-Moslem alliance would be very useful. The pope could not have known of the machinations within the Tartar world, and the West never appreciated the opportunity Hulagu's predicament offered.

Hulagu's death did not end the talk of alliance. His son Abaga's (1265–82) marriage to a daughter of the Byzantine emperor Michael VIII Palaeologus was a sign of his desire for Christian support against the Moslems.[55] In the first year of his reign, the new il-khan dispatched a mission to the West. The envoys eventually reached Clement IV's court, but nothing seems to have come of the mission. Any letters exchanged do not appear in Clement's registers.

The complexities of Christian-Tartar relations came out clearly at the Second Council of Lyons in the summer of 1274. One of the announced reasons for calling the council was to raise troops for the defense of Hungary against the Tartars. On the other hand, Abaga sent representatives to the council seeking Western Christian support for the il-khan's policies. As evidence of their master's desire for an alliance with the West, the envoys received baptism.[56] By this act, Abaga's representatives eliminated what Alexander IV had seen as a fundamental obstacle to alliances with the Tartars. As members of the Church, the il-khan's envoys could enter into alliance with the Christian nations of the West as equals.

In accepting baptism as a preliminary to an effective alliance, Abaga's envoys were only following in the footsteps of Michael VIII Palaeologus, who had previously signed the Act of Union designed to end the schism between Eastern and Western churches.[57] Submission to Rome was the price for the military aid against the Moslems that both the emperor and the il-khan desired. In the long run, the papacy's interest lay in the inclusion of all men within the fold of the Church. The immediate situation of the Greeks and the Tartars was thus seen as providential because the papacy could hold out the promise of military support in return for the conversions of the emperor and the il-khan. Ironically, as the papacy became less able to provide military aid for the Greeks and others who sought it, popes seem to have become more insistent on submission to the papacy before making promises of aid they could not provide.

We may wonder whether Abaga and Michael VIII Palaeologus ever fully appreciated that the papacy's major interest was in their souls and those of their subjects. Did they ever realize that the proffered military alliances were only means to an end? The Greeks, of course, often complained about the willingness of the papacy to take advantage of their situation to impose ecclesiastical unity as the price for aid against the Moslems, but they may not have grasped the nature of the papacy's interest. This is not to say that the papacy was uninterested in stopping the Moslem advance; Gregory X was obviously quite interested in doing just that when he called the Second Council of Lyons. As matters turned out, it was easier to promise spiritual salvation, through baptism or ecclesiastical reunion, than it was to provide military salvation through successful crusades.

Even within the ecclesiastical sphere, where, presumably, the papacy's supremacy was secure, there were serious obstacles to missionary efforts among the reunited and the recently baptized. Few clerics appear to have been willing to journey to the East in order to complete the conversion of infidels. The most obvious example of this problem appeared when the Polo brothers brought to Rome the khan's request for a hundred wise men from the West. After overcoming a number of obstacles, the Polo brothers began the return trip to China with two friars, both of whom refused to venture into the Tartar-dominated regions when the travelers actually reached them.[58] Even under the best of circumstances, it was difficult to find an adequate supply of missionaries willing to make the long trip into the unknown. The widely publicized stories of those who did make the trip and whose reports have appeared in print may lead to overestimating the numbers of missionaries who actually went eastward.

Nicholas III's pontificate (1277–80) saw a revival of interest in the mission to the Tartars. Apparently responding to Abaga's initiatives, a number of Franciscans went to the East bearing a papal commission to reconcile schismatics living in the il-khan's dominions with the Latin Church. Abaga had sent new envoys to the West, intending them for the court of the short-lived Pope John XXI (1276–77). Instead, Nicholas received them on their arrival and, as the il-khan had requested, sent new missionaries to Persia.[59] The letters Nicholas sent with the missionaries illustrated the current view of papal relations with the East. He pointed to the long history of missionary efforts in the East, hoping that the present missionaries would climax the years of effort with the conversion of the Tartars in Persia. Perhaps to encourage the missionaries, Nicholas told them that, according to Abaga, the great khan himself was already a Christian.[60] With this hopeful sign, the pope looked for the final ripening of the Christian harvest of souls in Asia. Such was Nicholas' optimism that a new diocese was erected there to administer the spiritual crop that the missionaries were expected to harvest in the near future.[61]

Papal letters also went out to Abaga and to the great khan, introducing the missionaries and seeking official support for their work. To the il-khan's request for an alliance to sweep the Moslems out of the Holy Land, the pope responded with a discussion of the need to baptize Abaga's subjects. Either Nicholas realized that he could not make any serious commitments to provide military forces for such an alliance, or he was skeptical of the il-khan intentions. These hesitations did not, however, stop the pope from making a request of Abaga. He asked that the missionaries be given safe conduct to enable those who planned to visit the great khan to do so.[62]

Like earlier travelers to Peking, the friars carried a letter introducing them to the khan and explaining their mission. It also contained a basic statement of Christian doctrine, modeled on Innocent IV's letter *Dei Patria*, which John of Plano Carpini brought to the khan. The letter outlined the nature of Christ's redemptive mission and explained the pope's responsibility as Christ's vicar for the salvation of all men. Nicholas went on to tell the great khan that he was writing because Abaga had informed him of the khan's desire to receive baptism.[63]

Nicholas' hopes for the khan's conversion were obviously not based on an accurate knowledge of the situation either in Persia or in China. Abaga's willingness to admit Christian missionaries and the baptism of his envoys to the West misled the pope. This was not unusual; papal letters often displayed a great optimism about the conversion of infidels that reflected not experience but hope. Furthermore, in the case of Nicholas' mission to the East, the hope of converting the khan was soon dead.[64] The il-khan himself was disappointed at the lack of specific proposals for a Christian-Tartar alliance. Perhaps the failure of the missionaries to obtain the safe-conduct the pope requested for the remainder of their journey was Abaga's response to a pope who asked for assistance without giving any in return.

Upon Abaga's death, civil war broke out in his domains. Eventually, the victor, Arghun, renewed contacts with the West, sending an embassy in 1285.[65] He wrote a long letter to Pope Honorius IV (1285–87) outlining a plan, attributed to Kublai Khan (1260–94), for a general attack on the Moslems in the Near East, in which he hoped the pope could arouse European interest. The rosy picture of a Near East free of Moslems was only part of the letter. There was also an undertone that may well have struck the pope as ominous. The new il-khan hinted that the Tartar universal mission took precedence over the papacy's claim to a universal mission. In the Tartar's opinion, God had destined them to take the Christians under their protective wing, a response similar to that which Innocent IV had received from the khan.[66] Not surprisingly, nothing seems to have come of this mission. Contact between the papacy and the Persian court broke off until the pontificate of Nicholas IV (1288–94).

Nicholas IV's reign was the high point of papal-Tartar relations during the thirteenth century. For a moment the decades of contact seemed about to flower. Again the impetus for alliance came from the East, not from the West: like Innocent IV's other successors, Nicholas IV seemed inclined to act only if the Tartars took the first step. This time, Rabban Sauma, a Nestorian priest, headed an embassy from Persia. The priest, whose previous adventures had brought him from Peking to Persia, visited Rome and went on to visit the French and English royal courts, eventually returning to Persia bearing letters for Arghun and the members of his family.[67] These letters did not offer any military aid to the il-khan; instead, following the practice of previous popes, Nicholas sent doctrinal statements designed to inspire the il-khan and his family to accept baptism.[68] The question of a grand alliance against the Moslems was avoided.

In 1289 Nicholas IV initiated one of the most famous missions to the East when he commissioned the Franciscan friar John of Monte Corvino to visit China. In doing so, the pope was no doubt working on the assumption that the khan was seriously interested in Christianity. What he did not know was that the khan had shown a similar interest in other religions as well.[69] The mission may also have been the eventual papal response to the khan's request, transmitted through the Polo family, for wise men from the West to visit his land. John of Monte Corvino took with him the usual letters of introduction to various Tartar leaders. The message contained in them was a purely religious one; Nicholas did not include any promises of military or diplomatic aid against the Moslems. The letters addressed to Arghun indicated that the new mission was the result of reports concerning the il-khan's interest in Christianity and contained some information about the background of the mission that explained the pope's interest in the matter and something of his knowledge of the situation in the East. The letter suggested that John of Monte Corvino had actually instigated the mission.[70] Nicholas received the proposal with interest because he recalled the earlier mission of Rabban Sauma.[71] Thus, Monte Corvino's mission, in an indirect way at least, could be traced to earlier Tartar initiatives, not simply to papal interest in missionary work. Elsewhere, Nicholas informed Arghun that Monte Corvino had described his warm reception in Persia and so encouraged the pope to dispatch this new mission.[72] The body of the letter to the il-khan also contained the usual restatement of Christian doctrine, the kind of statement the il-khan had seen all too often before. Confident about the eventual conversion of the il-khan and his subjects, the pope asked him to assist Monte Corvino on his way to the great khan's court at Peking.

John of Monte Corvino reached Peking only after the great khan, Kublai Khan, had died in 1294. As a result, the friar presented his letters from the pope not to a khan noted for his interest in Christianity but to his successor, Timur (1294–1307), an unknown quantity. Although the new khan proved tolerant of the friar's work, he lacked the personal interest in Christianity attributed to Kublai Khan. As in previous letters, Nicholas emphasized Monte Corvino's work as a missionary, not as a diplomat. The friar was interested only in the Tartars' souls. The letters made no proposal for an alliance against the Moslems.[73] In another letter, addressed to Kublai Khan's nephew, Caydo (d. 1298), the pope stressed Christ's universal redemptive mission and the pope's responsibility for completing Christ's work among men.[74] Clearly, the papal hope, like that of the Jesuits centuries later, was that once the leaders of the society became Christians, the remainder of the population would follow suit.[75] Nicholas' expectations about the imminent conversion of the Tartars were encouraged by the widespread belief that the upper ranks of Tartar society were already infiltrated by Christians or individuals sympathetic to Christianity.

In 1291 Nicholas sent another series of letters to the East. This time the pope concentrated his efforts on converting Arghun. The initiative for this activity seems to have come once more from the Persian court, whose leaders had not yet given up all hope of an alliance with the Latin West against the Moslems. As for Arghun's expressed hope for an alliance with the West, Nicholas had referred the request to King Edward I of England.[76] The pope's interest lay in the work of salvation, not in military affairs. Nicholas also addressed letters to Arghun's sons and their wives. The wives were apparently already Christians, Nestorians in all probability, and so the pope saw them as his natural allies in the missionary effort. In a letter to one son, the pope stressed Arghun's well-known inclination toward Christianity; in addition, Nicholas observed that one of Arghun's sons had already become a Christian, taking the name of Nicholas at baptism.[77] The only inducement the pope held out to the potential converts was the hope of eternal life, the reward of Christians. In another letter, this time to his namesake, Nicholas encouraged the convert to use his influential position to spread the faith among the Tartars of Persia.[78] To assist the neophyte, the pope included in this letter a basic statement of Christian doctrine, such as was generally given to missionaries working among schismatics and heretics. In this case, the pope may have been anxious to insure the orthodoxy of the convert's teachings as he strove for the conversion of his own people: there was the obvious danger that the convert, swept away with enthusiasm, would fail to appreciate the differences between the Latin Church and the Nestorians or other Christians he encountered. Should this happen, the papal mission would then only have spawned another schismatic community.

Nicholas also appears to have had some awareness of the practical difficulties involved in converting infidels to Christianity. He warned his Tartar namesake to refrain from insisting that his converts make significant changes in the external style of their lives, and pointed especially to changes in dress as something to avoid. He emphasized to the potential missionary to the Tartars of Persia the importance of not seeming to require cultural changes along with baptism, "lest a basis for dissension and scandal develop against you among your people."[79] Given the delicate balance between pro-Christian and pro-Moslem factions among the Tartars in Persia, such advice was prudent. There was no need to fuel the conflict with evidence that conversion to Christianity required accepting European styles of dress and culture as well. Nicholas' warning may have been linked to some knowledge of the Tartar disdain for the Nestorians who lived among them. The pope's suggestion was to emphasize that one could be both a Christian and a Tartar. If baptism required living and dressing like the despised Nestorians, the Tartars would not be likely to listen to the missionaries.[80]

The gradual slide of the Hungarian kingdom into the Tartar orbit gave Nicholas further reason to encourage the conversion of these infidels. Hungary could survive if only the Tartar pressure on Christendom's eastern flank was lessened. Nicholas was well aware of the difficult choice facing the Hungarians. In 1288 he wrote to King Ladislas IV, warning him not to accept an alliance with the infidel Tartars as the price for saving the kingdom. The Tartars were known enemies of the Christian faith who could not be trusted. If Ladislas did not turn away from the proposed alliance with the Tartars, and if he did not take back the wife he had repudiated, the pope promised that the next crusade against the Tartars would have as a secondary goal Ladislas' deposition for being an ally of those who would destroy Christendom.[81]

With Nicholas IV's death, papal interest in the eastern mission came to an end. This was due to the lengthy interregnum following his death in 1292; there was no pope, except for the few months of Celestine V's pontificate, until the election of Boniface VIII late in 1294.[82] Boniface's preoccupation with matters of internal Church policy and with the struggle with Philip the Fair over the taxation of the French clergy blocked any strong interest he might have had in the eastern mission. Furthermore, the situation in the East was not encouraging.[83] In 1291 the last crusader foothold in the Holy Land, Acre, fell to the Moslems. Boniface did call for a new crusade, and he did write to yet another band of Dominicans who were setting off for the East.[84] These activities were expected of a pope, but in Boniface's case, the interest seems perfunctory. One sign of a lack of interest on his part was the absence of any mention of John of Monte Corvino in Boniface's letters and his failure to send additional missionaries to support the great work in which the friar was engaged.

Conclusion

In the five decades following Innocent IV's death, the rudiments of a papal policy for dealing with infidels were emerging. The policy stressed missionary, not diplomatic and military, contacts, the infidels' conversion, not their martial situation. In the second place, the initiation of these missionary efforts depended upon the interest shown by the infidels themselves or, perhaps, that shown by potential missionaries interested in a particular area. The il-khans of Persia did more to encourage good relations between East and West than did any of the popes of this period. Finally, the papal policy reflected great fear of the infidels. The papacy feared not only the infidels dwelling outside of Europe—Tartars, Moslems, Lithuanians—but those within Europe—Jews and Moslems—as well. The result was a basic mistrust of the infidels, leading to the belief that alliances with them were not possible until they had become Christians. Thus, conversion logically had to precede alliance.

Even though the papacy could call upon an ever-increasing number of missionaries with firsthand experience of various infidel societies, and in spite of the occasional visits of infidels to the papal court, the papal letters of this period rarely reveal any accurate knowledge or understanding of the differences between Latin Christian and infidel societies. Nicholas IV's warning about the need to allow converts to continue to dress and act as they had done before baptism stands out precisely because it does reflect some awareness of the problems of cultural conflict that conversion could introduce.[85] The popes relied upon letters composed according to standard formulae to respond to infidels, and this practice allowed them little room to indicate an understanding of a specific situation.

The use of epistolary forumlae may also suggest a lack of continuity in papal relations with the infidels in these five decades. In the period between 1198 and 1254 there had been five popes, four of whom reigned for a total of fifty-two years. Between 1254 and 1304 there were fourteen popes, with an average pontificate of three and one-half years. The average length of these pontificates is even lower when the periods of interregnum are considered. As a result of this rapid turnover there was little opportunity for a pope to put his personal stamp on papal policy. Boniface VIII stands almost alone in being able, in the course of his lengthy reign, to put such a personal stamp on the papacy. Because pontificates were so brief, responses to unusual situations, such as letters from distant infidel rulers, had to follow earlier models simply because the pope had little personal experience in dealing with them. The role of the curial staff in such situations was therefore great. The result was the continual repetition of letters sent years earlier in what the curialists assumed were similar situations. By the end of the century the letters had acquired an almost archaic flavor.

The reduction of papal interest in the infidels to a formula did not mean corresponding reduction of papal claims to universal jurisdiction. Although such claims too were repeated in ritual formulae, they were no less serious than when they had first been uttered. The popes of the late thirteenth century continued to assert their responsibility for both those within the flock formed by the Church and those sheep as yet outside it. Their inability to implement the task assigned by Christ did not prevent them from continually asserting their desire to do so.

The strongest papal assertion of universal responsibility came near the close of this fifty-year period. Boniface VIII's famous bull *Unam sanctam* expressed the papal responsibility for the souls of all men in the starkest terms.[86] Too often scholars have interpreted this letter only in terms of Boniface's battle with Philip the Fair. *Unam sanctam*, however, did not deal directly with the specific issues dividing king and pope, but with a much broader issue: the threat the king's policies posed to the Church's essential unity. The language of *Unam sanctam* was the standard language popes and canonists had employed for a century to state the nature of the Church. In *Unam sanctam*, Boniface VIII placed a number of clichés about the Church end to end, intending that the French recognize that he was only asserting a traditional position.[87] Indeed, much of *Unam sanctam* had already appeared in Innocent IV's letter *Cum simus*, sent to the schismatic king of the Bulgarians in 1245.[88] Innocent was seeking the end of the schism and the Bulgarians' restoration to the body of the Church. Two decades after Boniface's death, John XXII (1316–34) reissued *Cum simus* to encourage the schismatic king of the Georgians to return to the Church's fold.[89]

Seen against the background of *Cum simus*, Boniface seems to have issued *Unam sanctum* to forestall a French schism. Thus, the bull focused not on the specific issue of ecclesiastical taxation but on the evil effects that Philip's claims would have upon the Church, the seamless cloak of Christ. In the minds of Boniface and his staff at least, schism must have appeared to be a real possibility. There had been previous schisms headed by German antipopes in the course of the medieval papal-imperial conflicts, battles well known to Boniface and his associates. More recently, the papacy had been involved in dealings with the schismatic Greeks, Armenians, and Georgians, each of whom represented a schism of long standing. Boniface and his contemporaries recognized the difficulty of ending a schism once it was fully established. The failure of the various celebrated ecclesiastical reunions of the thirteenth century must have impressed the papacy with the difficulty of restoring unity once it was lost. Thus, when the pope reminded the king that there was no salvation outside of the Church, he was not only firing a salvo in the running battle over the rightful jurisdictions of the two powers; he was asserting the nature of papal responsibility everywhere. *Unam sanctam*, then, was part of the papacy's effort to force recognition of its universal spiritual responsibility, not simply a vain attempt at obtaining assent to a theory of papal jurisdiction in secular affairs.

Thus, *Unam sanctam*, though ostensibly part of the medieval Church-State conflict, has broad significance for papal relations with infidels and schismatics. Although Boniface's pontificate contained little indication of a strong personal interest in the eastern mission, Boniface's words provided a striking statement of the basis upon which the mission stood. Ultimately, the papal interest in the infidels was spiritual in nature. To be sure, the language of *Unam sanctam* sounds outrageous in light of the papal inability to convince Philip the Fair of the dangers in the course he was pursuing or in light of the Latin inability to win over the Tartars during the thirteenth century. Nevertheless, Boniface's bull, too stridently perhaps, stated the papacy's own conception of the role Christ assigned to it. The wide gulf that separated the realities of papal policy from the rhetoric used to state these policies may never have been so clearly demonstrated as in Boniface VIII's issuance of *Unam sanctam*. Just as its claims failed to reflect the status of papal-French relations, so too, did they fail to reflect the status of papal-infidel relations.

SCHOLARS interested in European expansion have long argued that between the end of the Mongol mission in the early fourteenth century and the Portuguese capture of Ceuta in North Africa in 1415, Europe became isolated from the outside world. According to this argument, the medieval frontier had closed down by the mid-fourteenth century, not to reopen for a century.[1] Friederich Heer has even extended this argument about the physical constriction of Europe to Europeans intellectual and religious life as well.

> The continent which in the twelfth century was open and ex-
> panding by the mid-fourteenth century had become closed, a
> Europe of internal and external frontiers, where nations, states,
> churches (i.e. the various regional 'Gallicanized' churches) and
> intellectual systems already confronted one another—often in un-
> compromising and hostile attitudes—in the forms they were to
> retain at least until the mid-nineteenth century or even into the
> twentieth.[2]

The result of this line of argument is the conclusion that there was a sharp division between the medieval and the modern interest in the world beyond Europe. The medieval period of expansion may then be labeled an isolated forerunner of the great age of expansion that began with the conquest of Ceuta and flowered in the years following Columbus' voyages.[3]

The fourteenth century stands, then, like a desert, barren of interest for those concerned with the expansion of Europe. No one would deny, of course, that some evidence of European interest in the world beyond Europe's borders does exist for the fourteenth century: for example, the popularity of *The Travels of Sir John Mandeville* and *The Travels of Marco Polo*.[4] But the popularity of such travelers' tales does not in itself prove that such interest had any tangible effect on European contact with the outside world. The fact that Columbus possessed a copy of Polo's *Travels* annotated in his own hand is interesting, but it is not conclusive proof that knowledge of medieval travels in China strongly influenced Columbus.[5] Indeed, there is even stronger evidence indicating the failure of medieval travelers' reports to influence later missionaries. When the first Jesuits reached China in the sixteenth century, they did not know of their thirteenth-century Franciscan predecessors, nor did they know that an archbishopric once existed in Peking. They did not even realize that Marco Polo's Cathay was China; the journey in 1602–7, of a Jesuit lay brother, Benedict Goes, across northern India and into China along the route Polo described was required before this identification was made.[6] Even the Franciscan order appears to have forgotten about its heroic missionaries of the thirteenth and fourteenth centuries.[7]

Furthermore, the enemies of Christendom tightened the noose around Europe during the fourteenth century. The loss of Acre was not avenged. The one significant attempt at doing so, the crusade of Nicopolis of 1396, was a disastrous failure, reinforcing the opinion that Latin Christian initiatives in the eastern Mediterranean were dead.[8] The emergence of the Moslem Tamerlane's empire out of the remains of the Mongol empire further limited Christian missionary activities in the East. The political and ecclesiastical situation within Europe reflected additional weaknesses. The Black Death reduced the population by 25 to 50 percent, reducing the number of individuals available for missionary work as well as the pressure for land along the European frontier.[9] From 1305 to 1415, the Church was weakened first by the Avignon period of papal history and then by the Great Schism.[10] Internal and external circumstances contributed to pushing back the borders of Latin Christendom. The work of converting the infidels could clearly not be a major focus of papal attention.

All of these observations about the factors that limited European interest in the world beyond its borders in the fourteenth century are true. They do not necessarily prove, however, that European contact with the non-European world ended completely. What they do demonstrate is the increasing difficulty facing those Europeans who were interested in traveling eastward. While the Moslem and

Tartar pressure on Christendom's eastern flanks was increasing, Spanish and Portuguese crusaders were pushing successfully against the Moslems on the southwestern flank. The kings of Portugal, Castile, and Aragon may not have scored any glorious victories against the Moslems in the fourteenth century, but they were not forced to retreat from their earlier conquests, like the crusaders in the Near East. Likewise, the fourteenth-century popes may not have been very successful in converting the infidels and in raising crusades, but they did not stop asserting the traditional papal responsibility for the souls of infidels and the protection of Christendom. During this century, there was a decline in successful crusading and missionary activities in the Near East but a rising interest in those efforts when they occurred at the western end of Christendom. European expansion did not simply come to a close in this period; rather it gradually shifted its emphasis in response to the pressures in the East. The Portuguese capture of Ceuta in 1415 was not, therefore, a fortuitous event. It was the result of a century of activity in that area.

One way to appreciate the shift in interest is to view fourteenth-century contact with those beyond Europe from the papal perspective. The papal registers of the fourteenth century, whether at Avignon or at Rome, continued to reflect papal interest in the conversion of infidels and the defense of Europe from invaders. Furthermore, these registers continued to mention the existence of dioceses in the East, reminding curial officials of earlier missionary activities there. At the same time, these registers recorded the crusading efforts of the Spanish and Portuguese kings, reflecting papal interest in the shift of expansion to the south and west. From the center of the Christian world, the picture of expansion in the fourteenth century was mixed.

The most important evidence of papal interest in the lands beyond Europe during this century is a papal register devoted to "the business of the Tartars, the lands of *outre-mer*, infidels, and heretics."[11] For the most part, the papal registers are arranged chronologically, and so scholars interested in papal letters concerning a specific topic, addressed to a specific person or class of persons, and so on, must examine a long series of registers to discover the materials they seek. Furthermore, these registers do not contain copies of all the letters issued during a pope's reign, but only a selection of the letters regularly issued. Whether or not a copy of a particular letter was made for the register depended upon a number of factors. As a consequence, many papal letters survive not in the papal registers, but in the cartularies of those who received papal letters and in chronicles whose compilers for one reason or another chose to include such letters.[12] On the other hand, once compiled, the letters in the registers were not purged or edited, as is often the practice in modern bureaucracies.[13]

There are some exceptions to the general rule that registers were compiled as the letters were written and dispatched. Two topically constructed registers exist. The most famous is Vatican Register 6, a register containing letters concerning the disputed imperial election during the pontificate of Innocent III. This register has long been known and examined.[14] Less well known is Vatican Register 62, misleadingly identified as "a collection of letters relating to the Tartars." The register's compiler identified its contents more broadly, stating that it contained "letters or other writings from the reigns of Clement V, John XXII, Benedict XII, and Clement VI which dealt with the business of the Tartars, the lands of *outre-mer*, infidels, and heretics."[15] The 191 letters and parts of letters that compose the main section of Vatican Register 62 were addressed to a wide range of rulers and ecclesiastical officials, including the Byzantine emperor, the kings of Georgia and Armenia, various Tartar khans and members of their families, as well as the rulers of the major European kingdoms. They deal with matters of ecclesiastical reunion, defense against the Tartars and Moslems, the conversion of the Tartars, and the other topics associated with papal interest in the Near East. In addition there are some letters dealing with the conversion of the Lithuanians and four letters concerning the conquest of the Canary Islands. Taken as a whole, Vatican Register 62 outlined the frontier of Christendom from the northeast to the southwest. The great majority of the letters dealt with areas and situations that had interested the papacy for two centuries or more. The inclusion of letters involving the first attempts to bring the Canary Islands under European domination foreshadowed increasing papal interest in newly discovered regions.

By linking heretics, infidels, and eastern Christians in a single sentence at the head of Vatican Register 62, the compiler was obviously creating a connection between this register and the missionary bull *Cum hora undecima*. The letters contained in the register had been sent to the leaders of the peoples listed in the salutation of the bull. Both the register and the bull demonstrated the wide range of papal interest in the non-European world. Vatican Register 62 gives the specific details about papal contacts with those outside of Latin Christendom, while *Cum hora undecima* only outlined potential relations. Furthermore, both the bull and the register blend together schismatics, heretics, and infidels as if the differences among them were less significant than the differences that kept each of these groups from membership in the Latin Church. There were no gradations of distance from the fold, at least to the compiler of the register: one was either within it or outside it. Vatican Register 62 reflected the increasing papal tendency to view the world as divided into two flocks belonging to Christ. The result was to assume that all those outside the Church could be approached in the same manner by Christian missionaries.

There is no indication in Vatican Register 62 about who compiled it, nor is there any information about when he compiled it or for what purpose. As the compilation of such a volume required access to the papal files and to the services of clerks to make the copies, the compiler must have been a senior member of the curial staff. It is even possible that a pope requested this compilation in order to see what his immediate predecessors had done concerning the nations living along the European frontiers. The date of the compilation and its purpose may be connected to the practice of carrying only some files with the papal court as it traveled from place to place.[16] Two of the popes resident at Avignon returned to Rome before the permanent return there in 1378: Urban V (1362–70) between 1368 and 1370; Gregory XI (1370–78), between 1377 and 1378.[17] Neither pope chose to remain there permanently, although Gregory XI died in Rome before returning to Avignon as he had intended. For both trips, the curial staff prepared sets of files to travel with the pope so that the regular work of drafting and dispatching letters could continue without interruption. It is possible that one of these popes ordered the preparation of Register 62 because returning to Rome meant a reassertion of the papal universal mission associated with the city of Rome itself. A pope who returned to Rome might wish to announce publicly his return by renewing the missions to the East and the calls for a crusade. Urban V, for example, emulated his great thirteenth-century predecessors by announcing the reunion of the Greek Church with the Latin when the Emperor John V Palaeologus traveled to Rome to submit in 1370.[18] There is another possibility that deserves mention. Vatican Register 62 may represent the desire of an official, or a group of officials, at the papal court to reinvigorate papal interest in the work of preaching to those of Christ's flock who were not yet members of His Church.

Although scholars have known of Vatican Register 62 for centuries, they have paid little attention to it. Generally, scholars have cited it only when pointing to locations where copies of the texts in the original registers may also be found.[19] When viewed as a whole, however, not simply as another source of individual letters, Vatican Register 62 provides a picture of papal relations with the world beyond Europe in the first half of the fourteenth century through the eyes of a contemporary papal official.[20] Furthermore, the compiler did not simply copy all the letters in the files relating to the peoples along the frontiers. He selected the letters he believed to be important, providing a more personal evaluation of papal policy than a collection containing every such letter would have provided.

The existence of Vatican Register 62 reveals the desire of the popes at Avignon to follow in the footsteps of their thirteenth-century predecessors. At one time, scholars were inclined to see the Avignon period as marking a sharp break with the style and aims of the papacy during the previous century. One writer, for example, emphasized the "shameless subservience to France of the papal court at Avignon."[21] This, of course, was in contrast to the arrogance of the thirteenth-century popes in their dealings with kings and emperors. In recent years, some scholars have begun to point to the continuity between the policies of the popes at Avignon and their thirteenth-century predecessors. Above all, the papal residence in Avignon, once seen as exemplifying the weakness of these popes, has been placed in proper perspective. During the twelfth and thirteenth centuries, the popes lived outside of Rome much of the time. The lengthy papal stay at Avignon was different only in that the popes spent so much time in one location outside Rome.[22]

Even more important is the fact that the fourteenth-century popes were not very different from their thirteenth-century predecessors. Like them, the popes at Avignon often had legal training and saw themselves as following in the footsteps of the canonist-popes such as Innocent III and Boniface VIII. Clement V (1305–14) and John XXII (1316–34) added volumes to the *Corpus iuris canonici,* and Innocent VI (1352–62) was a noted law teacher before becoming pope.[23] In addition, these popes were served by a staff of legally trained officials just as the popes of the thirteenth century had been. The pope's role as the supreme judge of all Christians, a role the canonists of the thirteenth century had developed, flourished exuberantly in the court at Avignon. One measure of this growth is the number of papal registers from the fourteenth century. Whereas the surviving papal registers for the thirteenth century total only forty-seven volumes, the pontificate of John XXII alone produced fifty.[24] The seventy-seven volumes produced in the reign of Clement VI (1342–52) include over eighty-six thousand items.[25] While all of these letters do not, of course, concern judicial matters, the bulk of them do. The increasingly legal and judicial preoccupations of the papacy shaped the character of the Avignon papacy far more than did some supposed subservience to the king of France. These legal and judicial interests were a major part of the legacy of popes like Innocent III and Boniface VIII.

The Tartars

The popes at Avignon continued to perceive the Tartars precisely as their thirteenth-century predecessors had done. The advancing Tartar armies remained a serious military threat to the Christians of eastern Europe and those in Asia Minor. Moreover, the dream of converting the Tartars continued to tantalize these popes, and the hope of a great alliance between Christians and Tartars against the Turks was not yet dead. The letters in Vatican Register 62 considered briefly the Tartars' military threat to Christendom and did not deal with the possibility of a diplomatic alliance at all. These letters reflect the increasing papal emphasis upon the missionary opportunity that contacts with the Tartars provided.

The possibility that the Tartars would ally themselves with the Turks in the Near East concerned John XXII. In 1322 he noted that such an alliance had been formed to complete the destruction of the Armenian kingdom.[26] This was a frightening turn of events because for the past hundred years the Armenians and the Tartars had lived at peace. An alliance between the Tartars and the Turks would have posed a great danger to the eastern flank of Christendom. Although the pope could not provide any military assistance to the unfortunate Armenians, he may have believed that a strong show of interest in them would cause the Tartars to reconsider allying themselves with the Moslems.

Poland and Hungary also remained under constant pressure from Tartar armies. Benedict XII (1334–42) wrote to Usbech (1312–40), leader of the Golden Horde, which was then occupying Russia, asking him to end his raids against Poland and Hungary. At the same time, the pope admitted that the Tartars were not responsible for all of the conflicts along the frontier of Christendom. He suggested that if the Christian rulers who bordered the khan's lands attacked the Golden Horde, the khan should inform him so that papal pressure could be exerted on these Christian rulers to bring the dispute to a speedy, negotiated conclusion.[27]

For the most part, however, the letters contained in Vatican Register 62 deal with the conversion of the Tartars. These letters fall into three categories, reflecting three attempts to bring groups of Tartars to the baptismal font. The first consisted of letters that John XXII wrote announcing the appointment of a new archbishop of Peking in 1333. These letters went to the leaders of the Tartar empire. The second group of letters consisted of Benedict XII's correspondence with a Christian community within the Tartar empire that had written to him in 1333 seeking a bishop to serve it. The last group, also from Benedict XII, went to Usbech, khan of the Golden Horde, who had sent an embassy to Avignon seeking to alleviate Tartar-Christian conflict along the Golden Horde's borders with Poland and Hungary. The existence of these letters indicates the continuing papal belief that peaceful relations with the Tartars were possible. At the same time, these letters indicate that the initiative for contacts continued to come from the Tartar side.

The compiler of Vatican Register 62 chose to begin the story of papal relations with the Tartars with the appointment of a certain Friar Nicholas as archbishop of Peking in 1333. This was a curious starting point because that see had been established only in 1307, when two letters from John of Monte Corvino eventually reached the West. These letters informed the pope that the friar had indeed achieved his goal of reaching the great khan's court in Peking; unfortunately, he had arrived in 1294, after Kublai Khan had died. While Kublai was known to be interested in Christianity, he was succeeded by rulers who did not have such an interest. Furthermore, Monte Corvino had to labor alone during most of his first dozen years in Peking. His original companion on the journey had died in India before ever reaching China, and no one came from the West to replace him, even though the way to China was known to anyone who wished to make the journey.[28] For many years, the only other European in Peking was an Italian merchant residing there.[29] Eventually, another friar, Brother Arnold, a German, arrived in Peking and joined Monte Corvino in his work.

Fearing that the work of converting the Tartars would not be accomplished without further assistance from the West, Monte Corvino asked his brethren to send additional friars for the mission in China. These letters, written in 1305 and 1306, informed his superiors that he had indeed reached Peking and was alive and well, though feeling old age upon him. He described his missionary work in optimistic terms and declared that but for the opposition of the Nestorian clergy, he would have made even more converts. As it was, he had reconciled a Nestorian chief of the Ongut Tartars to the Latin Church, resulting in the restoration of many of the chief's subjects to the Latin fold as well. Monte Corvino also claimed to have made 6,000 converts in Peking itself and to have built a church for the Christians there. The converts would have numbered 30,000, he added, if the Nestorian clergy had not interfered with his work.[30] In spite of this glowing report about the flourishing state of Christianity in the capital of the Mongol empire, Monte Corvino's letters also indicate that he was exaggerating his success. He described a small Christian community that he had created by purchasing forty young boys and then raising them as Christians. They prayed together daily and recited the divine office. His major success was among this small body of youths he had purchased.

The arrival of these letters from John of Monte Corvino after so many years must have come as a great surprise to his superiors. When Clement V learned of the letters, he responded by appointing Monte Corvino archbishop of the newly erected see of Peking and sending several friars to work with him in the great task of converting the Mongol empire to Christianity.[31] In terms of the number of missionaries involved, the mission to China reached its peak in the early years of the fourteenth century.

Yet Vatican Register 62 made no mention of this correspondence, neither Monte Corvino's letters nor Clement V's response. The letters the compiler chose to include—those dealing with the appointment of Friar Nicholas as Archbishop of Peking—do not mention Nicholas' predecessors. The letters of introduction the new archbishop carried to the great khan and other Tartar leaders described him as a learned and virtuous man whom the pope had selected from among the ranks of many such men for the office of archbishop. The letters also mentioned several other friars traveling with Nicholas who would assist him.[32]

The new archbishop headed a clearly religious mission. He was not designated to negotiate a treaty with the Tartars, nor was he empowered to discuss diplomatic issues with the khan. His only responsibility was the salvation of souls. The letters Nicholas bore contained the optimistic rhetoric of previous letters to the eastern infidels. John XXII explained to the khan that word of his interest in Christianity had reached the West; if only the khan would act upon this interest and receive baptism, eternal life would be his. The pope pointed to the journey of Friar Nicholas to Peking as a sign of papal interest in the Tartars' salvation, and compared the sending of Nicholas and his associates with Christ's sending of His apostles to preach the Christian message in the farthest corners of the world. Recognizing that the Tartars had extensive contact with Christianity through the numerous Nestorians in their empire, the pope was careful to distinguish between the Nestorians and the true Christians. He asked the khan to receive and protect those Christians who professed the doctrines that "the Roman Church, the teacher and mother of all those who believe in Christ, teaches, preaches and believes," for outside of that Church "there is no salvation."[33] The pope expressed the hope that the friar's words would move the khan and his subjects to become Christians.

John explained Friar Nicholas' mission in more detail in a letter to another Tartar leader. He explained that as all men belonged to Christ's flock, the missionaries were anxious to instruct them in Christian truths so that they might receive baptism and thereby achieve eternal life. Expanding upon the image of the Church as Christ's flock, John described the friars as seeking the souls of "all those others who dwell outside of the catholic and apostolic church and who wander about in darkness."[34] Friar Nicholas had come to bring the light of Christ to the spiritually dark world in which the Tartars so far had dwelled. Again, John expressed his hope that the Tartar rulers would lead their subjects to the baptismal font.

Finally, John addressed a letter to the Tartar people in general, introducing the missionaries and explaining his personal interest in their salvation. He appealed to both the good will and the spiritual self-interest of the Tartars everywhere. The friars brought the message of salvation that would insure eternal life for the Tartars if they believed.[35] In spite of this general address to the Tartars, however, John and his advisors assumed that the eventual success of the mission to the Mongols depended upon the conversion of the khan and those of his immediate household. They may have recalled the reunion of Nestorians to the Latin Church achieved by John of Monte Corvino, the result of the friar's successful effort to convince their leader, George, of the error of the Nestorian way.

As far as the compiler of Vatican Register 62 was concerned, papal interest in or knowledge of Friar Nicholas and his associates ended once the friars had departed on their journey to the East. In 1334 John XXII wrote to the Hungarians, encouraging them to stand fast in the face of the Tartar assaults on their borders. This letter indicated pessimism about the state of missionary efforts among the Tartars.[36] Such pessimism was, of course, part of the traditional rhetoric of papal letters in such situations. It may also, however, reflect real pessimism about the fate of Friar Nicholas. It is interesting that the compiler of Vatican Register 62 did not include this letter in his compilation, perhaps because he was not anxious to discourage those who would read his work.

In 1338 papal interest in the eastern mission revived when an embassy from the great khan Togan Timur (1332–70) arrived at the papal court. The envoys requested a successor for John of Monte Corvino, who had died some ten years earlier.[37] The members of this embassy were Alans, a people who originally lived on the Black Sea but who were now in the service of the khan. Their people had been converted to Christianity by Monte Corvino. The translator for the group was a European known only as Andrew the Frank. The Alans informed the pope that since Monte Corvino's death they had not had a priest to serve them.[38] They knew nothing of Friar Nicholas' mission, suggesting that he never reached Asia.[39]

Benedict XII responded to their request for a priest by sending a series of letters introducing Nicholas and his companions once more and praising the khan for the continuing interest he had shown in Christianity. In another letter from this series, Benedict expressed his appreciation to Chansi, khan of Turkestan, for having received Nicholas and his associates on their journey. According to the pope's letter, Chansi had allowed the missionaries to rebuild Christian churches that had fallen into disrepair and even to build new ones.

In addition, he had tolerated the missionaries' preaching in his lands. The pope added that if Chansi would send an embassy to the West, he would be happy to receive it at the papal court.[40]

The letters to Khan Chansi and the other rulers of Turkestan indicate that the papacy had closer ties with the Tartars in that region than elsewhere. In a letter addressed to two of the khan's familiars, Benedict referred to a plot of land the khan had granted to a bishop of the Franciscan order, apparently a friar named Richard of Burgundy, for the construction of a church in the city of Armalech, near the modern city of Kuldja (Ining) in western China.[41] The pope apparently knew that the church had actually been built. In a letter to Usbech, the pope referred to another new church constructed in lands the Tartars ruled; an unnamed Franciscan had built it in a city within the lands of the Golden Horde.[42] These references suggest that although the mission to the Far East had not been successful, the Tartar lands nearer Latin Christendom were comparatively hospitable to Christian missionaries.[43] They also suggest that the papacy had more knowledge of missionary efforts in the East than the papal archives would indicate.

Perhaps assuming that the Tartars' interest in Christian missionaries was more serious than it really was, Benedict may have seen a Christian age dawning in Asia. Buoyed by the willingness of the Tartars of Turkestan and the Golden Horde to allow missionaries to function and to build churches, he requested the great khan to allow missionaries to do the same in his domains. As usual, the pope held out the promise of eternal salvation to the great khan if he would only take the missionaries' words to heart and receive baptism.[44] In a letter to Prince Fodim, the leader of the Alan embassy that had initiated this series of letters, Benedict mentioned that he had requested the great khan to allow the exercise of Latin Christianity throughout the Mongol empire. Benedict added that the Alans should strive to remain fervent Christians. Their example would impel the great khan to move from interest in Christianity to conversion, and with him would come the entire empire.[45] The Alans were, then, to be the spearhead of the mass conversion of the Mongol empire.

Here again, however, the compiler of Vatican Register 62 omitted what would appear to be a significant aspect of papal relations with the Tartars in the fourteenth century: the sending of a papal legate to the East with the returning Alans. The legate, a Franciscan named John of Marignolli, traveled by way of Armalech, where he rebuilt a church and preached for a time. In 1342 he reached Peking, where he remained until, in 1347, he returned to the West by way of India. In 1352 he reached Avignon and, presumably, reported on the state of Christianity in Asia. It is possible that Marignolli's report on China discouraged further papal interest in the Far East. Even as he was leaving, the uprisings that culminated in the overthrow of the Tartar dynasty in China had begun. The legate may have realized that earlier reports about the imminent conversion of the East were greatly exaggerated and that whatever success Christianity experienced in Asia was directly connected with the toleration the Tartars extended to all religions. Consequently, the collapse of the Tartar empire would mean the collapse of Christianity there as well.[46]

The final group of documents in Vatican Register 62 concerning Asia dealt with further papal contacts with Usbech, khan of the Golden Horde. The papacy took special interest in this khanate because of the pressure it placed on the frontier kingdoms of Poland and Hungary. In addition, Italian merchants from Venice and Genoa were active in the Horde's lands; the khan had even made a trade agreement with them. As a result, this Tartar region was better known and understood in the West than any other, or at least so we may presume. In 1340 the khan sent two of his nobles and a Franciscan to Avignon. In responding to the embassy, Benedict XII restated many of the points made in the letters sent two years earlier, thanking Usbech for the favor he had shown to Christians, and adding, of course, that such favor should be shown only to Christians who belong to the Latin rite.[47] The pope appears to have feared the growth of Nestorianism, and so he stressed the differences between Nestorians and Latin Christians so that the khan's tolerance would not be exploited by the undeserving Nestorians.

Knowledge of events in Usbech's lands was apparent in some remarks Benedict made about the khan's Christian subjects. A recent unsuccessful plot against the khan's life had included only three Christians. This, Benedict suggested, was evidence of the loyalty of the khan's Christian subjects. The pope suggested that the khan view the early discovery of the plot as providential, a sign of the Christian God's favor toward him. Receiving baptism would be a suitable response to this sign of divine favor.[48] Other letters sent at the same time to the khan's wife and son stressed the spiritual advantages accruing to those who entered the Christian fold.[49]

At the same time, Benedict wrote to the missionaries working among the Tartars. Possibly buoyed by what seemed to be an opportune moment in the history of attempts to make converts among the Tartars, he encouraged the missionaries not to flag in their efforts. He also sent them a traditional statement of doctrine, which, he said, should be the core of their teachings. This part of the letter suggests that Benedict was worried about the orthodoxy of the teaching of missionaries who had been away too long from the main body of the Church.[50]

In spite of the optimistic language, however, the missionary efforts in Asia that attracted the interest of the compiler of Vatican Register 62 were not successful. John of Monte Corvino's enthusiastic description of the numbers of converts he had made must have seemed incredible to John of Marignolli when he visited Peking two decades after Monte Corvino's death.[51] What seemed to the missionaries to be Tartar interest in Christianity was only toleration or, more likely, indifference on the Tartars' part. They may have been afraid to offend the representatives of some unknown god. Benedict XII and his successors knew that at least the Tartars would allow the missionaries entry. Some sort of peaceful relations with them could be established as long as the work remained on the spiritual level and did not enter the realm of diplomacy, in which the Christians and the Tartars had conflicting interests. The letters in Vatican Register 62 stressed the pope's spiritual responsibility and did not offer military or diplomatic alliances; such ties were the responsibility of Christian secular rulers. To some extent, Vatican Register 62 stressed the optimistic side of papal responses to the eastern mission. Perhaps the compiler avoided discussion of John of Marignolli's journey because, as suggested above, he did not wish to discourage yet another attempt to convert the Tartars.

At Opposite Ends of Europe

What gives Vatican Register 62 its special character is not the selection of letters concerning the Tartars and the Moslems in the East; these nations were well-known threats to Christendom and had traditionally drawn papal expressions of concern for the security of the frontiers of Europe. So, too, the numerous letters in this register that concerned the schismatic Christian nations of the East reflected traditional aspects of papal policy. It was the handful of letters concerning the Lithuanians at one end of Europe and the inhabitants of the Canary Islands at the other that underscored the grand theme of the register, the state of Christendom along all of its borders with the infidels. For the compiler, the Christian frontier with the infidel stretched in a great arc from the southwestern corner of Europe, along the coast of North Africa, up into the Balkans, along the Hungarian border, ending at the shores of the Baltic, where the Teutonic Knights faced the Tartars and Lithuanians. One curious omission in Vatican Register 62 was the lack of letters concerning papal relations with North Africa. The compiler may, however, have believed that the letters dealing with the defense of Cyprus and Armenia from the Mamelukes of Egypt filled that gap; or he may have felt that the Moslem states to the west were no longer a serious threat to Christendom and therefore required no attention from him. Juxtaposing the letters in Vatican Register 62 that deal with the Canary Islands and those that deal with Lithuania provides an insight into the difficulties the Latin Church faced when the Church's interest in converting infidels conflicted with Christian secular rulers' desire to obtain their land. Although obviously the compiler could not have been aware of it, this problem was to be an increasingly important one for the papacy over the next two hundred years as Europeans turned away from defending the eastern frontiers and turned westward toward the infidel cordon around them.

The continuing papal efforts to complete the task of converting the Lithuanians encountered difficulties because of the constant pressure of the Teutonic Knights on that nation. John XXII reviewed the history of papally directed missionary efforts there in a letter to King Gedemin (1316–41) of the Lithuanians. He admitted that King Mindowe and his subjects had relapsed into paganism "because of the cruel and wicked actions of the Master and the knights" of the Teutonic order.[52] The Knights' greed for land had overcome whatever inhibitions they might have had about invading the new converts' territory. The Lithuanians now found themselves in the awkward position of being attacked by those who were supposed to be their brothers in religion. The converts were outraged by this turn of events.

John could provide only slight consolation for Gedemin and his subjects. Since he could not successfully order the Knights to halt their attacks on the Lithuanians, in effect he advised the Lithuanians to turn the other cheek, ignore the Knights, and focus their attention on defending Christendom from the Tartars to the east. The Lithuanians had, after all, become Christians, and so Gedemin "should act as other Christian rulers act," defending Christendom from its enemies.[53] The pope was seeking a buffer between Christians and Tartars. There is nothing in Vatican Register 62 to indicate how the Lithuanian ruler received this request. He did, however, move to remedy the split with the Church by allowing Dominican and Franciscan friars to function within his realm, thus beginning the task of reuniting with the fold those sheep who had strayed away.[54] As was usual in papal efforts to convert infidels, the pope emphasized the king's role in leading his people along the road of salvation, reversing the path that Mindowe had taken. The only practical contribution the pope could make was to send two legates to direct the missionary efforts already under way.

Although there was little to be achieved by appealing to the Teutonic Knights, John did write to them about the situation in Lithuania. He told them about the work of restoring the Lithuanians to the fold and ordered them to live at peace with the Lithuanians. The two papal legates sent to the Lithuanians were instructed to "deal with every issue" between Gedemin and the Knights that involved "the worship of God, the exaltation of the faith, the honor of the apostolic see, the well-being of the Church, and the salvation of the souls and the bodies of the poor."[55] These noble goals, however, did not blunt the Knights' desire to extend their authority over the lands of the converts. The salvation of the infidels' souls was of much less interest to the Knights than was the possession of their lands.[56] The Knights were impervious to the argument that their treatment of the Lithuanians was the major obstacle in the task of restoring the lapsed Christians to the Church's fold.

John's instructions to his legates in Lithuania summed up the situation there. He informed them of what he saw as Gedemin's desire for baptism and his willingness to achieve the reunion of his people with the Church.[57] According to the pope, Gedemin was prepared "to obey us in all things like other Catholic kings," once his differences with the Knights were resolved.[58] The legates were granted powers similar to those generally granted to missionaries in

Cum hora undecima. The instructions also included a statement of basic Christian doctrine so that the legates could insure the absolute fidelity of the converts and those whom the missionaries reconciled to the Church's teaching.[59]

The papal emphasis upon absolute fidelity in doctrine, as well as unity of ritual, in these letters involving the Lithuanians had a special meaning. Gedemin's subjects included not only infidels and lapsed Christians, but also a number of Ruthenians, who were schismatics belonging to the Greek Church. The missionaries had to contend with the attraction the Greek rite held for some of the king's subjects as well as with the attractions the infidel way of life held for others. Thus, the legates were reminded that unleavened bread must be used for the Eucharist and that polygamy was forbidden to Christians. These reminders in the letters to Lithuania, were not simply restatements of traditional form letters; rather, they related to the particular situation the legates were expected to resolve.[60]

In spite of John's interest in the reconversion of the Lithuanians, the work went slowly. The prompt and complete reunion of the Lithuanians envisioned in the pope's letters did not materialize. Twenty-five years later, Clement VI was still engaged in the task, but a new obstacle to the reunion had emerged in the person of King Casimir III (1333–70) of Poland, who had invaded Lithuania in 1344.[61] Clement reminded the king that the Lithuanians were now Christians and thus not lawful prey for Christian armies, because they no longer posed a threat to Christendom.[62] Furthermore, at their baptism, the Church had guaranteed that the Lithuanians' property and possessions would be secure from attack by other Christians. At the same time, it was clear that the work of conversion was moving slowly. The archbishop of Gniezno was ordered to send missionaries to instruct the newly baptized people in the rudiments of the faith.[63] The pope also wrote to Duke Kerstutim of Lithuania, assuring him of the security of his people from further Polish harassment.[64]

At the other end of Europe, the relationship between the conversion of the infidels and the desire of Europeans for more land was the opposite of that in Lithuania. When Luis de la Cerda, a member of Castile's royal house and admiral of France, sought to acquire the Canary Islands for himself, he explained to Pope Clement VI his intention to convert the infidel Canarians to Christianity.[65] According to four letters in Vatican Register 62 announcing Luis' intention and the pope's approval of the conquest, the prince's purpose in conquering the islands was to "eliminate their wicked pagan error so that the glory of the divine name may be praised there and the glory of the Catholic faith might flourish." In this case, territorial aggrandizement and ecclesiastical aggrandizement would go hand in hand. In order to make this possible, Clement had created "Luis prince of those islands together with a grant of temporal proprietorship and lordship of those islands." The title and the grant of authority were to be hereditary in the prince's family. The pope justified this grant on the grounds that Luis came from a family long known for its interest in spreading the faith.[66] In the pope's view, the conquest of the Canary Islands was being undertaken only for the noblest of motives.

The compiler of Vatican Register 62 gave no reason for including these letters in his collection. It might be interesting to consider him prophetic about the future course of European expansion, but there is no basis for such an opinion. The list of rulers to whom Clement sent copies of these letters does, however, suggest some reasons for the compiler's interest in the Canaries. The letters went to the kings of Aragon, Castile, Portugal, France, and Cyprus, as well as to the city of Genoa and to Humbert of Vienne. The last named was a perennial crusader who had earlier considered joining Luis de la Cerda in a joint expedition against the Moors in North Africa.[67] The recipients of the letters were precisely those individuals and communities that had a strong vested interest in Christian control of the Mediterranean. The letters hint at the use of the islands as a base from which the African mainland could be invaded by a Christian army. The pope described them as lying off the African coast, perhaps assuming that they were comparatively close to the mainland, just as islands in the eastern Mediterranean lay off the edge of the Moslem world.[68] As the latter could be employed to launch an invasion of the Moslem world, so too the Canaries could serve a similar purpose at the opposite side of Africa.

Nothing came of this first attempt to conquer the Canary Islands, and Luis de la Cerda and Humbert of Vienne turned their attention to other projects. The interest of the letters lies in the nature of the papal grant that Clement made to Luis. In another curious omission, the compiler of Vatican Register 62 did not include a copy of the bull *Sicut exhibitae*, which Clement issued in November 1344, granting the Canary Islands to Luis. The bull explained the basis on which he had awarded lordship of the Canaries to the Castilian. The islands were to be held as a papal fief, a *feudem perpetuum,* with Luis and his heirs exercising *merum et mixtum imperium et iurisdictionem omnimodam temporalem.* In turn, Luis and his heirs were to perform liege homage to Clement and his successors for the islands.[69]

Sicut exhibitae was similar to the bull issued fifty years earlier awarding the islands of Gerba and Kerkeni to Roger Doria. It was also similar to papal grants awarding lands taken from the infidels to the Teutonic Knights, and it even bore some resemblance to the papal letters recognizing Lithuanian jurisdiction over lands in Russia. In some of these cases, a pope had accepted lands conquered in a presumably just war from the hand of the conqueror and then granted the lands back to the conqueror as a papal fief. Roger Doria and Luis de la Cerda no doubt were anxious to legitimize their conquests, or potential conquests, by obtaining a powerful overlord whose protection would secure them from attacks by other Christian rulers anxious to extend their domains. In the situation involving Lithuanian claims in Russia, the land in question was not held as a papal fief. The pope had, however, legitimized the Lithuanians' conquest of the region, thus putting it off limits to other Christian rulers. In those cases where the Knights had conquered infidel lands in a just war, the papal letters also served to legitimize the conquest and protect it from attacks by other Christians.

The case of the Canary Islands was somewhat different from these. The Canarians were not a military threat to Christians. They were not even an implicit threat by virtue of being Moslems. They had not, so far as the pope was aware, forbidden entry to Christian missionaries. They were peaceful infidels, apparently not the legitimate objects of a Christian invasion. If this was true, then on what basis could the pope authorize the islands' conquest?

In the first place, the conquest of the islands did not depend on a papal initiative. Luis de la Cerda had approached the papacy with a proposal to conquer the islands and bring the inhabitants to the faith. Apparently the pope did not know that the Portuguese also claimed the islands. Acting on the assumption that there were no Christian claims, Clement authorized Luis to invade the islands. The only issue remaining was whether the planned conquest violated the rights of the natives. The pope seems to have assumed that the conquest was a just one, just as the Lithuanian conquest of land in

Russia was just. He may have assumed that the Canarians would not admit peaceful missionaries. Luis promised to support missionary efforts among the islanders. From the papal perspective, the Castilian's promise of support for missionaries meant that the papacy's prime responsibility, the salvation of souls, would be advanced if Luis ruled the islands. Clement may simply have placed spiritual interests ahead of legal consistency.

There is another point to consider, however, before coming to a conclusion about Clement's role in the conquest of the Canary Islands. What would have happened if the pope had not reacted favorably to the proposal to conquer the islands? His refusal to authorize the conquest, even if backed by a vigorous anathema, would have had little effect. Clement, like several of his successors, may have been inclined to accept the inevitability of a Christian conquest of the islands. Having done so, he may have acted to insure some papal role in their administration by accepting them as a papal fief: as overlord, he could order the removal of the fief holder if he ruled badly. Presumably, if Luis de la Cerda or his successors treated the Canarians inhumanely, the reigning pope could replace him with a more suitable Christian ruler.

Taken as a whole, the letters contained in Vatican Register 62 reflected the themes governing papal policy toward infidel societies for a century. The compiler created a picture of a papacy still anxious to extend the Church beyond Europe by reconciling the schismatics and converting the infidels. The popes of the fourteenth century continued to employ the rhetoric of their thirteenth-century predecessors. While modern scholars see the popes at Avignon as but pale ghosts of their mighty predecessors, the Avignon popes themselves did not seem to feel that way about their power. At the same time, they did not possess the drive that caused Innocent IV to open relations with the Tartars. The popes at Avignon waited for infidel rulers to approach them, or they waited for adventurous crusaders like Luis de la Cerda to propose conquests that would extend the Church. Furthermore, although the papal rhetoric had not changed, the possibility of successful papal intervention in disputes between Christian rulers for control of particular regions had declined greatly. Papal pronouncements could not protect the Lithuanians from the Teutonic Knights, nor would *Sicut exhibitae* protect Luis de la Cerda or his heirs if some stronger Christian ruler desired the Canary Islands.

Iｆ the compiler of Vatican Register 62 had hoped to inspire
more interest in extending Christendom's boundaries at the papal
court, he failed. There was no great revival of interest in the
Mongol mission, in the reconciliation of the schismatics, or in the
task of preaching the gospel in such infidel lands as the Canary
Islands during the last half of the fourteenth century. The problems
facing the papacy, of which the Great Schism beginning in 1378
was only one among many, would not allow any of these popes the
luxury of concentrating on the expansion of the Church.[1] The
survival of the Church within Europe was a more immediate problem. Nevertheless, the late fourteenth-century popes did not completely forget the Asian mission or the other efforts to expand the
Church. The papal files continued to record occasional missionary
efforts from the mid-fourteenth century onward.

The Mission to Asia

John of Marignolli's successful return from China in 1353 inspired the announcement of another mission to China. According to
the Franciscan tradition, Pope Innocent VI (1352–62) requested the
order to select several friars for consideration as bishops for this
mission. The pope was guardedly optimistic about the possibility
of establishing the missionary church in China on a more permanent
footing. The scheduled appointment of several bishops would suggest a growing number of converts in various parts of the empire.
Marignolli may have reported to the pope that the great khan was
seriously interested in Christianity, but this is difficult to accept.[2]
Missionaries and the chroniclers who wrote of their efforts routinely
made such statements to encourage further missionary efforts. Signif-

icantly, nothing is known about this mission's fate; in fact, the friars selected for it may never have left Europe. Nor is there any evidence that such a mission ever even left Avignon. In spite of occasional brave words, Innocent VI did not do much to renew the eastern mission.[3]

The pontificate of Urban V (1362–70), however, saw a strong resurgence of papal interest in converting the infidels and ending the schism between Eastern and Western churches. In 1363, for example, he mediated a dispute between the two archiepiscopal sees that had been created in the lands of the Golden Horde.[4] In 1364 he reissued two letters, first issued by John XXII, concerning the Dominicans' work in the missionary vicariates of Aquilonia and the Orient.[5]

The climax of Urban V's interest in converting the infidels came in the years 1367–70 when he returned the papal throne to Rome. Symbolically, the return to the traditional headquarters of the Latin Church announced a renewed emphasis upon the papacy's universal mission, a role associated with Rome and obscured by the long sojourn in Avignon. When the pope reconciled the Byzantine emperor John V Palaeologus with the Latin Church in 1369, he was reaffirming the pope's position as supreme head of the Christian church.[6] He was again following in the footsteps of the great thirteenth-century popes who had tried to end the schism.

Against the background of the papal return to Rome and the reunion of the Byzantine emperor with the Latin Church, Urban's efforts regarding the conversion of the infidels in the East take on special significance. At the end of 1369 he reissued *Cum hora undecima* to encourage the friars to expand their efforts.[7] He also showed his interest in the mission more tangibly by ordering that 1,000 ducats paid by a noblewoman for commuting a pilgrimage vow be sent to assist the friars in Tartary.[8]

In 1370 Urban reissued another traditional missionary bull of John XXII's, *Super gregem dominicum*, which contained a number of principles concerning the canon law of marriage.[9] It was to provide guidance for missionaries dealing with converts who were married within the degrees of relationship forbidden to Christians or who were polygamous. The core of this letter came not from John XXII's chancery but from Innocent III's, from the decretal *Gaudemus*, issued in 1201.[10] At that time missionaries in the Holy Land were having difficulties with potential Moslem converts to

Christianity whose marriages did not always conform to the canonistic standards. To ease the missionaries' task, Innocent III exempted such converts from the requirement of obtaining a dispensation before marrying within the canonically forbidden degrees of consanguinity and affinity. In effect, this meant that Moslems, and other non-Christians, who had married within the second to fourth degrees could retain their spouses after receiving baptism. It is striking, however, that in the century and a half following the publication of *Gaudemus*, no further development of canonistic thinking about the marriages of infidels occurred. When Urban acted to ease the path of such converts, he could only apply the principles that Innocent III had set down under rather different circumstances.

Urban took another, more decisive step regarding the infidels of Asia, when in 1370, he sent yet another mission to the East. He appointed a Franciscan, Friar William of Prato, as archbishop of Peking and sent several other friars to accompany him.[11] As usual, the pope armed the new archbishop and his associates with several bulls announcing their coming and introducing them to the local rulers. These bulls were also drawn from letters found in John XXII's register, suggesting that by the end of the Avignon period, his letters were the standard models used by his immediate successors when writing to infidel rulers. The letter *Fidelium novella plantatio*, for example, instructed the missionaries in the proper way to administer baptism to schismatics and infidels.[12] Clearly ignorant of the political situation in China following the ouster of the Mongol rulers in 1368, Urban also sent with the friars a modified version of John XXII's letter to the great khan, *Accedit ad tuae*.[13] Urban's letter, *Ad alti tui nominis*, enthusiastically repeated the earlier letter's description of the numerous converts awaiting the friars' ministrations.[14] The khan himself was to lead the Chinese people into the Church's fold. The remaining letters the friars bore were also modeled on letters John XXII had sent in 1333. One went to the leading officials of the Tartar empire; another to the Tartar people.[15] Their theme was the papal responsibility for the souls of all men.

There is no evidence, however, that the mission Urban sent to China was any more successful in reaching its destination than Innocent VI's mission in 1358 had been. Like the earlier mission, William of Prato and his associates left no trace of their activities. It is, of course, possible that the missionaries reached the outer edge of the Tartar world only to learn of the empire's collapse. The ouster of the Tartars from China and the break-up of the Tartar hegemony in central Asia meant that the highways across Asia were no longer as safe for missionaries as they had been when the Tartars dominated the region.[16]

The apparent failure of Innocent VI and Urban V to maintain the Christian Church in China did not mean the end of missionary activity among the Tartars. Missionaries continued to work among the Tartars who lived along the boundaries of Christendom at the end of the fourteenth century, as letters in the registers of Urban V and of Gregory XI (1370–78) show.[17] There seems to have existed the hope that once the political situation in Asia stabilized, missionaries would be able to pass through the lands of the Golden Horde and on into China. This hope, of course, was based on a lack of accurate knowledge about Asia within papal circles.

The difficulty of travel through Asia in the late fourteenth and early fifteenth centuries should not be exaggerated. It is true, of course, that there is little evidence of Europeans traveling through Asia in this period, but there is some evidence that such travel was quite possible. In 1403 two priests claiming to be Christians of St. Thomas from southern India arrived at Pope Boniface IX's (1389–1404) court.[18] In 1407 three more such priests visited Gregory XII's (1406–15) court.[19] The references to these visitors are hedged with some doubt about their authenticity: Boniface's letter said of the visitors that "they claimed to be" from India, recalling that the papacy had previously received visitors who were not what they claimed to be.[20] Nevertheless, the popes who received these visitors appear to have assumed such journeys were possible: persons claiming to have come from India would not automatically be accused of lying.

Furthermore, European travelers did journey through parts of Asia at about the same time as the priests from India visited Europe. Europeans visited the court of Tamerlane in the fifteenth century as Franciscans had traveled to the Tartar khan's court in the thirteenth, and as did a Castilian knight, Ruy de Clavijo, leading to the exchange of letters between that Asian ruler and the king of Castile.[21] Finally, the Franciscans continued to record the existence of convents in China among their houses as late as 1400, suggesting that they believed contact with China was still possible.[22]

If travel across Asia remained possible from the 1350's to 1415, then the Black Death's effect upon the European population might provide a reasonable explanation for the decline of missionary activity in those decades. This explanation assigns a major role in European expansion to population pressures: with the sharp decline in Europe's population after the Black Death, the interest in Asia declined.[23] This argument is not of much use here, however, because the missionaries were not inspired by the desire for new lands to occupy but by the desire to win souls for the Church. While the clerical population of Europe obviously declined in about the same proportion as the general population, this would not necessarily mean there were fewer clerics available to serve as missionaries; there is no evidence that the popes of the late fourteenth century found such a shortage. Even before the Black Death reduced Europe's population by as much as one-half, few missionaries seem to have gone to Asia. The careers of John of Plano Carpini, John of Monte Corvino, and William of Rubruck should not obscure the fact that the Polo brothers were unable to meet the great khan's request for a hundred wise men from the West. Only two friars began the return trip with the Venetians, and neither completed it. While it is clear that other friars visited the Far East, leaving only the barest hints of their travels, their numbers were small. Finally, friars were still available for missionary work close to Europe even after the Black Death struck.[24]

If neither the collapse of the Mongol hegemony in Central Asia nor the Black Death brought the Mongol mission to a close, what did? An obvious but overlooked answer is that Asian rulers no longer requested Christian missionaries to visit their countries. The papacy had not initiated most of the missions to the East during the thirteenth and fourteenth centuries; they had been sent in response to requests, either from infidel rulers or from individual missionaries who had a desire to work in a particular infidel region. Had the khan's successors requested missionaries, some probably would have been sent.

The Chinese rulers who succeeded the khans identified Christianity with the period of Mongol domination, and so they persecuted the remaining Christians.[25] Under such circumstances, more missionaries from the West would not have been welcome. The rise of Tamerlane, a Turkish Moslem, to power in the ruins of the Mongol empire was an even more significant obstacle to missionary activity in Central Asia.[26] Tamerlane saw no reason to encourage Christian missionaries. His ascendancy meant that the Christian-Moslem duel for the souls of the people of Central Asia was won by the Moslems. As Tamerlane's lands lay astride a major route to the Far East, the road to Peking was effectively blocked. Despite this setback, knowledge of the mission to China was never completely lost in the West, although contact between China and the West was broken.

Poland, Lithuania, and Russia

Although the Far East was no longer an object of major missionary interest in the last half of the fourteenth century, the northeastern border of Christendom remained an active missionary area. The struggles between the Teutonic Knights and the kingdom of Poland for domination of Lithuania continued to complicate the contest for the souls of the inhabitants. The papal letters of this period continued to voice fears about an alliance between the Poles and the infidels against the Knights along the lines of the proposed Tartar-Hungarian alliance. The Knight's expansionist policies continued to antagonize their Christian neighbors. The Polish rulers felt justified in seeking allies anywhere they could, even if it meant allying with the infidels against the Knights.

In 1353 Innocent VI wrote to the duke of Masovia in eastern Poland asking him not to allow schismatic Ruthenians or infidel Lithuanians under his jurisdiction to harass the Knights.[27] The pope noted that the Knights had complained in their turn about the interference of the duke's subjects with the order's campaigns against the infidels; according to the Knights' version of the situation, the duke's subjects had warned neighboring infidels about the Knights' military preparations and assisted those fleeing from the Knight's attacks. The pope wanted the duke and the other Christian rulers in the area to redouble their efforts to convert the Lithuanians in their domains to Christianity so that the borders of Christendom would be secure. This papal request seems to have had some effect, for in 1356 the duke of Masovia asked the Hermits of Saint Augustine to establish three communities in his lands. They were to work for the conversion of the remaining infidels among the Lithuanians and the reunion of the schismatic Ruthenians with the Latin Church.[28]

At the same time, Innocent VI wrote to the Master of the Teutonic Knights concerning Polish charges about the Knights' activities. The Knights were accused of attacking the kingdom of Poland, and working to destroy its economy by diverting merchants from it. What was even worse from the king's point of view was that while he was occupied in defending his people from infidels, the Knights had invaded the duchy of Masovia, claiming they were its lawful overlords. In the king's opinion, the Knights had no basis for such a claim; they were simply taking advantage of Poland while the king and his people were defending Christendom against its enemies, whom the Knights' activities were materially assisting.[29]

When Innocent wrote to King Casimir of Poland about the situation, he cited the Knights' complaints about the king's military activities against them. According to the Knights, Polish armies had invaded their lands, and the king had allied himself with infidels and schismatics, enemies of the faith, to defeat the order's forces. The Knights also accused King Casimir of having allied himself with the Tartars who had recently devastated Hungary.[30]

If the eastern flank of Christendom was to be secure, the Knights and King Casimir would have to end their continual conflict. In 1359 Innocent instructed the archbishop of Prague to investigate the situation and bring the two sides together in order to mediate a solution. The chief obstacle was, of course, the conflicting claims of two Christian powers to the same lands. As long as this situation existed, the Lithuanians would remain unconverted, a threat to the military security of the Christians living along their borders. For both of these reasons, the papacy was anxious to see the Lithuanians converted.[31]

The situation in northeastern Europe did not improve during the succeeding pontificates. In 1363 Urban V called upon Christendom to assist in the defense of Poland from the infidels. Waves of infidels—Tartars, Lithuanians, and others—were pouring across the northern borders of Christendom.[32] Sometime later, the pope asserted that the Knights had taken advantage of the invasion of Poland in order to seize the lands of fellow Christians for themselves. He pointed specifically to their seizure of Tarbaten, a city that "lay on the edge of Christendom surrounded by infidels," as typical of their wickedness.[33] Instead of protecting the city and its inhabitants as became Christian warriors, the Knights fell upon the unfortunate inhabitants for their own aggrandizement.

In addition to seeking an end to the conflict between Poland and the Knights, Urban continued to press for the conversion of the infidels in the region. He exhorted King Casimir and the Knights to continue their efforts in this direction.[34] The papal goal depended greatly, of course, on the willingness of the Poles and the Knights to put aside their differences. The Christian rulers of the border regions had to support the missionaries if they were to succeed.

During the pontificate of Gregory XI (1370–78), papal attention focused upon reconciling schismatics and converting the infidels without the assistance of local Christian rulers. A band of Franciscans under the leadership of Nicholas de Crosna worked in Russia.[35] The bishops of neighboring dioceses were instructed to assist them in their work.[36] The pope later wrote directly to several Lithuanian princes, attempting to bring them back to the Christian fold and seeking to end their battles with the Teutonic Knights. Gregory XI repeated the traditional argument that outside the Church there was no salvation, but added a more practical reason for the Lithuanians to accept Christianity: once Christians, bound in unity of belief with the Teutonic Knights, the Lithuanians would inevitably be able to live in peace with them.[37] As occasional participants in the wars between the Knights and the king of Poland, however, the Lithuanians could be forgiven if they refused to believe that unity of belief automatically brought peace and brotherhood between Christian states. The theme of Christian unity also appeared in Gregory's letters to the king of Poland and the duke of Masovia.[38] He stressed the importance of ending conflict among Christians in order to bring peace to all of Christendom. No doubt he also hoped that the example of peace among Christians would inspire the Lithuanians to accept baptism.

During the pontificate of Urban VI (1378–89), Christian relations with the Lithuanians took a new and unexpected turn. In 1386 Ladislaus Jagellion, grand duke of Lithuania, married Hedwig, daughter of King Louis (1370–82) of Poland. Jagellion also accepted baptism and agreed to work for the conversion of the remaining infidels among the Lithuanians.[39] Although this solution to the problem of Lithuania paved the way for a permanent solution to the wars between Christians and infidels, and those among Christians for control of Lithuania, the papacy seems to have paid little attention to it: there seem to have been no letters between Urban and the Polish court about the marriage. The work of converting the infidels continued to move slowly, and battles with the Knights continued to plague the Polish kingdom. Peace along this frontier of Christendom was in sight, however, although the participants did not realize it.

During the early years of Boniface IX's pontificate (1389–1404) there was little papal interest in Poland, Lithuania, and Russia. Judging from his registers, he turned his attention to these regions only at the close of the fourteenth century. In 1399 he wrote to the minister general of the Franciscans about the Society of Pilgrims for Christ, a special body of Dominicans and Franciscans devoted to missionary efforts in the East.[40] He noted the approval that Urban V and Gregory XI had showered on the work of these friars in Russia and surrounding regions, and expressed the hope that these efforts would eventually lead to the creation of a great Christian kingdom that would serve as a base for the extension of Christianity eastward. The remaining years of his pontificate saw additional letters granting privileges to the society and its members. These letters continued to voice optimism about the possibility of converting the infidels. This language, already a century old, was made up of rhetorical phrases about the imminent conversion of the infidels that were no longer connected to the realities of the missionary effort.[41]

The king of Poland did not share Boniface's optimism about the Tartars' conversion. He still faced the threat of a Tartar invasion. Through the archbishop of Cracow, the king requested the pope to call yet another crusade for the defense of eastern Europe.[42] The pope authorized a tax to meet the planned campaign's costs. This letter contained traditional rhetoric about the Tartars, concerning not their imminent conversion but their great wickedness.[43]

In the years between Boniface's death and the calling of the Council of Constance in 1414, the papal registers again reveal little interest in the infidels dwelling along the northeastern frontier of Christendom. In 1410 Gregory XII (1406–15) authorized a Franciscan mission to the Lithuanians, Ruthenians, and Tartars.[44] In 1412 the antipope John XXIII (1410–15) issued a letter concerning a new diocese in Polish-controlled Russia.[45] This letter was another ringing reaffirmation of traditional papal teaching about the universal nature of the pope's responsibilities.

The Papacy and the Moslem World

The end of Christian states in the Near East did not mean the end of Christian interest in the Holy Land: pilgrims continued to visit the sites associated with Christ's life, and there were periodic calls for crusades in the region. By the late fourteenth century, papal interest in this region appeared more in letters dealing with pilgrims than in calls for yet another crusade. Furthermore, the comparatively peaceful situation in the eastern Mediterranean meant increased trade with the Moslems. As a consequence, the papal registers contained an increasing number of letters concerning peaceful trading contacts with the Moslems.

The Franciscan friars, who were most active in serving the spiritual needs of Christian pilgrims to the East, received papal letters authorizing them to establish communities in the Holy Land. Although such communities required the approval of Moslem authorities, this did not necessitate direct contact between the papacy and the Mamluk sultans who controlled the Holy Land: Christian secular rulers often acted as intermediaries. In 1363, for example, Queen Joanna of Sicily interceded with the sultan on behalf of some Franciscans whom Urban V had authorized to establish a house in the Holy Land.[46] In another case, the king of Aragon wrote in support of friars working in the Moslem-dominated lands of the Near East.[47] At the same time, Urban V did more than simply authorize the creation of such communities. He also issued a letter addressed to the Christian community at large requesting funds to pay for the purchase of property near Jerusalem.[48] The land was for a hospice to house poor pilgrims visiting the Holy Land. Urban issued several other letters seeking support for the friars involved in this pious work.

These peaceful contacts with the Moslem world stood in sharp contrast to the crusading impulses still found in Christian rulers. Peter I, Latin King of Cyprus (1359–69), planned a crusade against the sultan at a time when other Christian rulers sought to penetrate his lands peacefully. In October 1365 Peter I successfully attacked Alexandria and occupied the city for several months.[49] Urban V congratulated the king on his success, but suggested that he make peace with the sultan, since there were no funds available in Europe to support the initial success in Egypt.[50] Furthermore, King Peter's campaign had seriously interfered with trade between the East and

Europe. Much of this trade normally passed through Alexandria, and so merchants involved in it pressured the pope to withdraw support from Peter's adventures. Increasingly, trade took on greater importance for European Christians than renewal of the crusades.

The Moslem success in stopping the crusades of the late fourteenth century raised yet another problem for the papacy. Numbers of Christians living under Moslem rule were apostatizing. In 1372 Gregory XI wrote to the Dominicans and Franciscans working in these regions, instructing them to make special efforts to assist Christians living under Moslem rule and expressing special concern for the souls of those Moslems who had become Christians when the Christians were victorious in the Near East. Many of these individuals were returning to their earlier faith.[51] Three years later Gregory wrote again, in the same terms, to Franciscans working in Egypt, Syria, and the Holy Land, warning them about the growth of heresy and apostasy within the Christian communities in these lands.[52]

Papal letters of the late fourteenth century also reflect Christian contributions to the successful Turkish advance in the Near East. Gregory XI's registers contain repeated condemnations of Christians who assisted the Turks, the usual charge being that they sold arms and military supplies to the enemy.[53] In 1391 Boniface IX ordered some Christians excommunicated because they had assisted the Turks.[54] At the same time, economic reality forced the same pope to absolve various individuals who had been excommunicated for such dealings. Some Christians in the eastern Mediterranean lived by trading with the Moslems, and such trade sometimes included arms.[55] Unless Christians were willing to deal with the Moslems, various products Europeans desired would not be available in the West. Although papal policy emphasized the use of economic sanctions, in the long run Europeans would be more affected by them than the Moslems would be.

Closer to home, the popes of the late fourteenth century continued to express interest in the Moslems living in Christian Spain or along the edges of the reconquest. In 1376 Gregory XI wrote to Ferdinand I of Portugal (1367–83) about the King's planned campaign against the Moslems in Granada and Benamara (Beni Merid). To the pope, the campaign was a just war of defense against the traditional enemies of the faith, and the result of a successful campaign would be the extension of the Church throughout the rest of the Iberian peninsula and into North Africa. The pope instructed the king to build cathedrals, churches, and other ecclesiastical institutions in the reconquered areas. These should be adequately endowed once established, the pope added, presumably by gifts from the Portuguese king. Gregory also ordered the Portuguese to restrict the practice of the Moslem faith in the newly conquered territories, pointing specifically to the Moslem practice of having mullahs call the faithful to prayer. The sound of such calls would scandalize the Christians living among the conquered people, perhaps causing some to lose their faith. The pope added that such restrictions were not meant to force Moslem conversions to Christianity.[56] The Moslems were not to be forced to accept baptism—that is, not directly. Restrictions on the public practice of their religion were, in fact, pressures on the Moslems to convert, if only for the sake of avoiding inconvenience and harassment.

The restrictions Gregory XI suggested were, of course, traditional elements of papal practice toward the non-Christians living within Christian societies. Gregory XI was only following in the footsteps of Gregory IX and Innocent IV in this. Gregory's immediate predecessor, Urban V, had taken similar action concerning Jews living in Europe.[57] He had also issued a bull insisting that Christians not harass their Jewish neighbors. When Gregory XI instructed the king of Portugal about the treatment of Moslems in newly conquered areas he was insisting on the enforcement of traditional standards for dealing with conquered nonbelievers and indicating also that the proper Christian policy for dealing with infidels anywhere they were encountered was already in existence. The medieval papal policy and practice were universally applicable.

The Atlantic Islands

Increased Portuguese and Castilian pressure on the Moslems living along the southeastern fringe of Christendom increased interest in the islands lying off the African coast. By the end of the fourteenth century, Europeans had discovered not only the Canary Islands but the Madeiras and the Azores as well.[58] From the perspective of the various Iberian rulers, the islands might serve as a means of outflanking the Moslem cordon around Europe. To the papacy, these discoveries meant new fields for missionary activity. Both parties dreamed of linking up with Christian kingdoms believed to exist beyond the Moslem-dominated world.[59] In some respects, the dreams of expansion that the papacy once had concerning the East were revived when the Portuguese first moved out into the Atlantic. Just as medieval maps showed the earth as divided by a series of great rivers, the papacy saw Christendom as divided from the rest of the world by a band of territory the Moslems inhabited. If the Christians could circumvent the Moslem cordon, the Latin West would be able to link up with the enemies of the Moslems on the other side of the Moslem world. Latin Christians, united with the long-lost Christian communities believed to exist beyond the Moslem-occupied lands and converts from among the infidel nations, might be able to end the Moslem danger to Europe in one last great crusade.

The registers of Urban V reflect the slight but continuing papal interest in missionary efforts in the Canary Islands. Urban noted the great interest in such activities among both friars and secular clergy, and as usual, the papal letters painted the opportunities for making converts in the most glowing terms. The Canarians were described as "having no law, belonging to no religion, worshiping only the sun and the moon."[60] Apparently the primitive level of society on the Canary Islands and the fact that the people were not Moslems suggested to the pope that their conversion would be comparatively easy. Again, however, papal interest in this area of missionary endeavor was linked closely to the activities of missionaries and secular rulers who were already present in the area. The pope was not initiating new missionary activities there.

The Franciscans were also involved in missionary efforts in the Azores as well as in the Canary Islands. The order's records list a house in the Azores in 1400, although this community, like that listed for the same date in China, may represent a hope and not a reality.[61] The major attempt to conquer these islands and convert their inhabitants to Christianity was to come only after 1415. Nevertheless, the papal interest in the Canary Islands and the reference to the Azores reflected increasing interest in these previously unknown regions, regions the Moslems had not yet penetrated.

During the first half of the fifteenth century the papal role in the relations between Christian and non-Christian societies underwent a significant transformation. Where the papacy had once been at the center of contacts between Christian and infidel societies, if not always the initiator of such contacts, the popes increasingly found their role that of mediator between the conflicting interests of Christian states in infidel regions. The initiative for contacts with infidels came increasingly from Christian rulers anxious to expand their domains. The longstanding conflict between the king of Poland and the Teutonic Knights for control of Lithuania provided a model for the late medieval papal role in the expansion of European society. The expansionist policies followed by various Christian rulers inevitably led to conflicts not only with infidel societies but with other Christian rulers as well, when two Christian nations laid claim to the same area.

This gradual transformation had two advantages for the papacy. In the first place, as Christian rulers became interested in gaining control of infidel lands, it became possible to provide permanent protection and support for missionaries working among infidels. The papacy was able to insist upon the support of missionaries as the price of papal approval for expansion in a particular region. In the second place, for the popes of the fifteenth century to serve as mediators between Christian rulers in such an important matter as the occupation of infidel lands was to restore the papacy to a role in European political life that it had not played since the thirteenth century.[1] For the papacy, an institution badly scarred by the Avignon period and the Great Schism, the opportunity to become once more the court to which disputes between nations would be brought was a sign of the institution's renewed vitality and strength.[2] Disputes between Christian rulers concerning overseas conquests were not, of course, central issues in fifteenth-century conflicts between European rulers, and these popes were not at the level of political influence that Innocent III or Innocent IV had reached. European kings continued to seek the resolution of conflicts crucial to their personal interests in combat, not in the papal court. Nevertheless, their use of the papacy in matters involving overseas conquests was a sign of renewed willingness to see the papacy as having some role in the resolution of political conflicts affecting Christendom.

Alexander VI's (1492–1503) bull *Inter caetera*, issued in 1493, is the most famous example of papal mediation in a dispute between Christian rulers over conflicting interests in infidel-occupied lands. The pope's resolution of this conflict between Portugal and Castile over the recently discovered islands in the Atlantic Ocean and the previously discovered shore of West Africa was a reassertion of powers associated with the pontiffs of the thirteenth century. Although Alexander's mediation was the best-known example of such papal activity, it was not the only one. From the early decades of the fifteenth century, various popes acted in similar disputes as Europeans became more active in reaching out beyond Europe. There was a direct line of papal involvement in these issues during the fifteenth century, beginning with the Council of Constance (1414–17).[3] Among the issues presented to the council for resolution was the dispute between the Teutonic Knights and the kingdom of Poland. Twenty years later, another pope, Eugenius IV (1431–47), had to face the question of whether to award the Canary Islands to the Portuguese or to stand by while European slave traders raided the islands. In both cases, the traditional arguments about the rights of the natives played a significant role in shaping the papal response, and so did political realities. In addition, the proponents of Christian domination of infidels began to raise new arguments. The king of Portugal, for example, raised the question of whether Christians had a responsibility not only to baptize infidels but to civilize them as well. Although he was considering the primitive state of the Canarians when he made this argument, the papal response to this question was to have great significance over the next several centuries as Christians sought to justify their conquest of the non-Western world.

These discussions of the rights infidels could claim when facing conquest by Europeans generated some significant pieces of legal literature. The material from this early period did not have a direct effect upon the development of later discussions of these rights. It did, however, demonstrate that the legal principles found in the canonistic tradition were relevant to the era of European overseas expansion. For the next century and a half, the defenders and the opponents of European expansion drew upon the thirteenth-century legal materials concerning the rights of infidels to define the relationship that ought to exist betwen such people and Christians.[4] For the first time, canonistic thinking about the rights of infidels was applied directly to specific situations involving existing infidel societies. Acting in their capacity as chief judge of Christian society, popes were forced to decide whether the actions of individual Christian rulers were in keeping with the legal principles set down by Innocent IV.

Poland and the Teutonic Knights

The long-standing struggle between Poland and the Teutonic Knights provided the first major application of legal thinking about the rights of infidels to a specific situation. Because both parties based their claims to Lithuania on papal authorization and on spiritual motives, the papacy was the logical source for a solution of their conflict. The inability of either side to defeat the other completely added to the pressure for a diplomatic solution negotiated by the papacy. The marriage of Grand Duke Jagellion of Lithuania to the queen of Poland, leading to the union of the two nations in 1386 when the grand duke became Vladislav II (1386–1434) of Poland, did not stop the Knights from claiming Lithuania, nor did the Polish victory over the Knights at Tannenberg in 1410. The First Peace of Thorn, signed after Tannenberg, turned out to be only a truce in the long series of campaigns.[5] The growing strength of the Polish kingdom was making the Knights' position increasingly precarious. From their point of view, the legal basis for their stand was therefore increasingly important.

The conflict between the Knights and the Poles came before the Council of Constance. There was some irony in this circumstance because the Council dealt also with the teachings of John Wyclif, among whose doctrines was the opinion that the rightful possession of office, ecclesiastical or secular, was dependent upon the posses-

sor's being in the state of grace.[6] Inasmuch as the Knights justified
their attempts to conquer the Lithuanians on the grounds that, the
Lithuanians, being infidels, could not legitimately possess land and
office, the fate of Wyclif's teachings at the Council of Constance
had a bearing on the Knights' conquests. To understand the council's
debate on the conflict between Poland and the Knights, it is first
necessary to examine its treatment of Wyclif's ideas.

Wyclif's assertion that the valid exercise of secular or ecclesiastical office depended upon the spiritual state of the officeholder was
a crucial element of his program for ecclesiastical reform. The
primary goal was to reform corrupt clergy. By denying the validity
of sacramental actions performed by immoral and corrupt clerics,
Wyclif aimed at the traditional defense of such clerics, that their
moral failings did not invalidate their sacramental powers. Until
this defense was removed, the clergy would not be reformed.

Wyclif's linking of the validity of sacramental power with the
priest's moral state was not new. As his theological opponents were
well aware, this idea was the ancient Donatist heresy that had
flourished in North Africa during the fourth and fifth centuries.
Saint Augustine had led the intellectual assault on the Donatists,
becoming in the process the major defender of the opinion that the
validity of a sacramental action had nothing to do with the moral
worth of the priest who administers it: as long as the priest employed the proper form and had the right intention, the act was
sacramentally valid for those who received it.[7]

The essence of the Donatist opinion continued to reappear during
the Middle Ages. Periods that saw strong demands for ecclesiastical
reform generally produced examples of Donatist or pseudo-Donatist
ideas, and this was especially true when the demands for reform
focused on corruption among the clergy. Denial of the validity of
sacraments administered by sinful clerics was the most extreme
form of pressure that could be brought on unreformed priests. During the Investiture controversy of the twelfth century, some con-
gregations were encouraged to boycott masses said by priests
known to be simoniacs or to be living with women.[8] Although this
was obviously not true Donatism, official encouragement of such
actions may have contributed to a popular belief that the moral
worthiness of the priest and the value of his sacramental actions
were connected. The consequence was to encourage beliefs that
bordered on Donatism.

At any time, Wyclif's ideas would have posed a threat to the existence of the institutional Church. When he advanced them in the last half of the fourteenth century, they meant an even greater danger to the Church. The Great Schism had divided the papal office, the symbol of ecclesiastical unity. The addition of the Pisan line of popes in the early fifteenth century caused the papacy to appear ludicrous, and the demands for fundamental reform grew strident. Although Wyclif had been dead for almost thirty years when the Council of Constance was called, his ideas were a significant element in the intellectual armory of the reformers.[9] Members of the council were asked to consider a number of propositions drawn from Wyclif's works. Earlier, 267 such propositions had been condemned by ecclesiastical officials in England.[10] Supporters of the condemnation sought an affirmation of their decision from the council, and because of the long history of conflict over Wyclif's ideas, they were able to present it with a full statement of what they believed should be condemned in Wyclif's teachings. The members of the council who examined the English theologian's opinions were not required to read his works, however, with the result, that they have been accused of misunderstanding what he wrote.[11]

Crucial to the debate about the Teutonic Knights' attempted conquest of Lithuania was a statement Wyclif made about *dominium:* "no one is a civil lord or a prelate or a bishop while in mortal sin."[12] Given the superficial reading of Wyclif's works at the council, it is no wonder that his arguments could be understood as justifying Christian conquest of any lands occupied by infidels—the infidel rulers would not be in the state of grace and so could not legitimately possess lordship. A Christian army could invade and seize control of the lands which the infidel had usurped. Wyclif's *De civili dominio* could provide further support for such conquests. At one point, Wyclif illustrated his argument that *dominium* was lost as a consequence of mortal sin by pointing to God's expulsion of Adam and Eve from the Garden of Eden. They lost the enjoyment of the Garden because they sinned against God's command.[13] If the reader identified the pope with God and the infidels with Adam and Eve, he could find a perfect justification for dispossessing infidels in the contemporary world. Just as Wyclif's arguments could be employed to dissolve the structure of the institutional Church's, so too they could be employed to extend Christian domination over the entire non-Christian world.

A more careful reading of Wyclif's arguments, however, would reveal his preference for the conversion of infidels over their conquest. He emphasized Christian responsibility for the salvation of infidel souls rather than the conquest of infidel bodies.[14] Wyclif's arguments even sounded rather like those Innocent IV had advanced: Christians could use force against infidel societies only if the ruler refused to admit peaceful Christian missionaries into his lands.[15] He was not even enthusiastic about involving Christian secular rulers in missionary work. Rather than support missionaries in far-off lands, Christian rulers would be better advised to seek Church reform at home.[16] Besides, Christian rulers were inclined to seek the conquest of infidels only on the pretext of preaching to them.

Furthermore, Wyclif rejected a fundamental argument for conquering infidel societies when he rejected comparisons between the biblical wars of the Hebrews against their enemies to win the land God had promised them and fourteenth-century wars against infidels. For him, the Incarnation meant the end of religiously inspired wars. The God of the Old Testament ordered His people to wage war on their enemies, but in the New Testament, Christ ordered His followers to love all men.[17] Thus, contemporary Christians could not justify wars against infidels on the grounds that missionary efforts required them. Peaceful missionaries should be the first line of Christian advance into infidel lands. The Christian message was to bring eternal life, not temporal death, to those outside the Church.

The clearest evidence of the council's failure to grasp Wyclif's thinking, both on the issue of *dominium* and on the issue of infidel-Christian relations, is found in the council's treatment of the Bohemian heretic John Hus. The council condemned Hus for holding the doctrines for which Wyclif had been condemned. As in the case of the English heretic, the council condemned Hus on the basis of propositions drawn from his writings. The Bohemian had the distinct advantage, however, of being present to answer the charge of heresy in person. On the crucial issue of the relation between office and grace, for example, Hus denied believing that "a priest in mortal sin does not consecrate," a belief his accusers had attributed to him. He suggested that his accusers should actually read the works from which the charges were drawn: He claimed that careful examination of these works would show his belief in the validity of sacraments administered by a priest in mortal sin; the priest was personally unworthy to administer the sacraments in that condition, but it did not deprive his actions of their sacramental validity.[18]

Hus's denial of the charge that he accepted the most dangerous doctrine advanced by Wyclif did not save him from the stake. One of his most important accusers, the theologian Jean Gerson, insisted that Hus's opinions about *dominium* constituted "the most pernicious error" in all of the Bohemian's works. As a modern scholar has written, "Gerson hastily assumed that Hus shared Wyclif's view without taking the trouble to note Hus's qualification of it."[19] The same charge can be leveled against all those who condemned Hus, and a similar charge at those who condemned Wyclif. They did not seem to have understood their arguments completely or even to have tried to understand them.

The council's failure to consider Wyclif's argument in its full complexity and its unwillingness to consider Hus's qualification of the argument reflected the contemporary fear of the argument's implications for the Church. Because Hus linked ecclesiastical reform with ideas similar to those of Wyclif, he could not have avoided condemnation without recanting, not only in matters of doctrine, but in matters of reform as well. Even modified, Wyclif's ideas about *dominium* were too dangerous to be tolerated.

Fear of what Wyclif and Hus taught, or were believed to have taught, was not limited to ecclesiastical figures at the Council of Constance. Secular rulers who attended the council did not find such ideas about such ideas about *dominium* attractive either. Wyclif made sin grounds for depriving secular officials of their offices; priests and kings alike had to be in the state of grace if they wished to rule in a rightly ordered world. The immoral king was as incapable of issuing binding commands as the sinful cleric was incapable of administering the sacraments validly. Emperor Sigismund (1410–37), the prime mover of the council, and the guarantor of Hus's safety, was startled when he overheard some of the debate about *dominium*. Having heard Hus state that mortal sin rendered a secular ruler unworthy before the throne of God, Sigismund dryly responded that all men were sinners, and so all men must, therefore, be unworthy to possess *dominium*.[20] The emperor obviously equated Hus's notion of unworthiness with Wyclif's argument that mortal sin automatically deprived a man of office and lordship. The emperor's failure to appreciate Hus's argument cannot have been uncommon. The members of the council feared the implications of

Wyclif's ideas so greatly that they readily attributed them to ideas that were similar, although not identical, to Wyclif's. The result was the condemnation of a man who denied that he was a follower of the English heretic but whose ideas about ecclesiastical reform sounded similar.

Just as the Council Fathers placed John Hus's ideas within the framework of Wyclif's theological position, so too they placed the debate about the Teutonic Knights' attempted conquest of Lithuania in the context of the debate about *dominium*. Any argument about the right of Christians to conquer infidel lands raised questions about the justification involved. Were the Knights arguing that the Lithuanians as infidels had no right to possess land and lordship? Did *dominium* depend upon grace? Such arguments led inevitably to the question of whether the Knights, or their Polish enemies, were heretics, followers of Wyclif and Hus.

Representatives of the Knights and of the king of Poland exchanged angry polemics. The leading advocate of the Knights' position at the Council, the Dominican friar Johannes Falkenberg, described the Poles and Lithuanians as "heretics and shameless dogs who have returned to the vomit of their infidelity." Not content with these lurid charges, Falkenberg went on to accuse them of idolatry as well. In his opinion, the "king of Poland, since he is a bad ruler, is an idol and all Poles are idolators and serve their idol Jaghil."[21] The Polish representatives were no less vituperous. They accused the Knights of having deceived the various popes and emperors who had authorized the order's expansion in Lithuania, of having obtained papal and imperial blessings on their advance into Lithuania by falsely claiming that they were interested in saving infidel souls when in reality they were interested only in seizing land.[22]

If the quarrel between the Poles and the Knights had remained on this level of invective, it would not have contributed significantly to the development of legal thinking about the rights of infidels. Those who heard the debate at the Council of Constance were not interested in hearing two Christian parties hurl epithets at each other. The issue was far too serious for that. The crux of the matter was the legal issue of the infidels' rights: the Council was being asked to authorize either the Knights or the Poles to take charge of the Christianization of the Lithuanians.

The king of Poland's representative at the council made the most important contribution to the legal literature concerning relations between Christians and infidels. Paul Vladimiri, onetime rector of the University of Cracow and a noted canon lawyer, summed up the Polish position in a paper known as the *Opinio Hostiensis*. In Vladimiri's opinion, the question was whether or not infidels could possess *dominium*.[23] If they could, the Knights' wars against the Lithuanians were simply wars of aggression unless the Knights could demonstrate the existence of unprovoked Lithuanian attacks against Christendom. The Polish canonist framed the legal issue simply and clearly—too simply for the Knights' liking. He assumed that the Knights justified their conquests by employing the Hostiensian arguments: "It is the opinion of Hostiensis that at the coming of Christ all jurisdiction, rule, office and lordship was transferred from infidels to the faithful, since, as his opinion states, infidels are entirely incapable of possessing such things."[24] In reality, the Knights did not rely upon this argument to justify their expansion into Lithuania. Their stated goals were to convert the infidels and defend Christendom against its enemies. Their use of armed force in Lithuania was subordinated to their desire to convert the Lithanians. Furthermore, they also claimed both papal and imperial approval for their efforts. Consequently, Vladimiri was presenting the Knights' position unfairly by beginning his attack at Constance with the Hostiensian argument.

Having begun by identifying the Knights' position with Hostiensis, and by implication with Wyclif, Vladimiri plunged on to inform his hearers that Innocent IV's position on the rights of infidels was preferable to that of Hostiensis.[25] He pointed out that the majority of canonists followed Innocent, not Hostiensis, on this issue, and in support of this view quoted the opinion of Peter de Anchorano, whom he described as "the most famous doctor of both laws in Italy" and under whom Vladimiri had once studied. Anchorano described Hostiensis' position on *dominium* as absurd because it would justify acts of murder and robbery whenever Christians performed them against infidels. According to Anchorano's interpretation of Hostiensis' argument, even an infidel society's willingness to live at peace with Christians was not sufficient to insure its protection from Christian invasion.[26] Vladimiri contended that the council ought therefore to condemn Hostiensis' opinion, if only to maintain the good order of society. Although the canonist did not mention Wyclif's name in these opening remarks, his hearers could not avoid connecting the call for condemning Hostiensis' ideas on *dominium* with the condemnation of the English heretic's ideas.

Having presented the relevant legal theory, Vladimiri turned to the facts of the case. He painted a picture of devout Polish kings who had admitted the Teutonic Knights into their kingdom to convert the infidels to Christianity. The kings granted lands to these soldiers of Christ to support them while they worked among the infidels. To their amazement, however, the kings discovered that they had admitted and favored not pious missionaries but hypocritical ingrates. The Knights' noble protestations about converting the Lithuanians were only words. Their real goal was to obtain lands for themselves in order to create their own principality. The wickedness of the Knights was demonstrated by their attacks on the Lithuanians even after that people had indicated willingness to live at peace with the invaders. In addition, the Knights falsely portrayed the situation in Lithuania as a constant round of battles with fierce infidels in order to raise funds from among the pious supporters of crusades. These funds were then used to finance the order's expansion at the expense of the peaceful Lithuanians. The Knights used the same deceptive tactics when they sought papal and imperial approval for their work. Thus, Vladimiri concluded, the Knights' actions had a veneer of legality, a veneer composed of papal bulls and imperial privileges.[27]

After destroying the Knights' argument for their activities in Lithuania, Vladimiri presented the Polish view of the situation. According to him, Polish missionaries, not the Knights, were converting the Lithuanians. Indeed, the Knights had thrown obstacles in the way of the Polish missionaries, burning down the churches erected for the converts and interfering in various other ways with the work of converting and pacifying the Lithuanians. Not content with these wicked actions, the Knights had even attacked Poland itself.[28] Reduced to the simplest terms, Vladimiri's argument is the injunction "by their fruits you shall know them." The fruits of the Knights' activities in Lithuania were death and destruction. The root from which the poisoned fruit sprang was the order's lust for land belonging to others.

Vladimiri presented fifty-two statements supporting his accusations. The statements fell into two categories. The first dealt with the Knights' claim to papal approval for conquering Lithuania, and the second with alleged imperial authorization for the conquest. Each of these fifty-two opinions was in turn derived from Vladimiri's longer works about the powers of pope and emperor.

Vladimiri's discussion of papal power rested on Innocent IV's commentary on the decretal *Quod super his*. His major point was simply that all men belonged to Christ's flock, and so Christians must treat fellow Christians and infidels alike in keeping with Christ's instruction to Peter, "Feed my sheep." Vladimiri illustrated the relationship between Christians and infidels by pointing to the existence of Jewish communities within Christian Europe. Such people could not be legitimately ousted from Christendom simply because they were not Christians. As long as such people were willing to live in peace with their Christian rulers and neighbors, they could legitimately dwell among Christians without interference. Likewise, as long as the infidel Lithuanians were willing to live at peace with Christians, there was no justification for the Knights' attacks on them.[29]

Vladimiri's discussion of the right relationship between Christians and infidels followed the guidelines that Innocent IV had laid down. An infidel ruler could be forced to permit the entry of peaceful missionaries. Furthermore, Christians had a legitimate right to punish infidels who violated the law of nature. Vladimiri stressed, however, that only the pope could authorize Christian invasions of infidel societies for either reason. Christian rulers could not act on their own initiative in such cases.[30] Underlying this argument was Vladimiri's contention that the Knights had deceived various popes about the situation in Lithuania. They had adhered to the letter of the law by obtaining papal authorization for their efforts, but they had lied to the popes when seeking this authorization. The Knights never intended to seek the Lithuanians' salvation, only their territory.

The conclusion of Vladimiri's argument was obvious: the Knights lacked legitimate papal authorization for invading Lithuania. They had deceived several popes about their intentions, and they had acted contrary to Innocent IV's guidelines for Christian-infidel relations. The order's assertion that Clement IV's bull authorized their conquest of Lithuania was false because the authorization was based upon lies.[31] Such deviousness was especially wicked because the popes whom the Knights cited in their support had had to rely upon the Knights' description of the situation in Lithuania when issuing the letters authorizing the conquest. Now that Vladimiri had clearly demonstrated the Knights' evil intentions from the very beginning of their involvement in Lithuania, the veil of legitimacy was torn away from the Knights' wars. They were now exposed as wicked wars for territorial aggrandizement, deserving papal condemnation, not papal approval.

Vladimiri then turned to the Knights' assertion that they possessed imperial approval for their conquest of Lithuania. Did the emperor actually possess the right to authorize Christian conquest of infidel lands? The Polish canonist said no.[32] Having previously demonstrated that the pope alone possessed such authority, Vladimiri used this section of the *Opinio Hostiensis* to prove that the emperor had no legal basis to award Lithuania to the Knights. His argument began with the assertion that canon, divine, and natural law agreed that the pope alone held both spiritual and temporal jurisdiction.[33] Interestingly, Vladimiri did not choose to defend this argument by reference to the *Decretum* or the *Decretales*, nor did he rely upon the opinion of a noted canonist. He pointed instead to Boniface VIII's *Unam sanctam*, citing the famous last line of that bull, "that it is necessary for salvation to believe that every human creature is subject to the Roman Pontiff."[34] Vladimiri used Boniface's words to subject the jurisdiction of secular rulers to considerations arising from the overriding papal responsibility for the souls of all men. In this case, the papal responsibility for the souls of the Lithuanian infidels could be the only source of Christian temporal jurisdiction over them. Vladimiri also cited Aristotle in support of this position. In the *Politics*, Aristotle had argued that the good order of the world required that there be a single prince over all men. In Vladimiri's opinion, the only secular claimant to such universal jurisdiction, the emperor, had no jurisdiction in spiritual matters. Logically, then, the pope, the ultimate source of spiritual and temporal jurisdiction fitted Aristotle's description of the rightful ruler of the world.[35]

Thus, for Vladimiri, the emperor was not the lord of the world, as the Roman legal maxim described him, but only a ruler over a specific segment of humanity. There was no basis for an emperor to claim jursidiction over infidels as a consequence of his supposed universal jurisdiction. Unlike the pope, to whom he was occasionally compared, the emperor had no divinely authorized mission to all men, nor could the emperor claim to be freely chosen ruler of all men, nor could he claim universal jurisdiction by right of conquest. So, yet again, the Knights' claim to an imperial basis for their conquest of Lithuania proved false. The emperor could not give to the Knights that which he did not possess himself.

Having denied the emperor's claim to universal authority, Vladimiri went on to discuss the relationship between the papacy and the empire. He began with an unflattering description of the empire's origins in the Roman conquest of neighboring societies.[36] This underscored what he thought so wicked about the Knights' conquest of Lithuania, its origin in the lust for land. Taking an Augustinian line, Vladimiri was arguing that secular authority emerged from wicked motives, unlike ecclesiastical jurisdiction, which was derived from Christ's love for all men. The imperial power, rooted in wickedness, was clearly restricted to secular matters and clearly subject to the spiritual power. Vladimiri did not, however, deny the autonomy of the secular sphere. The emperor, like other secular rulers, was not directly subordinate to the pope in every matter; there were areas of secular jurisdiction normally exempt from ecclesiastical interference. In matters involving the salvation of souls, however, the pope remained the ultimate authority.[37] Secular rulers then came under his jurisdiction indirectly. The conquest of Lithuania, based on the Knights' stated desire to convert the infidels, belonged therefore to the papal sphere of jurisdiction, not to the imperial.

Finally, Vladimiri turned from legal theories about jurisdiction over infidels to contemporary situations occasionally seen as comparable to that of the Teutonic Knights in Lithuania. Some defenders of the Knights had compared their efforts to the work of the Spanish kings who were driving the Moslems out of Spain.[38] To Vladimiri, this was an invalid analogy because the wars in Spain aimed at reconquering lands Christians had once possessed and from which the invading Moslems had driven them in an unjust war of aggression. Lithuania, however, had never been a Christian land, and so Christians could not legitimately claim to be reconquering it.[39] The only possible claim the order could make to possession of Lithuania was by virtue of conquest. This was not, Vladimiri argued, a legitimate claim. The inhabitants had indicated their willingness to live peacefully with their Christian neighbors, and so the Knights had no justification for their conquest. What the Knights had done was steal the infidels' lands under the cover of religion. Vladimiri pushed the discussion further, apparently in response to the argument that even if the original conquest had been unauthorized, nevertheless good would come of it when the Lithuanians accepted baptism. This would imply coerced acceptance of Christianity, something canonists and theologians had long rejected as wrong. Conversion must come as the result of a voluntary acceptance of the faith, not as the result of conquest.[40]

The remaining propositions in the *Opinio Hostiensis* restated Vladimiri's basic argument that the papacy ought to insure just treatment for the Lithuanians and emphasized it with a novel use of the image of the pope as pastor of those outside the Church. Because of this divinely created responsibility, the Lithuanians had the right to expect fair and just treatment from the pope. He should, therefore, protect their natural right to property and lordship, just as he could punish them for violating the natural law when the occasion arose.[41] Protection of the infidels' natural rights was a logical corollary to Innocent IV's argument that the pope had the power to judge men by the law applicable to them. In the Lithuanian case, the infidels could require the pope to restrain Christians who were seeking unlawful conquest. This description of the pope's relationship to infidels obviously would extend papal authority well beyond imperial authority. Although Vladimiri did not mention it, this argument would strengthen the Polish position in Lithuania as well.

The conclusion of the *Opinio Hostiensis* was a ringing reaffirmation of the natural right of infidels to possess property and lordship. Not only was this conclusion legally sound; it was also the only practical conclusion. Otherwise, Christians would be in the morally absurd position of violating the divine prohibitions against murder and robbery in the name of spreading Christ's message.[42]

In December 1417 a commission appointed to settle the controversy between Poland and the Knights made its report to the council. The report generally agreed with Vladimiri's position. The committee members also specifically condemned Johannes Falkenberg's intemperate tract against the Poles, describing it as containing "many false, detestable, and damnable [statements] which are against the faith and against good morals."[43] Thus, Falkenberg, who had accused the Poles of heresy, came very close to being charged with heresy himself. Although the committee stopped short of condemning him as a follower of Wyclif, it is reasonable to assume that among Falkenberg's "errors against the faith" were the Wyclifite implications of the arguments he advanced to support the conquest of Lithuania. Even a fellow supporter of the Knights recognized the heretical implications of the Dominican's argument and wanted to disassociate the Knights from the taint of heresy involved.[44] Falkenberg's near-condemnation may also have stemmed from his highly polemical style, more suited perhaps to the pulpit than to the council. Rational arguments, especially those rooted in the legal tradition, were required, not impassioned but carelessly phrased accusations. Nevertheless, when all allowances have been made for Falkenberg's position, it is clear that the members of the committee were unwilling to give their approval to ideas seemingly tainted with Wyclif's heretical ideas. Any suggestion that *dominium* depended on grace, as the Knights' supporter appeared to argue, was sufficient to taint Falkenberg's position.

The Council of Constance brought to an end the line of argument about the dependence of *dominium* upon grace that the thirteenth-century canonists had developed. Following the condemnation of Wyclif's opinions, Hostiensis' views on *dominium* were no longer acceptable. In the future, canonists, theologians, popes, and secular rulers who sought to defend the conquest of infidel lands would have to march their troops through whatever loopholes they could find in Innocent IV's arguments about the natural right of infidels to possess property and lordship, or they would have to develop new arguments that avoided heresy.

The Canary Islands: To Civilize Primitive Man

Twenty years after the Council of Constance tried to resolve the conflict between the Teutonic Knights and the king of Poland, the papacy again faced the issue of the rights of infidels, but this time a new justification for conquest emerged, a justification destined to have a long life. The situation that led to its development was not unlike the one that led to Vladimiri's presentation at the council. As European nations began to expand more aggressively into North Africa and along the coast of West Africa, they began to quarrel about their claims to the new lands they encountered. The background of the conflict that led to the development of a new rationale for Christian conquest of infidel lands was the renewal of interest in the Canary Islands almost a century after Luis de la Cerda had announced his intention to conquer them. Portuguese and Castilian interest in the Canary Islands foreshadowed the role the papacy was to play in the great age of discovery and conquest that was to follow Columbus' voyages. As Europeans expanded into previously unknown regions, the papacy was increasingly involved in resolving disputes over new territories and providing legitimization of the conquests.

Although Clement VI had awarded the Canary Islands to Luis de la Cerda in 1344, it was not until the early fifteenth century that Europeans began to take a serious interest in occupying the islands. As Iberian sailors continued to move out into the Atlantic, however, they gradually encountered the other island chains as well. The Maderias and the Azores were discovered in the fourteenth century. In the fifteenth century, seamen found the Cape Verde Islands.[45] In addition, European explorers were beginning to move along the coast of Africa, and by the early fifteenth century, both Portugal and Castile were showing increased interest in the agricultural opportunities these regions presented. Both kingdoms claimed the Canary Islands by virtue of discovery. Seamen from these nations, as well as from the Italian maritime states, had sighted the islands and, on some occasions at least, landed on them. The Portuguese claim, for example, rested on landings by Portuguese seamen as early as 1341, three years before Clement's awarding of the islands to Luis de la Cerda.[46] The conflicting claims of the Portuguese and the Castilians to the Atlantic Islands were only a small part of the series of conflicts between the two kingdoms during the fifteenth century. The major interest in these wars was control of the Iberian peninsula. Nevertheless, the struggle for domination of the Atlantic Islands and the west coast of Africa was destined to have far-reaching consequences.[47]

The consequences of Christian interest in the Canary Islands had caused Pope Eugenius IV (1431–47) to ban further Christian penetration of the islands in 1434.[48] In 1436 he issued another bull, *Romanus Pontifex*, designed to end the struggle for control of the islands by awarding them permanently to Portugal.[49] This bull was the result of discussions within the papal court about the rights of infidels. It reflected not only legal theorizing about the rights of infidels, but also papal awareness of the political realities involved in European expansion overseas.

Eugenius had originally banned further Christian expansion into the Canary Islands in response to a plea from a bishop stationed there. According to the bishop, a number of Christian converts from among the native population had been terrorized by a party of European adventurers. These men had first attempted to land on an island still occupied entirely by infidels. The natives were too fierce, however, and repulsed the invaders, and so the Europeans then attacked Christian communities on two other islands, killing and wounding a number of converts and stealing their goods.[50] For the first time, Christian expansion on the southwestern flank of Christendom was presenting the conflict between spiritual and territorial goals that marked expansion in the northeast.

In 1436 King Duarte (1433–38) of Portugal wrote to Eugenius requesting that he lift the ban on Christian expansion in the Canaries. As matters stood, Christians were allowed to continue their conquest of those islands whose conquest had begun before the ban was imposed but not to extend their control to the remaining infidel-occupied islands in the chain. The king's letter began with a plea that the pope allow the Portuguese to continue the important task of converting the Canarians to Christianity. The work of conversion was, according to the Portuguese king, the fundamental reason for Portuguese activity in the Canaries. He went on to describe the extremely primitive existence the inhabitants of the unconquered islands led: "The nearly wild men who inhabit the forest [of these islands] are not united by a common religion, nor are they bound by the chains of law, they are lacking in normal social intercourse, living in the country like animals." Canarian society was so primitive that the people have "no contact with each other by sea, no writing, no kind of metal or money." In a word, the Canarians' way of life was little better than that of animals.[51]

King Duarte then went on to explain the source of Portuguese interest in the Canary Islands. The king's younger brother, Prince Henry (1394–1460), better known as Henry the Navigator, had initiated Portuguese missionary efforts among these unfortunate people. Henry's intention was to provide for these primitive people "civil laws and an organized form of government," as well as Christian baptism. The initial result of this missionary effort was the conversion of 400 Canarians, thus planting Christianity in a land where "the name of Christ had never been known." Less obviously, Prince Henry's work resulted in a strong Portuguese claim to control over the Canary Islands.[52]

The Portuguese efforts in the Canaries were not without faults. Referring to the attack that caused the papal ban on further European expansion in the islands, King Duarte explained that such unprovoked attacks were not typical of Portuguese expansion. In that case, however, the fierce resistance of the infidels, combined with the failure of a relief vessel loaded with food to arrive, pushed some of the invaders to extreme measures. They sailed to a Christian island, where the starving men seized whatever they could to sustain themselves. They observed that the men were so hungry that "scarcely even the wild goats were safe from their desires."[53] In the king's view, the circumstances of the attack should mitigate the penalty the pope imposed. The papal response was too severe a penalty for a single act. Furthermore, Duarte wanted the pope to appreciate the great expense the Portuguese people had borne in the work of spreading the Christian faith and the great difficulties Prince Henry and his associates had suffered in fulfilling this most noble of goals. The Portuguese had nothing to gain in a material way from their efforts among the Canarians, only the spiritual reward given those who sacrificed themselves to bring the gospel to the infidel.

Duarte also reminded Eugenius of the strategic importance of the Canary Islands. They lay off the coast of Africa, where the Portuguese were already battling the Moslems. The king appears to have been suggesting that Christian possession of the islands would secure the southwestern flank of Christendom from Moslem attack. Perhaps the islands might even be useful as a springboard for future Christian assaults against the Moslem world.[54]

Finally, Duarte raised a fundamental problem for the pope. In the event that Eugenius refused to lift the prohibition, could he enforce it? The king indicated that the Portuguese would obey the papal injunction, but would less virtuous persons do so? In Duarte's opinion, less devout men—pirates and slave traders, no doubt—would be inclined "on their own authority to wage war and to occupy the lands of the infidels."[55] He was apparently confident of the Europeans' ability eventually to overcome the Canarians' resistance to invaders, and since defeat for the natives was inevitable, the only question remaining concerned how the conquest was to proceed. Papal authorization of further Portuguese conquests in the Canaries would mean an orderly conquest motivated by the highest ideals and in accordance with papal guidelines. The result would be to the spiritual and the temporal advantage of the Canarians: not only would the Portuguese insure the conversion of the natives and their eternal salvation, but they would also protect the people from slavers who would only exploit them.

The king ended his letter with a ringing affirmation of the pope's universal jurisdiction, a power coming from God Himself. Duarte was obviously appealing to Eugenius' high sense of mission and his exalted notion of papal authority. At a time when papal power was under attack from the conciliar movement, which sought to reduce the pope's power and provide institutional restrictions on its exercise, a reminder of the exalted powers he alone held was welcome to a beleaguered pontiff.

> Although many will strive on their own authority to wage war and to occupy the lands of the infidels, nevertheless, because the earth and its fullness are the Lord's, Who left to Your Holiness the fullness of this power over the entire world, whatever is possessed by the authority and permission of Your Holiness is understood to be held in a special way and with the permission of almighty God.[56]

These words, reminiscent of Boniface VIII in the heyday of papal power, must have been especially cheering to Eugenius, who was thereby identified with the powerful figures of the thirteenth-century papacy.

The king's letter avoided discussion of the Canarians' right to continue in secure possession of their property and lordship and focused on the pragmatic reasons why the pope should authorize Portuguese conquest of these islands. At the same time, he did not completely neglect the question of infidel rights. Indirectly at least, his argument was that as the conquest of the islands by European Christians was inevitable, it was only reasonable to insure that the conquest proceeded in a fashion that would insure the spiritual and physical well-being of the native population. The Portuguese king was proposing to protect the natives from oppression and exploitation: a virtuous goal. The papal approval that the king was requesting was, in his view, only a guarantee that the Portuguese would not have to fight other Christian powers for control of the islands. The king and his heirs would serve as the pope's agents in the Canary Islands, acting in his name. Even if Eugenius was not convinced by this interpretation of the legal tradition concerning the rights of infidels, Duarte's letter provided other bases for authorizing the conquest. The fierce natives who occupied these islands would obviously not allow peaceful missionaries to land; so military protection would have to be provided if the Church's mission to the infidels was to be fulfilled. This argument would fall within the conditions for armed conquest of infidels that Innocent IV had set down. Finally, the king's letter raised, apparently for the first time, the responsibility of Christians to civilize primitive people as well as baptize them. Although Innocent IV had not raised this issue directly, his argument about natural law could be extended to fit the situation in the Canary Islands. People as primitive as the Canarians seemed to be could be assumed to be constantly violating natural law and therefore subject to papally directed punishment. Consequently, Eugenius would be able to authorize the planned Portuguese conquest of the Canaries while adhering to the legal tradition concerning the rights of infidels.

Until recently, there was only slight evidence that King Duarte's letter caused Eugenius to pay serious attention to the conquest of the Canary Islands. A Portuguese chronicler, Ruy de Pina, mentioned in passing that the pope had consulted with his cardinals before issuing his response, the bull *Romanus Pontifex*, to the king of Portugal.[57] Such a remark would ordinarily mean little because the chronicler was not privy to the activities of the papal court; it would be taken as a piece of rhetoric added routinely to characterize the papal decision-making process. A modern scholar working in the Vatican Archives, however, has discovered two documents that appear to be connected with Eugenius' deliberations about Duarte's request. The documents are legal opinions apparently solicited by the pope to determine the current state of legal thinking on the rights of infidels.[58] This discovery suggests that Ruy de Pina was correct when he claimed that Eugenius sought advice from his councilors before responding to Duarte's request. Perhaps the pope sensed the importance of his answer to future European expansion in the Atlantic islands and elsewhere.

The authors of the opinions, Antonio Minucci de Pratovecchio and Antonio Roselli, were well-known canon lawyers, not cardinals. Each was asked to respond to the same statement of the problem: "A certain Catholic prince or king who recognizes no superior [in temporal matters] wishes to wage war against the Saracens who do not possess or hold lands of that king but who hold land which belonged to other Christians as if in barbarism."[59] Although their opinions were discovered bound together with a copy of Duarte's letter to Eugenius, there is no evidence that the canonists actually read the king's letter. They may have been presented with a summary of the letter or simply with a brief statement summing up what the pope saw as the crucial points. Presented with a statement of the problem such as this one, the two canonists could respond only with arguments drawn from Innocent IV's commentary on the decretal *Quod super his*. Furthermore, not only did this statement of the problem virtually dictate the response they would make; it did not present the problem correctly. The Canarians were not Moslems, as the statement implied, and the Canary Islands never belonged to Christians. Each of these phrases was, however, capable of interpretation. The Canarians may have been described as Moslems because their islands were close to Moslem Africa. As for Moslem possession of Christian lands, the statement may refer to the grant of the islands to Luis de la Cerda.

Each canonist responded to the statement by framing a series of questions about specific aspects of the problem. Neither referred to the Canary Islands or to Portugal in his response. Both opinions began, however, by restating the original question so that it corresponded more closely to the situation in the Canary Islands: whether it was lawful to wage war against infidels who occupied lands that had never belonged to Christians.[60] The answer to this question was obviously the key to the problem, not only of the Canary Islands, but of Christian expansion beyond Europe in general. The remaining questions in the canonists' responses concerned such related issues as whether a ruler could tax his subjects for a war of the kind described and whether a soldier who killed another man in such a war was guilty of murder.[61] As might be expected, both canonists followed Innocent IV's line of argument. They differed, however, in the emphasis they placed on specific aspects of the general problem. Minucci, for example, dealt at some length with each of the subquestions, while Roselli devoted the greater part of his opinion to the fundamental issue of the infidels' right to possess *dominium*. Furthermore, each canonist's opinion has a distinct flavor. Minucci's opinion gives the impression of being a strictly academic exercise, developed without any serious consideration of the facts of the matter or any awareness of the significance of the problem. On the other hand, Roselli's opinion appears to have been a serious attempt to wrestle with a contemporary problem that had important long-range consequences.

Minucci began his response by restating Innocent IV's opinion that the pope had no right to authorize wars against infidels simply because they were infidels. Like Paul Vladimiri, he seems to have followed Peter de Anchorano's explanation for this prohibition. He observed that such a power, even if possessed by a pope, would nevertheless encourage the waging of wars against the infidels for financial reasons alone. Minucci went on to support the opinion that infidels possessed *dominium*, not by the terms of natural law, however, but by the terms of the law of nations, the *ius gentium*.[62] In Roman law, the law of nations described practices common to all societies, in contrast to the natural law, which described an ideal order. Minucci's resting of infidel *dominium* on the law of nations suggests that in the ideal order of things, infidel *dominium* would not be safe from Christian conquest; thus, he seems to have weakened the case for infidel possession of *dominium* to some extent by relating it to the law of nations.

Although Minucci recognized the existence of *dominium* in infidel societies, he also recognized the existence of some form of papal jurisdiction over infidels. Such jurisdiction was *de iure*, not *de facto*. Consequently, the pope could deprive infidels of their property and lordship under certain conditions. These conditions were the usual ones, such as the failure of an infidel ruler to admit peaceful missionaries to his domain or the existence of practices that violated the law of nature. Minucci followed Innocent IV's opinion so closely that he even discussed the legitimacy of a war aimed at restoring the Holy Land to Christian hands, a situation of no relevance to the problem he was considering.[63] His dependence on Innocent's opinion, to the point of irrelevancy, may have been the result of Minucci's being intimidated by his famous predecessor's reputation. His colleague, Antonio Roselli had described Innocent IV in his opinion as "he who was the light of the law and who knew the laws better than anyone else."[64] This reputation, when added to the Council of Constance's condemnation of ideas about infidel rights conflicting with Innocent's, may have been sufficient to force a canonist into a close adherence to that pope's opinion.

If Antonio Minucci had provided the only opinion about the rights of infidels, the pope could have felt assured that the canonists had not made any significant advances on this issue since Innocent IV had written his commentary on *Quod super his*. Antonio Roselli's opinion, however, though following Innocent IV's line of argument, was not restricted to a faithful repetition of the master's words. At the very beginning of his opinion, Roselli demonstrated his willingness to go beyond Innocent IV's arguments. Having focused first on Innocent's opinion about the right of all men to possess *dominium*, Roselli went on to cite Aristotle and Cicero in support of the natural rights common to all men. These pagan authors had asserted the natural right of all men to defend themselves from aggression, an assertion that Roselli equated with Innocent's argument about man's natural right to *dominium*. In addition, Roselli explained that Christians and infidels alike could protect their lives and possessions according to the *ius caritatis et diuinum*. Roselli thus linked pagan philosophers, canon lawyers, and Christian theologians in support of the natural law rights of infidels.[65]

Having first defended infidels' possession of *dominium*, Antonio Roselli went on to discuss the nature of *dominium* at some length. He distinguished between natural *dominium* and civil *dominium*, the former rooted in natural law, and the latter in the law of nations. Civil *dominium* was common to all men, Christian and infidel alike, because it originated with Adam's fall. The consequences of Adam's fall affected all his descendants, regardless of their relationship to the Christian Church. Christians could not, then, claim that the birth of Christ had deprived infidels of *dominium*, that is, civil authority, because it had never rested on being in the state of grace. It existed only because of the loss of grace by Adam.[66]

Roselli did not deny the existence of a basis upon which Christians could legitimately conquer infidel societies. Like Innocent IV and those who followed his reasoning, Roselli had no difficulty in explaining how Christians could lawfully deprive infidels of rule and property.[67] The pope's responsibility for the souls of all men could necessitate removing an infidel ruler's *dominium* for a higher good. In Roselli's view, those outside the Church were those not fed by Peter and his successors, the shepherds of Christ's flock. Such people were, of course, subject to the *diuinum dominium*, God's own power, in which Peter and his successors shared. To illustrate the relationship derived from the papal sharing in God's power, Roselli compared the pope to Abraham. The Hebrew patriarch had two families, one by Sara, the other by Agar. Abraham's patriarchal authority extended over both the Hebrews, the descendants of Abraham by Sara, and the peoples of the desert, the Saracens, descended from Abraham and Agar. Like Abraham, the pope shared in God's universal fatherhood of mankind, giving him the right to interfere in infidel societies on certain occasions.[68]

Having established the existence of *dominium* in infidel societies and the occasions upon which the pope could override that right, Roselli moved to a discussion of the opinion that *dominium* did not exist outside the Church. He focused his attention on Hostiensis' opinions on *dominium*, which, he argued, were held by others, such as the canonist Oldratus. Here again, Roselli drew upon the distinction between civil and natural *dominium*. Christ's coming could not have deprived infidels of *dominium* because He possessed natural *dominium*, not civil. The former ended when Adam sinned and was replaced by the latter.[69] To support the opinion that Christ did not participate in acts involving civil rule, Roselli pointed to Christ's refusal to give a judgment in an inheritance case brought before him. Regarding property, Roselli recalled Christ's statement that the animals of the fields had their lairs and the birds their nests, while the Son of Man had no place to rest his head. In his opinion, these cases proved Christ's lack of *dominium* in civil affairs. This being so, Christ could not have come and taken away *dominium* from anyone.[70] He concluded this section of his discussion by observing that the opinions of Hostiensis and Oldratus in this matter were designed only to extend papal power beyond its proper boundaries.[71] Papal lust for power was, in the final analysis, as reprehensible as the Knights' lust for infidel lands.

Although neither Minucci's nor Roselli's opinion was clearly related to the case that Eugenius IV was deciding, their opinions did provide the pope with the broad outlines of current canonistic thinking about the rights of infidels in the face of Christian expansion. These lawyers made it quite clear that although infidels possessed true *dominium*, this right was not absolute. The papal responsibility for all men's souls could supersede the infidels' right to *dominium* in certain circumstances. Both canonists also agreed that the pope alone was competent to authorize Christian armies to invade infidel lands.

In *Romanus Pontifex*, Eugenius authorized the Portuguese to oversee the conversion of the remaining infidels in the Canary Islands, regardless of where they lived. Taking his theme from

Duarte's letter, Eugenius stressed his role as Christ's vicar on earth. Because the earth and its fullness belonged to Christ, the pope, His vicar, could exercise Christ's authority over all and everything on earth.[72] The remainder of *Romanus Pontifex* restated traditional descriptions of papal power and responsibility. The bull did not reflect any specific points expressed in the opinions of Minucci and Roselli, nor did it discuss specific aspects of the situation in the Canary Islands. The pope focused closely on the general theme of universal papal authority, a theme that no canonist or king could reject.

The exchange between Eugenius IV and Duarte brought together the basic elements of the debate over the rights of infidels that was to occur over the next two centuries. Popes, canonists, theologians, philosophers, and, of course, Christian rulers were concerned about the justice of the conquests being made as Europeans began to reach out and discover new lands. The papal claim to universal responsibility for the souls of men, the claims of various Christian rulers to lands occupied by infidels, and the legal opinion that infidels possessed *dominium* formed three parts of an equation that needed resolving. As the opinions of Roselli and Minucci made very evident, the lawyers' theories about the rights of infidels did not always fit the realities of the situation to which they were applied. Furthermore, secular rulers and their legal advisors were quite capable of developing new justifications for overseas conquests that would fall within the categories of just conquest that the lawyers had already created. The existence of a primitive way of life among the Canarians would justify their conquest so that they might be raised to a civilized one to prepare them for the message of the gospel. The fierce nature of such people would obviously justify the use of Christian armies for the protection of the missionaries eventually sent to preach to them. Fierce, primitive infidels were as much obliged to admit peaceful missionaries as were the rulers of advanced infidel societies.

Eugenius IV's response to the Portuguese king's request for authorization to conquer the Canary Islands was not simply a legalistic evasion of the fundamental legal and moral problems involved in European expansion overseas. It must have been quite clear to the pope that European conquest of the Canary Islands, and of other lands occupied by infidels who did not pose a direct military threat to Christendom, would proceed with or without papal approval. The king's reference to wicked men who would not heed any papal prohibitions against such conquests could be applied to any number of figures; the king of Castile was not the only other Christian ruler anxious to expand his domains at the expense of infidels. There were also private individuals who would be willing to exploit the infidels. With an optimism not necessarily justified by the actual military conditions, Eugenius appears to have been resigned to European military conquest of the Canarians. The issue was not whether the Europeans could conquer the natives but when the conquest would be completed. The problem was bound to grow worse as the European exploration of the Atlantic and the movement along the west coast of Africa proceeded.[73] The pope had no forces available to him to block European advances in those areas, even if he wished to do so.

Eugenius recognized the papacy's need to ally itself with the advancing conquerors in order to insure fulfillment of the papacy's primary responsibility, the salvation of all men's souls. Previous popes had taken advantage of similar wicked deeds to further the papal mission. Innocent III had professed his dismay at the crusaders' capture of Constantinople in 1204, but he used that conquest to force the reunion of the Eastern Church with Rome.[74] There was strong precedent for Eugenius' actions with regard to the Canary Islands.

Furthermore, Eugenius may have felt that as long as Christian kings were anxious to obtain papal approbation for their expansionist activities, there remained an opportunity for the papacy to influence the direction of the conquest. If possession of a papal license was attractive to secular rulers, then possibly the threat of losing that approval would serve as a brake on the rulers' activities. By playing off one king against another, the pope would be in a position to ameliorate the effects of the conquest upon the conquered. Under such circumstances, primitive peoples, such as the Canarians, would eventually move to a more sophisticated cultural level.

Finally, Eugenius may simply have recognized that European conquest of the border regions would continue with or without papal approval. His choices were limited. He could condemn any such conquest but be unable to enforce the condemnation except in the spiritual order, or he could participate in the expansion. Since the Portuguese professed only the highest motives for their actions—

motives the same as those that inspired the papacy itself—the only path was that of participation in the hope that this would lead to the infidels' salvation. The choices were not pleasant ones—impotent condemnation or participation in conquests that were obviously inspired by less noble goals than those the Portuguese stated.

THE later fifteenth century saw a strong upsurge in European contacts with the peoples who lived beyond the borders of Christendom. Although the fall of Constantinople in 1453 and the subsequent advance of the Turks through the Balkans brought an end to major Latin attempts to convert the people of the Near East, this contraction of Christendom in the East was counterbalanced by the continuing Portuguese and Spanish expansion into the Atlantic. Following the capture of Ceuta and the renewal of interest in the Canary Islands, the Portuguese began the conquest and settlement of the Madeira Islands in 1420. By the 1430s they had discovered the Azores and in 1456 the Cape Verde Islands. Under the direction of Henry the Navigator, Portuguese seamen were slowly moving down the west coast of Africa, establishing outposts along the shore. In addition, although the settlement of the conflict between the Teutonic Knights and the kingdom of Poland by the Second Peace of Thorn in 1466 did not lead to the expansion of Christendom in the northeast, it did lead to the stabilization of the border between Latin Christendom and its eastern neighbors.[1] From the papal point of view, the likelihood of extending the Church's jurisdiction over infidels was gradually improving toward the end of the fifteenth century.

In these years, the papacy's role in European dealings with the non-Christian world was changing. The fall of Constantinople put the final nail in the coffin of papal crusading policy. The goal of saving the Eastern empire from the advancing Moslems, first announced by Urban II in 1095, had failed completely. In reality, of course, the papacy had lost its leadership role in the crusades during the thirteenth century, long before Constantinople fell. The rhetoric of the crusade continued to appear in papal letters, but the actual direction of the later attempts at crusading was in the hands of secular rulers. Likewise, the Second Peace of Thorn resulted not from acceptance of the papacy's judgment on the status of Lithuania but from a decisive war between the two parties. During the exploration and conquest of Africa and the island chains of the Atlantic, the Portuguese and the Castilians informed the papacy of their activities in traditional rhetorical forms that stressed their desire to spread the word of God. They acted, however, according to their own dynastic interests, seeking papal approval for courses of action already undertaken. Clearly, the day when popes could initiate policy toward the peoples beyond Christendom had passed. The temporal interests of European secular rulers, not papal spiritual interests, were directing the course of European contacts with infidels.

This did not mean that the papacy simply lost interest in the traditional forms of missionary work among the infidels. Papal registers continued to record letters appointing bishops to sees in North Africa and settling difficulties involving the Franciscans working in the Holy Land.[2] The friars continued to serve the spiritual needs of those Christians who lived under Moslem rule as well as the physical needs of the pilgrims who visited the places sanctified by Christ's life and death.[3] The missionary bull *Cum hora undecima* was also reissued, several times, for example, by Eugenius IV in 1433.[4] The privileges contained in it were reconfirmed in 1452 by Nicholas V.[5] Both popes emphasized that they were reissuing a bull with a history reaching back to the early fourteenth century. A link with the great mission to the Mongols appeared in 1448 with the appointment of a new bishop for Peking, the diocese created in the early fourteenth century.[6] Although the newly appointed bishop never visited his diocese, the fact that the appointment was made indicated that the earlier mission at least survived in memory.

The papacy played a much more active role in the appointment of bishops for the new dioceses created by the Portuguese conquests of the Canary, Madeira, Azores and Cape Verde island chains. Here the papacy trailed in the wake of the Portuguese advance. Missionary sees were created as the conquests proceeded, so that the establishment of these dioceses confirmed papal acquiescence in the work of conquest.[7]

The continuing series of conflicts between the Portuguese and the Castilians, who also claimed the Canaries, might have allowed the papacy to play a more directive role in the conquest.[8] In a wider sense, this conflict was not over control of the islands but rather over control of the trade between Europe and the Guinea coast of Africa. Each king sought a monopoly of the trade. Because the initial justification for the conquest of these regions was the desire of the Portuguese and the Castilians to spread the Christian faith, it was inevitable that the papacy would be drawn into the conflict. The result was a series of papal letters outlining the zones within which each kingdom would have exclusive responsibility for the work of Christianizing the natives. Each would, in other words, serve as the pope's agent in a specific region, fulfilling the pope's responsibility for the souls of the infidels living there.

A major stage in the delineation of zones was reached in 1454 when Pope Nicholas V issued the bull *Romanus Pontifex*, awarding the Canary Islands to the Portuguese over the objections of the Castilians, and justifying Portuguese expansion in terms of the traditional theory of the just war.[9] The bull outlined papal responsibility for the souls of men, extending to every corner of the world so that "the sheep divinely committed to Us might be brought to the Lord's one fold." The Portuguese role in this work lay in the efforts of their king to stop "the savage excesses of the Saracens and of other infidels" so that they might be brought into Christ's fold.[10] Nicholas traced the history of the Portuguese in Africa from their successful campaign against Ceuta up to the present. He found the Portuguese willingness to work for the defense of the Church and its expansion into areas where the name of Christ was previously unknown an admirable quality. The hoped-for result of this work would be the eventual union of Latin Christians with those Christians who lived beyond the Moslem world. Then the Moslems would be crushed as in a vise by the two branches of the one Church.

Because of the noble ends the Portuguese had espoused, Nicholas V gave Alfonso V of Portugal the right

> to invade, search out, capture, vanquish and subdue all Saracens and pagans whatsoever, and other enemies of Christ wherever they live, along with their kingdoms, dukedoms, principalities, lordships, and goods, both chattels and real estate, that they hold and possess. . . .

Alfonso was also empowered

to reduce their persons to perpetual slavery and to take for him-self and his heirs their kingdoms. . . .[11]

By stressing that these lands were occupied by enemies of the Christian faith, Nicholas was able to define these conquests as the product of a just war of defense against known enemies of Christendom. He also implied that missionaries would be unwelcome in these lands, and so Christians could justifiably use armed force to protect the preachers of the gospel there. The vistor in such a just war was within his rights in seizing the goods and power of the conquered. Furthermore, it was also acceptable to sell into slavery infidels defeated in a just war.[12]

Nicholas' bull was more, however, than a general letter approving a just war. It also contained specific information about the territorial boundaries within which the Portuguese would have exclusive responsibility for the conversion of the infidels. The region assigned to the Portuguese ran from the capes of Bojador and Nao, along the Guinea coast, and on through the south. The bull also granted the Portuguese a general license to acquire any lands "in the more distant and remote parts" that they could take "from the hands of infidels or pagans." Furthermore, the Portuguese were to have a monopoly of all trade with Saracens and infidels who dwelled in these lands.[13] Nicholas joined the exclusive right to trade with the regions specified in *Romanus Pontifex* with the Portuguese responsibility for providing clergy and building churches in the newly conquered lands. The costs that the Portuguese would bear in the missionary work upon which they had embarked would be repaid from the profits of the trading monopoly.

Presumably, *Romanus Pontifex* reflected the Portuguese version of the situation in West Africa.[14] Nicholas had to assume, in the absence of any other views, that the Portuguese were telling the truth. The Castilians, who had their own interests to pursue in the Atlantic, continued to harass the Portuguese in spite of Nicholas' bull. In 1479 the rulers of these kingdoms brought the first phase of their duel for control of West Africa to an end with the Treaty of Alcaçovas. The Castilians recognized Portuguese jurisdiction over the Guinea Coast, the Azores, the Madeiras, and the Cape Verde Islands. In turn, the Portuguese recognized Castilian possession of the Canary Islands.[15]

The course of European conquest in the Atlantic was similar to that of the conquest and Christianization of Lithuania. In both cases, the rights of the infidels took second place to the question of which of two conflicting Christian powers would dominate their lands, and in both cases the eventual conquest of the infidels was taken for granted. What was at stake was the final organization of the conquest. At the same time, the popes continued to act as if their court could resolve disputes between Christian rulers.

Two and a half centuries of legal and papal thinking about the responsibility of the pope for the souls of all men and about the right of non-Christians to govern themselves free of outside interference came to a climax in the fifty years following Columbus' momentous voyages. Columbus himself was deeply rooted in the medieval tradition of maritime development and in the medieval crusading tradition.[16] It should, therefore, come as no surprise that when Columbus' contemporaries came to analyze the consequences of his work, they did so in terms of the medieval legal tradition concerning the rights of infidels. Columbus presented his contemporaries with two very traditional questions: what were the rights of the infidels whom he encountered, and under what, if any, circumstances could Queen Isabella of Castile lay claim to the lands recently discovered.

When Columbus returned to Europe from his first voyage to the New World, he threatened to revive the conflict between Castile and Portugal that was supposed to have been settled by the Treaty of Alcaçovas. Forced by bad weather to put in at the first port he sighted, Columbus landed in the Azores. The Portuguese governor at first assumed that these Castilian ships had been engaged in an illegal trading voyage in West Africa, in violation of the treaty of 1479. Consequently, he began to arrest Columbus and his men, but after arresting some sailors and interrogating them, the governor accepted the Castilian story about having sailed directly west to lands not included in the papal grant to the Portuguese.[17] The discovery of the new lands created the same problems as had the earlier discoveries. The result was yet another series of papal bulls and, eventually, another treaty between Portugal and Castile, all designed to allocate jurisdictional zones to the two Iberian kingdoms. Because the papacy had been employed previously to resolve such issues, it was only logical to appeal to Pope Alexander VI (1492–1503) for a resolution of the matter.

The papal resolution of the problems that Columbus' discoveries presented was contained in three bulls, *Inter caetera* and *Eximiae devotionis*, both dated 3 May 1493, and a third bull also entitled *Inter caetera*, dated 4 May 1493.[18] These bulls covered approximately the same material, but there were some significant differences among them. In essence, all the bulls continued the work done in *Romanus Pontifex*. They created a zone within which the Castilians would be responsible for establishing churches and supporting missionaries. Strictly speaking, these bulls did not, as is often said, divide up the world between Castile and Portugal. They simply recognized that both kingdoms had asserted responsibility for converting the infidels in the lands they had discovered. As chief of the ecclesiastical structure, the pope was allocating spheres of ecclesiastical responsibility. At the same time, it is important to note that the letters obviously reflected the Castilian view of how the newly discovered lands should be treated. Although it is occasionally remarked that these bulls favored the Castilians because Alexander VI was himself from Valencia and therefore unduly inclined to favor his own countrymen, there is no need to assume collusion between the pope and the Castilians.[19] As we have seen, the papacy generally acted on the basis of the facts presented to it. Papal letters of authorization then contained a restatement of those facts and a conclusion based on them. For example, *Romanus Pontifex* had reflected the Portuguese view of the situation in the region of Guinea even though Nicholas V was not himself Portuguese.

In the prologue to both versions of *Inter caetera*, Alexander VI traced the history of Castilian crusading activity up to the conquest of Granada, the last step in ridding Spain of the Moslems who had conquered it seven centuries earlier. Having completed the reconquest, the rulers of Aragon and Castile could now begin their long-desired campaign to extend the bounds of the Church by bringing the word of the gospels to those nations that had not yet heard it. Describing the inhabitants of the lands Columbus had discovered in terms obviously taken from the explorer's own reports, Alexander portrayed them as a primitive but peace-loving people who seemed quite willing to accept the Christian faith.[20] The pope also recognized the Castilian determination to bring these people under Castilian domination in any event. As a result, the bulls he issued did not deal directly with the rights of the infidels. Rather, they focused on the narrow question of ecclesiastical jurisdiction within the new-found lands. After all, the agents of these kings were already occupying the lands in question. Alexander's bulls simply took advantage of the fact of the conquest to fulfill the papal responsibility for converting the infidels. Again, the papacy assumed that the conquest would be successful. In addition, Columbus' description of the people he met as primitive and simple would encourage papal support for the conquest in order to protect these simple people from exploitation by wicked Europeans, just as Eugenius IV had accepted the Portuguese claim that they would protect the Canarians.

In return for converting, civilizing, and protecting these newly encountered people, the pope granted dominion over these lands on the same terms on which his predecessors had given the Guinea coast of Africa to the Portuguese. The Castilians were to have a monopoly of trade and dominion, as the Portuguese did in the regions assigned to them. Again, the profits of the trading monopoly would recompense the Castilians for the costs of the missionary work and justify the exclusion of all other Christians from the region unless they possessed a license from the Castilian government.[21]

These bulls also contained a clause limiting the regions open to Castilian conquest to areas not actually possessed by other Christian rulers. Taken in isolation, this clause appears to assume that infidel *dominium* was invalid while the *dominium* of Christians was valid. In the context of the preceding papal letters, however, it would seem that this was not the case. If the Castilians encountered another Christian land, they could not claim it on the grounds they were spreading the faith and establishing the Church there. The existing Christian ruler would be responsible for insuring the spiritual well-being of his subjects, so that there would be no need for the Castilians to interfere. Again, the lawyers who actually drafted these bulls were careful to avoid a direct denial of infidel *dominium*.

The bulls Alexander issued in the spring of 1493 indicated that the papacy had acquiesced in the Christian conquest of the infidel world. At the same time, it had not given up all hope of influencing the course the conquest would take. As long as Christian kings continued to have conflicting claims to newly discovered lands and continued to bring these problems before the papal court to secure papal approval for what they were doing, the papacy would be in a position to exercise some influence on how the conquerors dealt with the people they conquered. As long as European rulers sought to justify their conquests by describing them as a program to extend the boundaries of the Church, the papacy would continue to play a role in the work of conquest. No secular ruler would deny that conquests based on spiritual motives belonged to the spiritual sphere, and so the pope as the supreme judge in spiritual matters was an essential part of Spanish and Portuguese overseas expansion.

The papal role in determining the course of expansion also depended on the existence of conflicts between Christian kingdoms that could be resolved by the papal court. Once such disputes were resolved to the satisfaction of the parties involved, the opportunity for papal intervention was ended. When the Portuguese and the Castilians signed the Treaty of Tordesillas in 1494, they settled their differences about the direction in which each would continue to expand. This treaty ended the last Portuguese hesitations about a permanent agreement with Castile. The parties agreed to change the line of demarcation between the zones assigned to each from 100 leagues west of the Azores or the Cape Verde Islands to a line 370 leagues west of the Cape Verde Islands.[22] There was no further need to seek papal decisions until the discovery of Asia necessitated a determination of the line of demarcation through the Pacific Ocean. Eventually Leo X had to issue the bull *Praecelsae devotionis* in 1514 to settle the matter.[23] His solution drew the line of demarcation through the Atlantic from pole to pole, thus allowing the Portuguese to lay claim to any infidel lands they discovered in the Pacific. Such a solution was obviously unacceptable to the Castilians, especially after a Castilian expedition led by Ferdinand Magellan discovered the Philippine Islands. Finally the Castilians and Portuguese worked out their own solution to the problem of jurisdiction in the Pacific without papal intervention. The Treaty of Sargossa in 1529 provided the basis for the solution, although opposition to it continued to exist in some Castilian quarters.[24] Again, the political and economic interests of the countries engaged in overseas expansion took precedence over the spiritual interests of the papacy.

In spite of the tendency to resolve jurisdictional disputes without papal involvement, the Castilians in particular remained sensitive about the legitimacy of the conquest. This sensitivity was not simply hypocrisy. There was a wide gulf between the way the government at home perceived the progress of the conquest and the way it actually took place on the frontier. The interests of the government were not identical with those of the conquistadores. The "Spanish struggle for justice in the conquest of the Americas," as Lewis Hanke described it, was also linked to the monarchy's traditional policy of insuring orderly absorption of newly won territories into the royal system of government.[25] The royal goal was to prevent the creation of a noble class capable of flouting the monarchy. As a result, the Castilian government's protestations about the abuses of the conquistadores and its assertion of interest in the spiritual well-being of the Indians were related to its own interests. Furthermore, the Castilians found it useful in European politics to continue seeking papal approval for their activities.

One gauge of the Castilian desire to prevent ecclesiastical criticism of their American conquests and to justify these conquests in terms of the legal tradition about the rights of infidels was the *Requerimiento* issued in 1512.[26] This was one of the most striking legal documents issued during the course of the conquest of the Americas, and it has generated a good deal of scholarly literature. A long line of critics, beginning with Bartholomew de Las Casas in the sixteenth century, has noted that this one document compressed into a narrow compass the combination of high-sounding motives, legal chicanery, and brute force that made the conquest of the Americas possible.[27] One modern scholar has summed up the *Requerimiento* as another "useless legalism" designed only to hide the brutal realities of the conquest.[28] Although from a modern standpoint such criticism is understandable, in the context of the medieval legal tradition within which the Castilian court operated, the *Requerimiento* made sense.[29]

The *Requerimiento* contained a statement of Christian beliefs and an explanation of the Spanish presence in the Americas. Before troops launched an attack on infidels, a priest was to read the document to them. Critics from Las Casas to the present have been scandalized by the vision of a friar reading this statement to an audience composed of trees or empty huts, or hurling its words at the backs of fleeing, uncomprehending Indians, terrified by the sight of armed strangers. There is no evidence that the text was ever translated into any American tongue so that the natives might have some opportunity to understand it.[30]

If the Indians had understood the words flung at them, they would have learned that the Christian Church claimed to be responsible for their spiritual well-being. Missionaries had come to preach the Christian message, and the infidels must admit them. Furthermore, King Ferdinand of Aragon and his daughter Queen Joanna of Castile, acting on behalf of the head of the Christian Church, had sent soldiers to protect the missionaries. The pope had also appointed Ferdinand and Joanna temporal overlords of these people so that the work of conversion could proceed smoothly. Should the infidels refuse to admit the peaceful missionaries, the Spanish troops who accompanied them could then legitimately march in, first to force their admission, and then to protect the missionaries while they preached.[31]

Scholars have long agreed with Las Casas' opinion that the *Requerimiento* embodied Hostiensis' opinion that infidels did not possess *dominium*. According to this view, the legal basis alleged for the Spanish conquest was that infidels were the usurpers of land and lordships that could rightfully be held only by Christians. The point of the *Requerimiento*, however, was that the infidels did have *dominium* and that the Spanish had to justify their invasion by demonstrating the unwillingness of the Indians to admit peaceful missionaries. Thus, the *Requerimiento* demonstrated the Castilians' reliance upon Innocent IV's views on the rights of infidels, not those of Hostiensis.

Las Casas himself recognized the theological impossibility of defending the conquest of the Americas according to Hostiensis' argument concerning the rights of infidels. He admitted to being puzzled by the fact that Juan Lopez de Palacios Rubios, a noted lawyer generally identified as the author of the *Requerimiento*, had relied on the Hostiensian argument.[32] Las Casas could not explain why a learned lawyer would rest the conquest on a legally and theologically unsound basis. The problem lay with Las Casas, however, not with Palacios Rubios. The friar did not appreciate that the Innocentian opinion about the rights of infidels did not absolutely forbid an invasion of an infidel society. Both Hostiensis and Innocent IV had concluded that Christians could lawfully invade and subdue an infidel society; they differed on the grounds that would justify the invasion.

Las Casas also seems to have been of the opinion that the purpose of reading the *Requerimiento* was to inform the Indians of the choices open to them: acquiescence or conquest. If this was the case, then the document was clearly a useless piece of legal ritual because the Indians could not possibly have understood it. In the light of the long debate about the rights of infidels, however, and in the light of the debate about Wyclif's opinions, the *Requerimiento* appears to have a different purpose from that which Las Casas attributed to it. The legally trained officials who staffed the Castilian government feared the charge of heresy that the argument that the infidels had no right to *dominium* might evoke. The purpose of the *Requerimiento* was to demonstrate to the papacy that the Castilian invasion of the Americas was based on the refusal of the natives to admit missionaries. The Castilians may have feared that the Portuguese or some other Christian people would inform the papacy that the Castilian conquest was illegal. Then the papacy would be asked to withdraw its approval of the Castilian conquest and grant another nation the monopoly of Christian contacts with the Americas. Having been involved in such a legal dispute with the Portuguese during the fifteenth century, the Castilians were well aware of the possibility of such an appeal to the papacy. If the Spanish conquest seemed to be based on the condemned doctrines of John Wyclif, the papacy would be within its rights in withdrawing its license from the Castilians and transfering the responsibility for converting the Indians to another Christian ruler who would proceed with the missionary work on terms acceptable to the papacy.

It is also clear that Palacios Rubios recognized the existence of true *dominium* in infidel societies. In a treatise he wrote about the nature of the Spanish claims to the Americas, *De las Islas del Mar Oceano*, Palacios Rubios emphasized that infidels did possess *dominium* and that Christians could not legitimately deprive them of their lands and their power simply because they were not Christians. The Spanish could invade the lands of infidels only for just cause.[33] As a way of emphasizing his adherence to the position of Innocent IV on this issue, the Castilian also noted that the coming of Christ had no effect on infidel possession of *dominium*. Thus, Palacios Rubios was well aware that the Castilian crown could not legitimately base its claims to the Americas on the opinion of Hostiensis. It would be necessary to use the opportunities provided by Innocent IV's opinion for that purpose. That is, such conquest had to be based on spiritual motives approved by the papacy.

Las Casas was correct in seeing some Hostiensian elements in Palacios Rubios' work, although this was only in a minor part of it. Following Hostiensis, the Castilian lawyer denied that infidel rulers could exercise lawful authority over Christians.[34] This opinion was widely held among the canonists, and apparently among philosophers as well, but it was not the only opinion on the matter; Innocent IV, for example, considered such a situation imprudent and dangerous to the faith of the Christians involved, but not an invalid exercise of infidel authority. In the long run, however, Palacios Rubios stressed the overriding responsibility of the pope for the souls of infidels as justification for the conquest of the Americas, and in so doing, he was hewing to the line of argument Innocent IV had charted.

The *Requerimiento* alone did not end the discussion of the legitimacy of the Castilian overseas conquests. Intellectuals, such as Francis Vitoria, and critics of the conquest, such as Bartholomew de Las Casas, continued to bring the issue to the attention of Charles V and his associates at the highest level of government. Primary Professor of Sacred Theology at the University of Salamanca, Vitoria was only one of many scholastic philosophers and theologians in sixteenth-century Spanish universities who criticized the conquest.[35] His *De Indis*, based on lectures given at the university, was a major contribution to the debate about the legitimacy of the conquest. Las Casas' works, though better known because of his vivid polemical style, were drawn from the same intellectual wells as Vitoria's. When Las Casas faced the theologian Juan Gines de Sepulveda in debate at Valladolid in 1550, the arguments of both the defenders of the conquest and its opponents were presented publicly to the leading figures of the kingdom.[36] Defenders of the conquest, such as Sepulveda, argued on Aristotelian grounds that the inhabitants of the Americas were inferior to Europeans and were, therefore, clearly designed by nature to be slaves.[37] In refuting this argument, Las Casas, like Vitoria before him, relied on the earlier canonistic discussion of the rights of the infidels.

Although Vitoria's *De Indis* was first published posthumously in 1557, it contained material he had presented in a series of lectures as early as 1532. Even then, these lectures were not the first scholarly treatment of the rights of the infidels in the face of Spanish conquest of the Americas. They reflected the continuing interest of Spanish intellectuals, lawyers, and bureaucrats in the legality of the conquest upon which their rulers had embarked. In an oblique reference to the lawyers' interest in the legitimacy of the conquest, Vitoria suggested that they were not the best-qualified persons to evaluate the situation:

> it is not for jurists to settle this question or at any rate not for
> jurists only, for since the barbarians in question . . . were not in
> subjection by human law, it is not by human, but by divine law
> that questions concerning them are to be determined. Now,
> jurists are not skilled enough in the divine law to be able by them-
> selves to settle questions of this sort.[38]

In Vitoria's opinion, the conquest of the Americas presented far
more than a narrow technical problem of jurisdiction. It was primarily a problem involving moral and spiritual matters that priests,
not lawyers, were best able to resolve. This opinion foreshadowed
the position Vitoria was to take on the legality of the conquest. The
papal responsibility for the souls of all men and the spiritual needs
of the Indians were the fundamental questions involved in any consideration of the legitimacy of the conquest. The temporal interests
of the Spanish crown were not important.

In spite of warning his readers about the insufficiency of legal
arguments, however, Vitoria drew heavily on the works of the
canon lawyers in the arguments presented in the *De Indis*. His debt
to them appeared clearly in the major theme he chose to develop in
considering whether the Spanish conquest of the Americas was
valid. He focused on the question of *dominium*: did the Indians
possess it, and under what, if any, circumstances could the Spanish
deprive them of it?

Vitoria's discussion of *dominium* began with a consideration of
the Aristotelian argument that some men are natural slaves, an argument often employed by those who defended the conquest.[39] The
Dominican rejected this argument on the grounds that all men
shared the same nature, so that some could not be natural slaves
while others were natural masters. Therefore, the Indians were as
capable of possessing *dominium* as the Spaniards were.

Vitoria then turned to the problem of whether sin affected legitimate possession of *dominium*: could men who were "sinners or were
unbelievers or were witless or were irrational" legitimately possess property and lordship?"[40] As he pointed out at the beginning of this discussion, the argument that *dominium* rested on grace was an old one,
reaching back to the Waldensians of the late twelfth century. The
focal point of Vitoria's discussion was the work of John Wyclif,
which, he noted, had been condemned at the Council of Constance.
Although Wyclif's opinions were not completely clear, Vitoria
pointed out that they were understood to mean "that the barbarians

had no dominion, because they were always in mortal sin."[41] Following the Fathers at Constance, Vitoria denied that mortal sin deprived a man of either natural *dominium*, that which ultimately is derived from God, or of civil *dominium*, that which is derived from human law. He pointed to the numerous wicked rulers to whom the ancient Hebrews were subjected with divine approval. Furthermore, Vitoria pointed out that since spiritual power, surely more important that civil authority, was not lost because of mortal sin, therefore civil *dominium* could not be lost by mortal sin either.[42]

In addition to the traditional arguments about the effect of sin on *dominium*, Vitoria presented a less common one, based on a decretal of Boniface VIII. In his *Cum secundum leges*, Boniface defended punishing condemned heretics with the loss of their property.[43] The basis for this practice was a Roman law authorizing similar punishment for those convicted of certain crimes. If crimes against the state could justify loss of property, so could heresy. Other lawyers extended the argument to infidels as well. Vitoria denied, however, that the fact of being a Jew, a Saracen, or some other kind of non-Christian meant that a man could not possess *dominium*. He argued that the loss of property by a heretic was the result of conviction of a crime by lawful authority, a judicial punishment. The conviction did not mean that the infidel had no right to *dominium* simply because he was an infidel.[44] He added that if heresy deprived a man of *dominium*, then a Catholic in a German Lutheran principality could not buy land from a Lutheran, a situation that would make normal business dealings impossible.[45] Consequently, from both theoretical and practical arguments based on the European experience, Vitoria concluded that:

> the barbarians in question cannot be barred from being true owners, alike in public and in private law, by reason of the sin of unbelief or any other mortal sin, nor does such sin entitle Christians to seize their goods and lands. . . .[46]

Having considered the general question of the right of infidels to *dominium* in the first part of the *De Indis*, Vitoria moved on to discuss the claims that had been put forth in defense of Spanish conquest of the Americas. He noted that defenders of the conquest alleged fifteen arguments, of which Vitoria defined seven as having no validity. Here again, the arguments revolved around the issue of *dominium* and involved the arguments developed by the canonists as well as by theologians and philosophers.

Of the seven claims that Vitoria judged invalid, five were deeply rooted in the canonistic tradition. Two of these claims were based on arguments concerning universal temporal jurisdiction by the Holy Roman Emperor and by the pope. Two other claims concerned the right of infidels to possess lordship and property and to select their own rulers. Finally, Vitoria discussed whether the Indians' refusal to accept the Christian faith was sufficient grounds to justify a Christian conquest.

The description of the emperor as the lord of the world came from Roman law and had passed into the writings of the canonists.[47] This argument was of special interest to the Castilians because their own king, Charles I, was also the Holy Roman Emperor Charles V. Vitoria approached this issue by asking whether there ought to be a single ruler over all mankind, an opinion held by some canonists, Roman lawyers, and political writers, such as Dante.[48] He also considered whether the coming of Christ might have had some effect on this issue. Citing Aquinas, but with overtones of Innocent IV as well, Vitoria concluded that there was no basis for assuming the necessity of a single government over all men. He described *dominium*, primarily the right of men to govern themselves, as the natural possession of all men.[49] He concluded therefore that there were no grounds for justifying the Christian conquest of the Americas on the basis of universal imperial jurisdiction.

Moving to the argument that the pope possessed universal jurisdiction in temporal affairs, Vitoria identified this assertion with Hostiensis and his followers.[50] If the pope was the true lord of the world in temporals, he would, of course, have the right to grant the Americas to the Castilians or any other Christian nation, but the Dominican argued that the pope's jurisdiction was restricted to spiritual matters. He pointed to Innocent III's argument that the king of France had no superior in temporal matters, an opinion often quoted by the canonists as evidence that the pope lacked any universal authority in temporals. If the pope did possess such power, the king of France would be subject to the papacy in temporals, something Innocent III's decretal denied.[51]

Vitoria went even further on the issue of papal jurisdiction over infidels in this section of the *De Indis*, denying papal spiritual jurisdiction over those outside the Church. He pointed out that the pope could not excommunicate them, nor could he impose the canonical laws of marriage on them. To this extent, he would not follow Innocent IV's line of argument about the pope's responsibility for those outside the flock of the Church. As a consequence, Vitoria concluded that one could not assert a Christian claim over the Americas on the basis of some universal jurisdiction belonging to the papacy.[52]

Logically, then, Vitoria denied that the refusal of infidels to accept the Christian faith would justify their conquest by Christians. He seems to have been envisaging the reading of the *Requerimiento* to assembled infidels when he discussed this point. In his opinion, simply reading a statement of Christian doctrine to the infidels was not a sufficient basis for claiming that they had failed to heed Christian preaching. Furthermore, if the infidels did accept baptism immediately upon hearing the *Requerimiento* read to them, it would indicate either lightness of mind or fear of Spanish retribution on their part, neither of which was a suitable basis for becoming a Christian. Presumably, therefore, any power that caused the acceptance of Christianity by infidels under these conditions would not be doing Christ's work and consequently would have no basis for claiming domination over the infidels involved.

On the question of punishing the infidels for violations of the law of nature, Vitoria again refused to go as far as Innocent IV had gone. In his opinion, ecclesiastical jurisdiction extended only to those who had voluntarily joined the Church; even in the case of sins against the law of nature, the pope has no special jurisdiction over infidels.[53] He seemed to reject here the notion that the law of nature was known to all men, and, therefore, that all men knew when they violated it, the position of Innocent IV. Vitoria also pointed out that since he had earlier rejected the assertion that the pope could make laws for the infidels, he could not now argue in support of a papal right to punish infidels for violations of law.

Vitoria also considered the claim that the Indians voluntarily submitted themselves and their *dominium* to the invading Spaniards.[54] If true, this would justify Spanish domination of the Americas because the transfer of *dominium* would have been based on the right of all societies to select their own rulers, as Innocent IV had argued. Vitoria needed no battery of authorities to reject this claim. He pointed out that even if a group of infidels did submit, they did so only because they feared the consequences of not doing so.[55]

Such submission was no more valid than was conversion to Christianity based on fear of Spanish troops. Kings, like baptism, could not be imposed by force or fear of force.

When Vitoria turned to the legitimate claims the Spanish could allege in support of their conquest of the Americas, he continued to use the arguments of the canonists as well as those of theologians and philosophers. As might be expected, the core of the arguments supporting the legitimacy of the conquest was the papal responsibility for converting all men. Underlying the right of missionaries to preach in infidel lands was not papal responsibility for all men, however, but, interestingly enough, the natural right of men to travel where they wished without interference. If the Indians refused to admit peaceful foreigners—not only missionaries but merchants and other kinds of travelers as well—the Spanish had the right to seize control of the infidels' lands and power.[56]

Having admitted a universal right to travel freely anywhere, Vitoria then went on to discuss the implications that this might have for missionary work among the infidels. The Spanish could claim the Americas on the grounds the pope had given them exclusive responsibility for the souls of those who lived there. If the work of conversion so required, the pope could even order the removal of the infidel rulers and their replacement with Christians. To illustrate this, Vitoria argued that if the infidels used violence against the missionaries or otherwise hindered the preaching of the gospel, then the Christians could lawfully declare war against them. Here again, he was agreeing with Innocent IV's opinion.

Vitoria then considered the possibility that an infidel ruler might persecute those of his subjects who had become Christians.[57] Again, following Innocent IV, he recognized the right of the coreligionists of such persecuted Christians to come to their aid in a just war. Vitoria was also careful to add that such armed assistance could spring not only from shared religious fellowship but from the natural friendship between two groups of people. In this way, the Spanish might come into possession of an infidel society with the approval of at least some of its members.

The conversion of a significant number of infidels could also lead to Spanish domination of the entire society if the ruler did not become a Christian voluntarily. Rather than risk the possibility that the ruler might at some point in the future order the persecution of Christians, the Castilians could remove the infidel ruler and install a

Christian ruler in his place. Here again, the higher good, the salvation of souls, would prevail over the lesser good, the *dominium* lawfully possessed by such a ruler.[58] One interesting corollary of this papal right to deprive infidels of *dominium* lawfully theirs, according to Vitoria, is that the pope might also put pressure on such an infidel ruler by declaring all Christian slaves held by him and his subjects freed even though such slaves were acquired and held legitimately. In effect, Vitoria seems to have been suggesting arousing a slave revolt in lands where infidels ruled.[59]

In spite of the earlier argument denying the Spanish the right to conquer the Indians because they were violating the law of nature, Vitoria developed an argument supporting a Christian conquest of an infidel society in which the infidel rulers were tyrannizing their subjects. Even without papal authorization, a Christian ruler could invade such a land and bring it under his own control for the good of the people who were so abused. Vitoria pointed to human sacrifice and the killing of innocent victims for the purpose of cannibalism as sufficient cause for removing an infidel ruler.[60] Here he explicitly cited Innocent IV's argument concerning the right of Christians to intervene in cases where infidels violated the law of nature. Although he did not resolve the contradiction between his opinion here and his previous rejection of similar arguments, Vitoria seems to have distinguished between sins committed by private individuals and a society's policy of tolerating the murder of numerous innocent people. Even if the victims themselves agreed to submit voluntarily to such a death, they lacked any right to do so. Vitoria seems to be verging on the argument that as the purpose of government is the security of life and property, any ruler who deprived his subjects of life, except as the consequence of having committed a crime, violated the pact that should exist between ruler and ruled. No group of people could voluntarily renounce their right to live. Under such circumstances, Christians could intervene to protect the people from being killed even if they did not wish to be so protected.

Yet another possible basis for Castilian domination of the Americas lay in the voluntary submission of the infidels to the Spanish. If the natives, becoming aware of the virtues of the Spanish, freely chose the king of Castile as their ruler, they could legitimately do so.[61] Here again, Innocent IV's argument about the right of all societies to select their own rulers could serve as a basis for Spanish control of the New World. This, of course, would mean the deposition of an infidel ruler who had until that point held his office legitimately. Vitoria was asserting, once again, a contract theory of government in which the ruler held office only as long as the people wished.

Finally, Vitoria considered the claim that the infidels were unfit to govern themselves at a human and civilized level. In language very similar to that employed by King Duarte of Portugal over a century earlier, Vitoria described such people as lacking laws and officials, any sort of learning and artistic work, even organized agricultural activity, as well as craftsmen of all kinds. He admitted the value of such an argument and the precedents for it. Such people could be fairly compared to children, and they required care and guidance just as children did.[62] At the same time, he was not convinced of the validity of such a claim as a basis for the conquest of the Americas.

In general, Vitoria seemed skeptical about the legitimacy of the American empire emerging under Charles V. Like Innocent IV, he saw such conquests as valid only if they were undertaken with the right intention and carried out for the welfare of the Indians, not for the profit of the Spanish. What was obviously lacking in this discussion for the most part was firsthand knowledge of the situation in the Americas. Even if the Spanish conquest was directed by only the highest principles, the actual work of the conquest might be carried out in such a way as to vitiate the noble intentions underlying it.

Bartholomew de Las Casas more than made up for Vitoria's lack of firsthand knowledge of the conquest. When he came to attack the Spanish role in the Americas, Las Casas filled his polemics with evidence about the progress of the Spanish conquest derived from his own career as a colonist before his religious conversion and ordination. As a polemicist, he drew first upon his own experience to impress upon the Spanish rulers the evils that their invasion of the Americas had caused. He did not, however, rely solely on vivid tales of Spanish atrocities in the Americas to persuade the government to change its policy toward the overseas possessions. Like Vitoria, he approached the legally trained bureaucrats who administered the empire through arguments based on the legal tradition about the rights of infidels. Furthermore, he stressed legal, not theological, arguments "because they would carry more weight than the speculations of the theologians."[63]

In one of his later writings, the *De thesauris in Peru*, Las Casas took the fundamental canonistic position on the right of infidels to *dominium* and then developed it even further than the canonists had done. Starting with Innocent IV's conclusion that all human societies had the right to select their own rulers, Las Casas added the legal doctrine of *quod omnes tangit debet ab omnibus approbari:* that is, "what affects all must be approved by all." In so doing he linked two important legal traditions that reinforced each other. Legal theorists had long agreed that major decisions affecting an entire society required the consent of all those who belonged to that society. Although the audience to which Las Casas was directing his criticism of Spanish policy might not have given a great deal of thought to Innocent IV's views on *dominium* and the right of a society to select its own leaders, its members would know the legal tag *quod omnes tangit* and what it signified.[64] From both these arguments, Las Casas was able to deny any papal right to deprive an infidel ruler of his office and replace him with a Spanish ruler. Like Vitoria, Las Casas concluded from this line of argument that the only way a Spanish ruler could legitimately claim domination of the Americas would be if the native population freely selected him as their ruler in preference to their present one.

Turning to Alexander VI's bull *Inter caetera*, the friar was then able to refute the argument that the bull awarded temporal jurisdiction over the Americas to the Castilians. According to Las Casas, what the bull granted was spiritual jurisdiction over the mission territory described therein. This reading of the bull transferring the lands of the Indians "with all their lordships and jurisdictions" to Castilian control assumes that although the bull appears to transfer the temporal *dominium* of these people to the Castilians, the words do not mean what they appear to say.[65] Again turning to the legal tradition for support, Las Casas denied to the pope any right to issue grants prejudicial to the rights of a third party without consulting that party. Consequently, Alexander could not have deprived the Indians of their temporal lordship and their property in the Americas.[66] Here again, Las Casas' selective use of legal arguments may have led him to overlook the full implications of Innocent IV's opinion about infidel *dominium*. If the Indians were defined as having refused to allow peaceful missionaries to preach the gospel in their lands, the pope could indeed deprive their leaders of *dominium* because the right to lordship included the responsibility to insure the physical and the spiritual well-being of one's subjects. Refusal to admit missionaries would be harmful to the spiritual health of the Indians. The protection of the missionaries could be insured only if the Spanish government took possession of the region. Where Las Casas saw an absolute barrier to a legitimate Spanish conquest, the legal tradition saw a hierarchy of goods with the pope as the ultimate judge of which right was primary.

The work of men like Palacios Rubios, Vitoria, and Las Casas was a major effort to shape Spanish colonial policy along the lines first set down by the medieval canonists. The effects of the conquest were obviously not those envisioned in legal theorizing about the rights of infidels and the papal responsibility for the souls of all men. It is, however, important to realize that the interest of the Spanish government lay in having an orderly, peaceful conquest. Because the conquest of the New World was understood as an extension of the reconquest of Spain, the government wished the newly won territories to be integrated smoothly into the Spanish system of government. Just as the kings of Spain had wanted proper papal authorization for their expansion in order to have a clear title to their work in Spain, these kings and their servants wanted a legally correct settlement of the Americas. To that extent, the lawyers, the popes, and the Castilian government agreed that the conquest should proceed only along lines that would safeguard the rights of the natives from the depredations of the conquistadores. As long the the Spanish did not feel secure in their possession of the Americas, the government gave at least lip service to the opinions of the canonists. It is no coincidence that the *Requerimiento* fell into disuse in the 1540s as the work of conquest passed from a tentative probing of the American mainland to an established fact. Although the government never completely rejected the theories of the lawyers about the rights of the infidels and the corresponding responsibilities of the Christians for their well-being, the interests of the Spanish empire came to dominate the work of conquest, gradually displacing the spiritual goals originally announced as the basis for it.

CONCLUSION

THE three hundred years from Innocent IV to Bartholomew de Las Casas formed a coherent period in the development of European attitudes toward non-Europeans. This period stands between the era in which the crusades, based on the theory of the just war, dominated European relations with non-Europeans and the era of modern international law, which is concerned with both war and peace among nations. Innocent IV's commentary on *Quod super his* was the first serious consideration of the possibility that European Christians could live at peace with non-Christians. By grounding the right to possess property and lordship on the natural law that is common to all men, Innocent IV provided a theoretical basis for securing the rights of infidels in the face of European expansion. At the same time, Innocent IV was also clearly working within the tradition of the just war. Although peaceful relations with infidels were possible, he was primarily interested in the defense of Europe from invading infidels, and so the theory of the just war played a large role in his thinking about the rights of infidels *vis-à-vis* Christians.

Although it might be possible to describe Innocent IV as the father of international law, there would be little purpose in doing so. The narrow focus of his work and the brevity of his commentary provided too small a foundation upon which to construct a broad theory of international law and international relations, at least as these terms are understood in the modern world. The argument that Innocent IV, rather than Grotius, Vitoria, or Vladimiri, deserves to be called the father of international law misses the point about the medieval contribution to the creation of international law. The important questions that need to be answered are how did Christian Europeans view their infidel neighbors during the Middle

Ages, and in what legal framework did they place these perceptions. Only then should we ask what effect, if any, did this tradition have upon the development of modern international law.

The fundamental difference between the medieval approach to international law and the modern approach is that for medieval thinkers the issue was essentially an ecclesiological one. For Innocent IV and those who followed him, the key to Christian European relations with those who were neither Christian nor European was the nature of the Christian Church. Innocent IV had defined the Church as including all men—potentially, if not in actuality. The mission of the pope was to insure that the gospel was preached to the infidels so that they would become full-fledged members of the Church, as was their rightful destiny. Modern international law concerns the relations between states, not between an ecclesiastical institution and individuals that are its potential members.

Furthermore, the medieval papal and legal approach to those outside the Church was rooted in the long tradition of conflict between the spiritual and temporal powers within Europe. In the two centuries from Gregory VII to Innocent IV, popes and lawyers had dealt at length with the relations that should exist between the two powers. The debate was not about which sphere had priority, because both sides agreed that the spiritual power was superior to the secular. The crux of the debate was the extent to which the representatives of the spiritual power could interfere in the secular sphere. At one extreme were a few thinkers like Alanus, who argued that as *dominium* rested on grace, sinners could not possess lordship or property in a Christian society. This position virtually erased the distinction between the spiritual and the temporal jurisdictions, leaving the spiritual authority as the only source of legitimate power. Such a blunt assertion of spiritual authority was too extreme for the majority of canonists and popes. The idea of the pope as the priest-king of Christian society, while attractive to some thinkers, was obviously not the role Christ descirbed in the gospels. In the final analysis, Alanus' position was unacceptable because there were things that were Caesar's and things that were not. The rejection of Alanus' views meant that the conquest of the infidel world could not be justified on the grounds that infidels could not legitimately possess *dominium* because they were not in the state of grace. Wyclif's later use of similar ideas made the dangers of Alanus' position quite obvious. The result was that another argument would have to be developed to justify the conquest of infidel societies in canonistic terms.

The canonists, by examining Christian-infidel relations only in ecclesiological terms, were building their discussion of international law and relations on a framework that was too small to bear the weight of a fully developed theory of international law. Even the inclusion of the theory of the just war did not broaden the intellectual basis sufficiently to enable the canonists to develop such a theory. The result was that even if the canonists had intended to develop a theory of international law from canonistic materials, they lacked an adequate theoretical base.

The second major weakness in the medieval canonistic approach to relations with non-Christians was the failure of the popes and the lawyers to assimilate the ever-increasing European experience of dealing with non-European and non-Christian societies. Innocent IV's commentary on *Quod super his* was accepted as the fullest treatment of the problem imaginable, just as *Cum hora undecima*, reissued virtually unchanged, was the fullest statement of missionaries' powers, and *Gaudemus* remained the basis for dealing infidel marriages. It would be possible to attribute the practice of constantly repeating old positions to the extremely heavy workload of the papal staff; the use of standard formulae is, of course, a regular bureaucratic practice. This cannot be the complete explanation, however; nor can the lack of development be attributed solely to the fact that papal-infidel relations were only a small part of papal activity. One is left with the impression that the popes and lawyers were so much intimidated by the work of their great thirteenth-century predecessors that they hesitated to move beyond their conclusions. The fourteenth- and fifteenth-century figures seem to have felt inferior to their thirteenth-century counterparts much as medieval philosophers remained for centuries intimidated by Aristotle. Given the comparatively low estate of the late medieval papacy, the thirteenth-century papacy may well have seemed a golden age to popes dwelling in Avignon or facing the Great Schism and the conciliar controversy. Likewise, the later canonists may well have been overwhelmed by the great mass of opinions, commentaries, and other legal materials they were expected to master before moving on to working out their own creative solutions to legal problems. One of the curious aspects of late medieval canon law is the increasing length of the commentaries written on the *Decretales*. This is often said to illustrate the mentality of the canonists in this period, who collected the opinions of their predecessors without adding significantly to the body of legal thought.[1] The commentary written by Innocent IV, on the other hand, was relatively short, usually published in a single volume, a sharp contrast to the two or more volumes that later canonists filled.

The failure of the late medieval popes to develop their predecessors' initiative regarding infidels clearly paralleled the decline in papal power that occurred during the fourteenth and fifteenth centuries. The struggles with the French monarchs and the Church's internal crisis occupied a great amount of papal administrative and intellectual energy. At the same time, however, the men who occupied the papal throne during these decades were generally competent administrators. They may not have been the intellectual and administrative equals of Innocent III or Innocent IV, but neither were they nonentities. Furthermore, the personal failings of individual popes could be made up for by the work of the curia, and the papal staff continued throughout the period to function as a well-oiled administrative machine in its daily operations. But although the decline in papal power was probably not as great as some scholars have claimed it was, the increased bureaucratization of the papacy may have contributed to the failure of the popes to respond more imaginatively to the problems posed by the infidels. The great mass of regular correspondence moving through the papal Curia in the late Middle Ages would have hampered those figures, like Innocent III and Innocent IV, who had contributed greatly to making the papal court a focal point of bureaucratic activity. The amount of such activity may even have masked from those who were actually engaged in it the decline in real power that the papacy was undergoing. Nevertheless, the correspondence of the popes who ruled in these centuries reflects that decline.

There was yet another reason for the failure of the popes and lawyers of the late Middle Ages to develop further the work of their thirteenth-century predecessors regarding infidels. The initiative in dealings with non-European societies was passing to secular rulers. Popes after Innocent IV did not initiate contacts with infidel societies; they responded to ambassadors from such societies or to requests from potential missionaries. The next sign of this decline in papal interest was the undertaking of conquests of infidel lands by secular rulers who then sought papal approval for their activities. The increasing role of secular rulers in overseas expansion paralleled the general increase of royal power at the time. The assertiveness of the thirteenth-century popes toward secular rulers was a reflection of the kings' weakness as much as of the popes' strength. When the secular rulers had secured their positions by reducing the power of their nobles, they could then more easily ignore papal injunctions. It also became easier to assert initiative in the work of expansion. Rulers such as Duarte of Portugal were willing to base their desire to expand overseas on the traditional grounds of converting the infidels and protecting Christendom from infidel invasion. Nevertheless, it is also quite clear that these rulers saw political and economic gains for themselves and their subjects in these efforts. Gradually, the medieval motives for expansion, expressed in religious terms, gave way to secular justifications. As a result, by the mid-sixteenth century, the papacy no longer issued letters authorizing expansion, because no secular ruler was requesting them.

Another sign of the change can be seen in the description of the regions open to European conquest. Where Columbus and his predecessors had been authorized to occupy territory not presently occupied by Christians, during the sixteenth century explorers sailed with royal letters authorizing them to occupy lands not presently ruled by European princes.[2] This verbal change summed up the transfer of leadership in expansion from the papacy to the secular rulers of Europe. It was no longer the spiritual jurisdiction that set the rules for contact with the peoples beyond Europe; it was the secular rulers. It was no longer the spiritual mission of preaching salvation that was supposed to guide explorers and conquerors; it was the desire to avoid wars with other Christian rulers that determined which lands were open to European invasion. By the time that Vitoria and Las Casas condemned the conduct of the Spanish conquest of the Americas, the legal arguments they employed were irrelevant to the actual situation. The royal lawyers who heard or read their arguments understood these views because they also had been educated in that legal tradition. The actual practice of conquest, however, had gone beyond the canonistic legal framework. Vitoria and Las Casas were anachronisms. It is no wonder that at the same time, other thinkers, generally Protestants, were looking for another, more suitable basis for dealing with the problems that European encounters with the non-European world had created.

In the last half of the sixteenth century, men like Balthazar de Ayala (1548–84) and Alberico Gentili (1552–1608) began paving the way for Hugo Grotius (1538–1645) to write the *De Iure Belli ac Pacis*, the foundation of all modern thinking on international law and relations.

The new international law, however, was not completely distinct from the old. Grotius and his immediate predecessors had read many of the same writers that had shaped the canonistic theory of relations between states. He had also read the works of Vitoria and Joannes de Legnano, among others. Furthermore, in discussing the right of Europeans to punish those who violated the laws of nature, he admitted his debt to the work of Innocent IV: "Thus far we follow the opinion of Innocent and others who say that war may be waged upon those whose sin is against nature."[3] Grotius set the issue of international law and relations in a broader perspective than had Innocent IV or the other canonists, but there are clear links between the two schools of thought. Contrary to some modern opinions, Grotius also retained some of the moralizing flavor of the canonists' work on infidels, as the statement about the right to punish the violators of the natural law demonstrates. As was the case in so many aspects of sixteenth- and seventeenth-century life, the medieval substructure was just beneath the surface, not always perceptible from the vantage point of the twentieth century, but obvious when looked at from the medieval perspective.

APPENDIX: A NOTE ON MEDIEVAL ATTITUDES AND MODERN RACISM

The current American debate about the relations between whites on the one hand and blacks and Indians on the other has generated a great deal of literature touching on the origins of white European attitudes toward nonwhite, non-European peoples. In one way or another, much of this work touches upon the question of what effect, if any, medieval attitudes toward such peoples had on the formation of modern racial attitudes. Three important books sum up the current state of scholarship: David Brion Davis, *The Problem of Slavery in Western Culture* (Ithaca, N.Y.: Cornell University Press, 1966); Winthrop D. Jordan, *White Over Black: American Attitudes Toward the Negro, 1550-1812* (Chapel Hill, N.C.: University of North Carolina Press, 1968); and Francis Jennings, *The Invasion of America: Indians, Colonialism, and the Cant of Conquest* (Chapel Hill, N.C.: University of North Carolina Press, 1975).

These three authors argue that American attitudes toward non-Europeans spring from roots deep within the European cultural tradition. They differ, however, in the way they perceive these roots and their effects. Davis, for example, devotes a great deal of attention to the justifications for slavery, especially the enslaving of black Africans, developed by theologians and philosophers. Jordan, on the other hand, points to the literary tradition that described the "wild man," a hairy, beast-like creature who lived on the fringes of civilized society. When this myth was combined with European encounters with manlike apes in Africa, it was possible to assert that Africa was inhabited by humanlike creatures who were biologically inferior to Europeans.

While Davis and Jordan point to what might be termed racist attitudes among Europeans—that is, the belief that certain kinds of people are biologically inferior to Europeans—Jennings takes another tack. In his opinion, Europeans viewed other peoples not as biologically inferior, but as culturally inferior. The white, European Christian world represented civilization, while those who were not Christians and who did not accept European standards of behavior were savages or uncivilized people whom the Europeans could legitimately conquer in order to raise them up to civilization. This line of argument, unlike that of Davis and Jordan, suggests that Europeans did not see non-Europeans as different biologically from themselves; thus, in that sense, Jennings would seem to deny that Europeans were racists.

All three scholars assume, on the basis of limited research on the question, that the attitudes of modern Americans toward the nonwhite population are derived from medieval experience. In fact, however, medievalists have done little work on the problem of racial attitudes. Jordan used Richard Bernheimer's *Wild Men in the Middle Ages* (Cambridge: Harvard University Press, 1952) to develop his argument about the medieval basis of racism, but Bernheimer's work described the literary figure of a human creature who had degenerated to a more primitive level of existence: the wild man is not a biologically inferior being.

Most of the research on European racial attitudes deals not with the Middle Ages but with the sixteenth century. As a result, it is not possible to declare flatly at this point whether Jennings or Davis and Jordan are correct about the origins of modern attitudes, or, indeed, if any one of them is. Much more research by medievalists will be necessary before the answer can be found. The argument in the present volume is closer to that of Jennings in that it does not find racial thinking at the heart of papal and legal responses to the non-European world. For a discussion of the way in which ideas about cultural inferiority may have been transformed into a theory of biological inferiority, see James Muldoon, "The Indian as Irishman," *Essex Institute Historical Collections* 111 (1975): 267–89.

NOTES

Introduction

1. The basic positions in these debates are conveniently summarized in: Karl H. Dannenfeldt, ed., *The Renaissance, Medieval or Modern*, Problems in European Civilization (Boston: D. C. Heath, 1959); Denys Hay, ed., *The Renaissance Debate*, European Problem Studies (New York: Holt, Rinehart and Winston, 1965); Lewis W. Spitz, ed., *The Reformation: Basic Interpretations*, Problems in European Civilization, 2d. ed. (Lexington, Mass.: D. C. Heath, 1972).

2. See, for example: Boies Penrose, *Travel and Discovery in the Renaissance, 1420–1620* (Cambridge: Harvard University Press, 1955; reprint ed., New York: Atheneum, 1962); C. R. Boxer, *Four Centuries of Portuguese Expansion, 1415–1825* (Berkeley: University of California Press, 1961); J. H. Parry, *Europe and a Wider World, 1415–1715* (London: Hutchinson University Library, 1966).

3. See James Muldoon, ed., *The Expansion of Europe: The First Phase* (Philadelphia: University of Pennsylvania Press, 1977), pp. 4–7.

4. C. R. Boxer, *The Portuguese Seaborne Empire, 1415–1825* (New York: Knopf, 1975), p. 37.

5. For a survey of this literature, see James Muldoon, "The Contribution of the Medieval Canon Lawyers to the Formation of International Law," *Traditio* 28 (1972): 483–97; and Kenneth J. Pennington, Jr., "Bartolome de Las Casas and the Tradition of Medieval Law," *Church History* 39 (1970): 149–61.

6. The present state of the study of medieval canon law can be seen in the *Bulletin of Medieval Canon Law*, published annually since 1971 by the Institute of Medieval Canon law; and in Walter Ullmann, *Law and Politics in the Middle Ages: An Introduction to the Sources of Medieval Political Ideas*, The Sources of History: Studies in the Uses of Historical Evidence (Ithaca, N.Y.: Cornell University Press, 1975), pp. 119–89.

7. John Calvin, *Institutes of the Christian Religion*, ed. John T. McNeill, trans. F. L. Battles, Library of Christian Classics, vols. 20, 21 (Philadelphia: Westminster Press, 1960). Under "Gratian, *Decretum*," there are one and a half columns of references given in the author and source index. There are only three references to the *Decretales*.

8. Garrett Mattingly, *Renaissance Diplomacy* (Boston: Houghton

Mifflin, 1955; reprint ed., Baltimore: Penguin, 1964), p. 246 (page references are to the 1964 edition).

9. See Muldoon, "The Contribution of the Medieval Canon Lawyers," pp. 488–91.

10. Frederic W. Maitland, "Moral Personality and Legal Personality," *The Collected Papers of Frederic William Maitland*, ed. H. A. L. Fisher, 3 vols. (Cambridge: Cambridge University Press, 1911), 3: 304–20 at 310.

Chapter 1

1. *Corpus Iuris Canonici*, ed. Emil Friedberg, 2 vols. (Leipzig: Bernard Tauchnitz, 1879–81), vol. 1, *Decretum*, C.23 q.4 c.17, *Infideles*. It is worth noting that the title of this *causa* is *De re militari et bello*.

2. Ibid., C.28 q.1 c.10, *Iudaei*, c.11, *Iudaeorum filios*. These appear in the *causa* headed *De nuptiis et coniunguo cum infideli*. Concerning the Church and the Jews, see Edward A. Synan, *The Popes and the Jews in the Middle Ages* (New York: Macmillan, 1965); Salo Wittmayer Baron, *A Social and Religious History of the Jews*, vol. 9, *Under Church and Empire*, 2d ed. (New York: Columbia University Press, 1965).

3. *Corpus Iuris Canonici*, vol. 2, *Decretales*, 5.6, *De Iudaeis Sarracenis et eorum servis*; 5.7, *De Haereticis*; 5.8, *De Schismaticis. et ordinatis ab eis*. Subsequently, the *Decretales* will be identified as X, a standard abbreviation derived from its originally being described as the *Liber extra*.

4. Ibid. 5.6.2, *Multorum ad nos*; 5.6.3, *Iudaei de civitate*; 5.6.7, *Consulit*.

5. Ibid. 5.6.6, *Ita quorundam*.

6. Ibid. 5.6.12, *Quod olim*.

7. James A. Brundage, *Medieval Canon Law and the Crusader* (Madison: University of Wisconsin Press, 1969), pp. 189–90. See also Michel Villey, *La Croisade: essai sur la formation d'une théorie juridique* (Paris: J. Vrin, 1942).

8. The most recent study of the medieval theory of the just war is Frederick H. Russell, *The Just War in the Middle Ages*, Cambridge Studies in Medieval Life and Thought, series 3, no. 8 (Cambridge: Cambridge University Press, 1975). In addition, see James T. Johnson, *Ideology, Reason, and the Limitation of War: Religion and Secular Concepts, 1200–1740* (Princeton: Princeton University Press, 1975).

9. On the relationship between medieval and early modern theories of international relations, see Muldoon, "The Contribution of the Medieval Canon Lawyers, pp. 496–97. The standard introduction to the study of medieval international relations is François L. Ganshof, *The Middle Ages: A History of International Relations*, trans. Rémy Inglis Hall (New York: Harper & Row, 1970).

10. Although Innocent IV was one of the most important figures in both the history of the papacy and the development of canon law, he has not attracted a biographer. The standard study of his life and career is Horace K. Mann, *Lives of the Popes in the Early Middle Ages from 590 to 1304*, 18 vols. (London: K. Paul, Trench, Trubner, 1902–32), vol. 14. Brief treatments are to be found in: *Dictionnaire de droit canonique*, ed. R. Naz, 7 vols. (Paris: Letouzey et Ané, 1935–65), 7:1029–62; *New Catholic Encyclopedia* (hereafter *NCE*), 15 vols. (New York: McGraw-

Hill, 1967), 7: 524–25, "Innocent IV, Pope." See also Vito Piergiovanni, "Sinibaldo dei Fieschi Decretalista: Ricerche sulla vita," *Studia Gratiana* 14 (1967): 125–54; Marcel Pacaut, "L'autorité pontificale selon Innocent IV," *Le Moyen Age* 66 (1960): 85–119; J. A. Kemp, "A New Concept of the Christian Commonwealth in Innocent IV," in *Proceedings of the Second International Congress of Medieval Canon Law*, ed. Stephan Kuttner and J. J. Ryan, (Vatican City: Biblioteca Apostolica Vaticana, 1965), pp. 155–59; J. A. Cantini, "De autonomia judicis saecularis et de Romani Pontificis plenitudine potestatis in temporalibus secundum Innocentium IV," *Salesianum* 23 (1961): 407–80. There is a very useful survey of recent literature dealing with Innocent IV's views on papal power: Carlo Dolcini, " 'Eger cui lenia' (1245/46): Innocenzo IV, Tolomeo da Lucca e Guglielmo d'Ockham," *Rivista di Storia della Chiesa in Italia* 39 (1975): 127–48.

11. A convenient introduction to the Mongol mission is I. de Rachewiltz, *Papal Envoys to the Great Khans* (Stanford: Stanford University Press, 1971).

12. X.3.34.8. Brundage, *Medieval Canon Law*, p. 77; James Muldoon, " '*Extra ecclesiam non est imperium:*' The Canonists and the Legitimacy of Secular Power," *Studia Gratiana* 9 (1966): 551–80 at 572–75.

13. Innocent IV, *Commentaria doctissima in Quinque Libros Decretalium* (Turin: Apud haeredes Nicolai Beuilaquae, 1581), 3.34.8, fol. 176v: "Pro defensione. Hoc non est dubium, quod licet Papae fidelibus suadere, et indulgentias dare, ut Terram sanctam, et fideles habitantes in ea defendant . . . , sed nunquid est licitum invadere terram, quam infideles possident, vel que est sua?" A partial translation of this commentary is available in Muldoon, *The Expansion of Europe*, pp. 191–92; and also in Brian Tierney, *The Crisis of Church and State, 1050–1300* (Englewood Cliffs, N.J.: Prentice-Hall, 1964), pp. 155–56.

14. Innocent IV, 3.34.8., fol. 176v: "Quod autem Papa facit indulgentias illis, qui vadunt ad recuperandam terram sanctam, licet eam possideant Saraceni, et etiam inducere bellum, et dare indulgentias illis qui occupant Terram sanctam: quam infidels illicite possident."

15. Ibid.: "unde licitum est Papae ratione Imperii Romani, quod obtinet, illud ad suam iurisdictionem revocare, qua iniuste expoliatus est . . . et haec ratio sufficit in omnibus aliis terris, in quibus Imperatores Romani iurisdictionem habuerunt, licet posset dici quod hoc iure scilicet ratione Imperii non possit, cum ecclesia non habeat Imperium nisi in Occidentem, 96 dist. Constan."

16. *Decretum*, D.96 c.14, *Constantinus*. The fundamental study of the Donation of Constantine and its place in medieval legal thought is Domenico Maffei, *La Donazione di Cosantino nei giuristi medievali* (Milan: A. Giuffrè, 1964).

17. Maffei, *La Donazione di Cosantino*, pp. 3–22; R. W. and A. J. Carlyle, *A History of Mediaeval Political Theory in the West*, 6 vols. (Edinburgh and London: William Blackwood and Sons, 1903–36), 2: 213. Concerning the application of the Donation to papal claims to jurisdiction over islands lying off the European mainland, see Luis Weckmann, *Las Bulas Alejandrinas de 1493 y la Teoría Política del Papado Medieval* (Mexico City: Editorial Jus, 1949). Weckmann's views were strongly criticized when he first presented them. See the review of *Las Bulas Alejandrinas* in *Speculum* 25 (1950): 306–11 by C. J. Bishko.

18. Innocent IV, 3.34. 8., fols. 176v–77r: ". . . Imperator potest facere ex aliis redictis causis, vel ad minus imperator potest facere ut Rex Hierusalem ad quem regnum illud de iure venit." Concerning Frederick II's claim to the title king of Jerusalem, see Thomas C. Van Cleve, "The Crusade of Frederick II," in Kenneth M. Setton, ed. *A History of the Crusades*, vol. 2, *The Later Crusades, 1189–1311*, ed. Robert Lee Wolff and Harry W. Hazard, 2d ed. (Madison: University of Wisconsin Press, 1969), pp. 429–62 at pp. 442–43, 455–56; Mary Nickerson Hardwicke, "The Crusader States, 1192–1243," ibid., pp. 522–56 at pp. 541–45; Ernst Kantorowicz, *Frederick II, 1194–1250*, trans. E. O. Lorimer (London: Constable, 1931; reprint ed., 1957), pp. 184–89; Thomas Curtis Van Cleve, *The Emperor Frederick II of Hohenstaufen: Immutator Mundi* (Oxford: Clarendon Press, 1972), pp. 222–26.

19. Concerning Frederick II's marriage and the claim it gave him to the Holy Land, see Van Cleve, "The Crusade of Frederick II," pp. 442–51; Kenneth M. Setton, *The Papacy and the Levant (1204–1571)*, vol. 1, *The Thirteenth and Fourteenth Centuries* (Philadelphia: American Philosophical Society, 1976), p. 55.

20. For Innocent IV's views on the just war, see Russell, *The Just War*, pp. 192–94, 293–303; and his "Innocent IV's Proposal to Limit Warfare," *Proceedings of the Fourth International Congress of Medieval Canon Law*, ed. Stephan Kuttner (Vatican City: Biblioteca Apostolica Vaticana, 1976), pp. 383–99.

21. Innocent IV, 3.34.8., fol. 176v: "sed nunquid est licitum invadere terram, quam infideles possident, vel que est sua?"

22. Ibid.: "Et nos respondemus, quod in veritate domini est terra, et plenitudo eius, orbis terrarum, et universi, qui habitant in ea . . . et haec a principio seculi fuit communis, quousque usibus priorum parentum introductum est." Roman law included a text that declared that by the *ius naturale* all things were originally held in common, but that in practice, according to the *ius gentium*, private property existed. The text is in the *Corpus Iuris Civilis*, 2 vols. (Geneva: Apud Petrum et Iacobum Chouët, 1621), vol. 1, *Institutiones*, 1. 2. The most convenient introduction to the problem of what is the natural law is Alexander Passerin d'Entrèves, *Natural Law: An Introduction to Legal Philosophy* (London: Hutchinson, 1951); see also Carlyle and Carlyle, *A History of Mediaeval Political Theory*, 1: 33–54. For the influence of Roman law on Innocent IV, see Gabriel Le Bras, "Innocent IV Romaniste: Examen de l'Apparatus," *Studia Gratiana* 11 (1967): 305–26, esp. pp. 316–17. A basic introduction to the problem of *dominium* as the medieval philosophers and theologians treated it is to be found in Ewart Lewis, *Medieval Political Ideas*, 2 vols. (New York: Knopf, 1954), 1: 88–139.

23. Innocent IV, 3.34.8., fol. 176v: "Et ideo licebat cuilibet occupare, quod occupatam non erat, sed ab aliis occupatam occupare non licebat, quia fiebat contra legem naturae, qua cuilibet inditum est, ut alii non faciat, quod sibi non vult fieri, habuerunt etiam specialia dominia per divisiones primi parentis, sicut apparet in Abraam, et Loth, quorum unus accepit ad unam partem et alius ad aliam." Genesis 13: 6–12.

24. Ibid.: "super homines autem . . . super servos nullus habuit dominium nisi de iure gen. vel civili. natura enim omnes homines, libri sunt."

25. Ibid.: "super familiam suam habebat iurisdictionem omnem a

principio, sed hodie non habet, nisi in paucis et modicis." Here again Innocent IV was drawing upon Roman law: *Digest*, 48.19.11, and *Codex*, 8.47.1–10.

26. Innocent IV, 3.34.8., fol. 176v: "Item per electionem poterunt habere Principes sicut habuerunt Saul, et multos alios."

27. Ibid.: "possessiones et iurisdictiones licite sine peccato possunt esse apud infideles. haec enim non tamen pro fidelibus. sed pro omni rationabili creatura facta sunt."

28. Ibid.: "dicimus, non licet Papae, vel fidelibus auferre sua, sive dominia sive iurisdictiones infidelibus, quia sine peccato possident."

29. There is an extensive modern literature on the political and legal thought of the medieval papacy. Fundamental works dealing with this literature are: Walter Ullmann, *Law and Politics in the Middle Ages*, Brian Tierney, "Some Recent Works on the Political Theories of the Medieval Canonists," *Traditio* 10 (1954): 594–625; and "The Continuity of Papal Political Theory in the Thirteenth Century. Some Methodological Considerations," *Mediaeval Studies* 27 (1965): 227–45; John A. Watt, "The Theory of Papal Monarchy in the Thirteenth Century: The Contribution of the Canonists," *Traditio* 20(1964): 179–317; W. D. McCready, "Papal *Plenitudo Potestatis* and the Source of Temporal Authority in Late Medieval Papal Hierocratic Theory," *Speculum* 48 (1973): 654–74. In addition, there is an extensive bibliography in Helmut G. Walther, *Imperiales Königtum Konziliarismus und Volkssouveränität: Studien zu den Grenzen des Mittelalterlichen Souveränitätsgedankens* (Munich: Wilhelm Fink, 1976).

30. Innocent IV, 3.34.8., fol. 176v: "Item alibi pasce oves meas, etc. . . . omnes autem tam fideles, quam infidels oves sunt Christi per creationem, licet non sint de ovili ecclesiae."

31. Ibid.: "Papa super omnes habet iurisdictionem. et potestatem de iure, licet non de facto."

32. Ibid.: "De Christianis autem non est dubium, quod eos iudicare potest Papa, si contra legem evangelicum facerent."

33. Ibid.: "Item Iudaeos potest iudicare Papa, si contra legem evangelii faciunt in moralibus, si eorum prelati eos non puniant, et eodem modo si haereses circa suam legem inveniant, et hac ratione motus Papa Greg. et Inn. mandaverunt conburi libros talium, in quo multae continebantur haereses, et mandaverunt puniri illos, qui praedictas haereses sequerentur vel docuerunt." Synan, *The Popes and the Jews*, pp. 111–15.

34. Ibid.: "credo, quod si gentilis, qui non habet legem nisi naturae, si contra legem naturae facit, potest licite puniri per Papam, arg. Gen. 19. ubi habes quod sodomitae, qui contra legem naturae peccabant, puniti sunt a Deo . . . si colant idola, naturale enim est, unum et solum Deum creatorem colere, et non creaturas." For a discussion of what the medieval canonists and theologians thought constituted the sin of the inhabitants of Sodom, see John T. Noonan, Jr., *Contraception: A History of its Treatment by the Catholic Theologians and Canonists* (Cambridge: Harvard University Press, 1965), pp. 5, 226.

35. Innocent IV, 3.34.8., fol. 177r: "Item licet non debeant infideles cogi ad fidem, quia omnes libero arbitrio relinquendi sunt."

36. Ibid.: "potest Papa iuste facere praeceptum, et constitutionem, quod non molestent Christianos iniuste, qui subsunt eorum iurisdictioni, immo quod plus est, potest eos eximere a iurisdictione eorum, et dominio

in totum . . . si male tractarent Christianos, posset eos privare per sententiam iurisdictione, et dominio, quod super eos habent. . . . tamen mandare potest Papa infidelibus quod admittant praedicatores evangelii in terris suae iurisdictionis, nam cum omnis creatura rationabilis facta sit an Deum laudandum . . . si ipsi prohibent praedicatores praedicare, peccant, et ideo puniendi sunt."

37. Ibid.: "tamen magna causa debet esse, quod ad hoc veniat, debet enim Papa eos, quantum potest sustinere, dummodo periculum non sit Christianis, nec grave scandalum generetur."

38. Ibid.: "licet Papae eis aliquid mandare, si non obediant, compellendi sunt brachio seculari, et indicendum est bellum contra eos per papam, et non per alios."

39. Ibid.: "Sed dices, quare non eodem modo licet eis repetere terram istam, scilicet Italiam, vel alias ubi dominati fuerunt infideles?"

40. Ibid.: "Sed dices nunquid et eodem modo debet Papa admittere illos, qui vellent praedicare legem Machometi?"

41. Ibid.: "Respon. quia domini harum terrarum cum populis eorum conversi sunt."

42. Ibid.: "si populi conversi essent, sed domini remanerent infideles, quod Papa bene posset domino infideli dominium et iurisdictionem dimittere super fideles."

43. Ibid.: "Item propter periculum posset cogi dominus ad recipiendum pretium vel commutionem."

44. *Codex* 7.13.1–4.

45. The Pauline Privilege was widely used in the sixteenth century to resolve the marital problems of infidel converts: see John T. Noonan, Jr., *Power to Dissolve: Lawyers and Marriages in the Courts of the Roman Curia* (Cambridge: Harvard University Press, 1972), pp. 342–46, 352–57.

46. Innocent IV, 3.34.8., fol. 177r: "Sed quaeres quo potest ecclesia Romana, et omnes aliae ecclesiae et etiam alii Christiani licite tenere, que tenent in occidente, et alibi, cum Imperatores Romani armis per violentiam haec omnia occuparunt, et ita constat, quod mala fide tenent?"

47. Ibid.: "Responsio. omnes generaliter clerici et laici possunt secure tenere et bona fide, quecunque tenent, quia nescimus, utrum illi, qui occuparunt praedicta, usi fuerint iure suo in occupando, debemus credere, quod usi fuerint iure suo, quam forte recuperaverunt, quod prius per violentiam amiserant, vel forte per munera, vel donationes ad eos pervenerunt legitime."

48. Ibid.: "quia si non constat, quis fuerit dominus ante occupationem Papae facienda est restitutio tanquam vicario Christi, et ecclesiis aliis, que per Papam possidentur, et eius auctoritate: nam Papa et ecclesiae nomine omnium hominum omnia possident."

49. Ibid.: "Respon. non: non enim ad paria debemus eos nobiscum iudicare, cum ipsi sint in errore, et nos in via veritatis, et hac pro constanti tenemus."

50. The role of Bernard of Clairvaux in this development has received a good deal of attention in recent years. Among the more important discussions of his role are: Walter Ullmann, *The Growth of Papal Government in the Middle Ages*, 3d ed. (London: Methuen, 1970), pp. 426–37; Gerhart B. Ladner, "The Concepts of 'Ecclesia' and 'Christianitas' and their Relation to the Idea of Papal 'plenitudo potestatis' from Greg-

ory VII to Boniface VIII," *Miscellanea Historiae Pontificiae* 18 (Rome, 1954): 49–77, esp. pp. 57–59. Ladner's article provides a survey of the literature on the question and reaches a conclusion opposite to that arrived at by Ullmann.

51. On the conflict between Innocent IV and Frederick II, see: Carlyle and Carlyle, *A History of Mediaeval Political Theory,* 5: 293–317; Karl Hampe, *Germany under the Salian and Hohenstaufen Emperors,* trans. Ralph Bennett (Totowa, N.J.: Rowman and Littlefield, 1973), pp. 293–300; Kantorowicz, *Frederick II,* pp. 578–91, 618–24, 635–36, 666–67; Van Cleve, "The Crusade of Frederick II," pp. 458–68, 484–97.

52. G. Le Bras, Ch. Lefebvre, J. Rambaud, *L'age classique, 1140–1378: sources et théorie du droit,* Histoire du Droit et des Institutions de l'Eglise en Occident, vol. 7 (Paris: Sirey, 1965), pp. 410–11.

53. Hostiensis, *Lectura quinque Decretalium,* 2 vols. (Paris, 1512), 3.34.8., fol. 124v: "Mihi tamen videtur quod in adventu Christi omnis honor et omnis principatus et omne dominium et iurisditio de iure et ex causa iusta, et per illum qui suppremam manum habet nec errare potest omni infideli subtracta fuerit ad fideles translata."

54. The importance of Alanus in the development of canonistic thought was first discussed by Walter Ullmann, *Medieval Papalism* (London: Methuen, 1949), pp. 10–11. Subsequently a number of Alanus' glosses were published and his thought discussed at greater length in A. M. Stickler, "Alanus Anglicus als Verteidiger des monarchischen Papsttums," *Salesianum* 21 (1959): 346–406.

55. On Donatism, see W. H. C. Frend, *The Donatist Church* (Oxford: Clarendon Press, 1952); G. Willis, *St. Augustine and the Donatist Controversy* (London: Society for the Promotion of Christian Knowledge, 1950); Herbert A. Deane, *The Political and Social Ideas of St. Augustine* (New York: Columbia University Press, 1963), pp. 4, 34–36, 175–97.

56. Hostiensis, 3.34.8., fol. 124v: "Regnum a gente in gentem transfertur propter iniusticias et iniurias et contumelias et diversos dolos." The line is from Ecclesiasticus 10:8.

57. Ibid.: "et hoc in personam Christi filii dei vivi qui non solum sacerdos fuit: sed et rex."

58. Ibid.: "Huius autem regni et sacerdotii principatum perpetuum commisit filius dei petro et successoribus eius."

59. Ibid.: "unde constanter asserimus quod de iure infideles debent subiici fidelibus. non econtra."

60. Ibid., fol. 125r: "Concedimus tamen quod infideles qui dominium ecclesie recognoscunt sunt ab ecclesia tolerandi: quia nec ad fidem precise cogendi sunt. . . . Tales etiam possunt habere possessiones et colonos christianos: et etiam iurisdictionem ex tolerantia ecclesie."

61. Ibid.: "Alios autem infideles in pace degentes: et etiam illos quod servos tenemus non per bellum: non per violentiam aliquam sed tamen per predicationem dici converti debere. Et si predicatores non admittant ipsos posse compelli per papam." For Hostiensis' views on the just war, see Russell, *The Just War,* pp. 129–43, 181–94, 201–12.

62. Hostiensis, 3.34.8., fol. 124v: "potest papa solus et non alius nisi de iure suo concederet bellum eis indicere. et contra eos seculares brachium invocare."

63. Hostiensis had such an exalted opinion of the pope's powers that Joannes Andreae remarked he apparently believed the pope could square

the circle. Joannes Andreae, *In quinque decretalium libros novella commentaria* (Venice: 1581; reprint ed., Turin: Bottega d'Erasmo, 1963), 2.1.2: ". . . Host. fatetur tamen, quod quandiu papa vivit, dominus dicitur, et potest mutare quadrata rotundis."

64. Hostiensis, 3.34.8., fol. 125r: "Sed cum hodie principes Christiani inter se bella et guerras propria temeritate moveant."

65. Concerning the life and career of Joannes Andreae, see Le Bras, *L'age classique*, pp. 327–28.

66. On the importance of the *consilia* literature, see: Peter N. Riesenberg, "The Consilia Literature: A Prospectus," *Manuscripta* 6 (1961): 3–22; and Guido Kisch, *Consilia. Eine Bibliographie der juristischen Konsiliensammlungen* (Basel: Helbing and Lichtenhan, 1970).

67. Oldratus de Ponte, *Consilia* (Venice: Franciscus Zilettus, 1571), consilium 72, fols. 72–73: "An contra Sarracenos Hispaniae sit bellum licitum."

68. Ibid.: "et hoc etiam tenuit Inn. in c. quod super his. quod ubi terra fuerit aliquo tempore Christianorum bellum sit licitum. Ipse tamen magis stricte locutus est in materia ista. nam tenet quod iurisdictio, et dominium etiam possit hodie esse penes infideles. Ho. tamen tenet contrarium. Et salva veritate videtur, quod opinio Host. sit verior. sed ratio Innocen. videtur habere locum in omni terra, quae hodie a Sarracenis possidetur."

69. Ibid.: "De Christo enim verificatur, quod omnes reges terrae adorabunt eum, et omnes gentes servient ... et ideo dicit Host. quod hodie non est iurisdictio, nec dominium nec honor, nec potestas poenas infideles: nam per adventum Christi translata sunt in Christianos."

70. Ibid.: "omnia enim subiecta sunt Christo, oves, et boves, et pecora campi.... Per oves enim intelligemus Christianos, quorum in tempore Salvator dicit se esse pastorem, et fuit pastor bonus, quia animam suam posuit pro ovibus suis.... Sed per boves et pecora campi intelligimus Saracenos, qui tanquam bestiae. ratione carentes relicto Deo vero colunt idola, et vide in frumento in verbo Saracenis."

71. Ibid.: "Et videtur, quod eis volentibus in pace, et quiete vivere non sit molestia inferenda."

72. Ibid.: "Sed quod contra Sarracenos illos bellum sit licitum, probatur sic. quia aut ipsi impugnant Christianos.... Nam tunc licitum est vim vi repellere.... et adhuc dico, quod bellum debet eis inferri, quia verisimile est, quod quandocunque ipsi opportunitatem habebunt, oppugnabunt, et persequentur Christianos, et ecclesiam."

73. Ibid.: "Et Saraceni ad literam vocantur bestiae, quia et Ismael pater eorum vocatus est a dominio Onager, et fuit ratio: ut dicit Metodius, quia futurum erat, quod qui de genere suo discenderent, omnem bestiarum rabiem supergrederentur, et mansuetarum numerus conteretur ab eis.... Et licet istae bestiae, quo ad pastum Petro non videantur commissae, sunt tamen pedibus eius subiectae, quo ad dominium, et potestatem." Concerning the practice of describing the Saracens as descendants of Agar and Ishmael, see Norman Daniel, *Islam and the West: The Making of an Image* (Edinburgh: Edinburgh University Press, 1960), pp. 79–80, 127–28; James Kritzeck, *Peter the Venerable and Islam* (Princeton: Princeton University Press, 1964), pp. 79, 86, 150, 161, 170, 192; R. W. Southern, *Western Views of Islam in the Middle Ages* (Cambridge: Harvard University Press, 1962), pp. 16–17.

74. Oldratus de Ponte, *consilium* 72: "Nam tota illa provincia His-

paniae fuit Christianorum, et fuerunt ibi ecclesiae, monasteria, et alia pia loca ... et isti Saraceni violenter occupaverunt ea, nos spoliando permissione divina propter peccata nostra." The status of Spain attracted the interest of several canonists in the thirteenth century. See Gaines Post, " 'Blessed Lady Spain'–Vincentius Hispanus and Spanish National Imperialism in the Thirteenth Century," *Speculum* 29 (1954): 198–209. Professor Post revised this article; see his *Studies in Medieval Legal Thought: Public Law and the State, 1100–1322* (Princeton: Princeton University Press, 1964), pp. 482–93.

75. Oldratus de Ponte, *consilium* 264, fols. 126–27: "Illa videtur probabilior sententia, quod princeps absque legitima causa pacificos Iudaeos, Saracenos, et alios paganos de terris suis non possit expellere.... Sed ipse nollet de regno expelli: ergo non alios de regno expellat.... Expellere ergo tales absque ratione contra praecepta charitatis aperte est."

76. Ibid.: "Et quod non possint, nisi persecutores fuerint, expelli, facit bene a sensu contrario.... Et innocentia, maxime regum, est nemini malum inferre...omni Christianae inest religioni lenitas, et mansuetudo, et crudelitas ei contraria est signanter . . . Item . . . pagani, et Iudaei inter oves Christi computantur creatione.... Cum ergo papa eos pascere debeat et verbo, et exemplo, et humanitate non rebelles, non ergo debet eos impugnare, nec permitter, ut laedantur.... infideles non terroribus, non asperitatibus, non violentiis sunt trahendi ad fidem, neque expulsionibus, sed blanditiis, et muneribus, ut integra sit forma iustitiae, et libertas arbitrii."

77. Ibid.: "Unde sicut infideles Saraceni, vel alii inter nos habitantes a nobis sunt pro suis sceleribus puniendi ... sic sine causa non sunt expellendi, vel puniendi."

78. Giovanni da Legnano, *Tractus De Bello, De Represaliis et De Duello*, ed. Thomas Erskine Holland, Classics of International Law (Oxford: Oxford University Press, 1917), pp. x–xviii; Muldoon, "The Contribution of the Medieval Canon Lawyers," pp. 411–12; Le Bras, *L'age classique*, p. 332.

79. Legnano, *Tractus De Bello*, pp. 91–93.

80. Ibid., p. 92: "quia ad fidem non cogendi non sunt, cum omnes alii non incorporati sint reliquendi arbitrio suo."

81. Ibid., p. 93: "... Papa facere praeceptum quod non molestent christianos subditos."

82. Ibid., p. 92: "Eadem civitas est ecclesia, unus Rex est Christus, duo populi sunt clerici et laici, duae vitae, spiritualis et carnalis, et duo principatus, Sacerdotium et Imperium, tamen unum est principale, scilicet Pontificatus."

83. Ibid.: "Sic igitur Papa de iure habet iurisdictionem super infideles, licet non de facto. Hinc est quod si gentilis, habens solum legem naturae, peccat contra legem naturae, puniri possit per Papam."

84. Ibid.: "Ex quibus infertur quod Papa, tanquam verus Princeps, potest bellum indicere infidelibus, et indulgentias concedere propter recuperationem terrae sanctae."

85. Maffei, *La Donazione di Cosantino*, p. 222.

86. Petrus de Ancharano, *Consilia sive iuris responsa* (Venice: Apud Nicolaum Bevilaquam, 1568), *consilium* 15, fols. 8–9. Paul Ourliac and Henri Gilles, *La période post-classique (1378–1500)*, part 1, *La problé-*

matique de l'époque les sources, Histoire du Droit et des Institutions de l'Eglise en Occident, vol. 13 (Paris: Éditions Cujus, 1971), p. 88.

87. Petrus de Ancharano, *consilium* 15: "... Potestas temporalis civitatis cesene dicit quod cognitio et punitio talis delicti spectat ad ipsum ita quod non dicit nec potest spiritualis iudex de hoc se intromittere."

88. Ibid.: "Videtur prima facie quod cognitio et punitio huius criminis spectet ad ecclesiasticum forum constat enim quod delinquenes in rem ecclesiasticam efficitur de eius foro sicut si delinqueret in personam, nam utroque casu sacrilegium committit et est tanquam sacrilegus puniendus est.... nam iudei et omnes infideles subsunt pape et super eos potestatem et iurisdictionem habet maxime cum delinquunt contra legem nature."

89. Ibid.: "Constitutiones etiam canonice hoc expresse statuunt scilicet quod iudei prosilientes in contumeliam creatoris per principes seculares condigna animadversione compensant.... Nam dico quod iudei immediate sunt de iurisdictione iudicis secularis sicut alii laici ... unde in defectum iudicis secularis vel propter eius negligentiam fatendum est quod iudex ecclesiasticus posset procedere vel ad hoc iudicem secularem cogere."

90. Ibid.: "quod constitutionibus canonicis non arctantur mediate vero subsunt papae etc. qui preest omnibus christianis."

91. Ibid., *consilium* 243, fol. 129: "ut dixi propter bonum publicum quod ex hoc sequitur videtur tale decretum posse defendi. providetur enim necessitatibus subitorum non valentium aliter reperire pecunias mutuo cum enim pecunie omnis obediant et per ipsam omnia estimentur."

92. Ibid.: "hinc est quod propter necessitatem multa regulariter prohibita iure divino iure humano conceduntur ut furtum homicidium et similia." Concerning the medieval attitude toward usury, see John T. Noonan, Jr., *The Scholastic Analysis of Usury* (Cambridge: Harvard University Press, 1957); and J. Gilchrist, *The Church and Economic Activity in the Middle Ages* (London: Macmillan, 1969), pp. 62–70, 104–15.

93. Petrus de Ancharano, *consilium* 271, fols. 141–42: "iudei sarraceni vel alie secte reprobate possunt dici fideles et devoti sanctae Romanae ecclesiae si nobiscum conversantur et vivunt et hinc est quod ecclesia eos in suis ritibus et cerimoniis tolerat."

94. Niccolò de Tudeschi, *Commentaria in tertium Decretalium Librum* (Venice: 1578), 3.34.8., fols. 168r–168v: "Sed quia tex. videtur hic approbare pugnam Christianorum contra Sarracenos, potest probabiliter dubitari, nunquid Principibus Christianis sit licitum movere bellum contra infideles, et eis auferre dominia et principatus, et alia bona. Inn. multum exquisite tractat." Concerning Panormitanus, see Ourliac and Gilles, *La période post-classique,* p. 89.

95. Niccolò de Tudeschi, 3.34.8., fol. 168v: "Ita quod licite infideles acquisiverunt dominia; ideo molestari sine causa non debent a Christianis."

96. Ibid.: "Item Imperator saltem quoad exercitium habet iurisdictionem super universum Orbem, et est dominus mundi."

97. Ibid.: "quedam sunt crimina ecclesiastica: et in istis Papa exercet iurisdictionem in infideles, sicut exercet contra fideles."

98. Ibid.: "In criminibus vero non ecclesiasticis, Imperator exercebit iurisdictionem."

99. Alexandrus Tartagnus, *Consilia,* 7 vols. in 4 (Venice: Apud Haeredes Alexandri Paganini, 1610), Liber 6, *consilium* 6, fol. 5: "Super praemissa dubitatione, scilicet an dispositio. cap. quanquam ... quatenus

invalidat testamenta manifestorum usurariorum, locum sibi vendicet in Hebraeis manifestis usurariis." Concerning Alexandrus Tartagnus, see Ourliac and Gilles, *La période post-classique,* pp. 89, 91. The decretal referred to is in the *Corpus Iuris Canonici* vol. 2, *Sextus,* 5.5.2, *Quanquam.*

100. Alexandrus Tartagnus, Liber 6, *consilium* 6: "quaerit, quid possunt ordinarii locorum contra Iudaeos ratione usurariae pravitatis."

101. Ibid.: "quod respectu poenae quae olim imponebatur ... quod priventur sepultura, nec ad communionem admittantur, et excommunicatione astringantur usque ad condignam satisfactionem, nil possunt quia non possunt excludi de corpore ecclesiae ... et quia quoad spiritualia, nil ad nos de his quae foris sunt."

102. Ibid.: "Confirmo alia ratione, nam ubi habemus legem Mosaicam, non debemus ab ea discedere quoad actum celebrandum per Iudaeum sine Christiano, et solum debet attendi ipsa lex Mosaica, non autem lex humana, nisi quatenus expresse lex humana prohiberet Iudaeis.... Praeterea secundum eum lex Mosaica est specialis lex Iudaeorum, ergo derogat generali et communi.... tunc inter Iudaeum et Christianum servatur lex Christiana."

103. Ibid.: "quod infideles degentes in terris Christianorum sunt de foro iudicis secularis, non ecclesiasticis, quia constitutionibus canonum non ligantur ... licet quando negligentes essent iudices seculares, possent iudices ecclesiastici indirecte punire infideles."

104. Ibid.; *consilium* 99, fol. 53: "quod non sint subiecti ecclesie, scilicet ubi ecclesia non habet temporalem iurisdictionem, et ita procedit illa authoritas, nihil ad nos etc. tamen bene sunt subiecti principibus habentibus iurisdictionem temporalem, quia tales Iudaeos punire possunt."

105. Concerning Wyclif and the revival of Donatist ideas in the fourteenth century, see below, Chapter 6.

Chapter 2

1. Carlyle and Carlyle, *A History of Mediaeval Political Theory,* 5: 318–19; LeBras, *L'age classique,* pp. 243–45.

2. "...si hostis Dei et amica demonum, gens impia Tartarorum." Innocent IV, *Plenae lacrimis* et, *Epistolae saeculi XIII e registis pontificum romanorum,* ed. G. H. Pertz and C. Rodenberg, *Monumenta Germaniae Historica, Epistolae,* 3 vols. (Berlin: Weidmann, 1883–94), 2: 3–4; *Les registres d'Innocent IV,* ed. E. Berger (hereafter Berger), 4 vols. (Paris: E. Thorin, 1884–1920), no. 30; A. Potthast, *Regesta pontificum romanorum inde ab anno post Christum natum MCXCVIII ad annum MCCCIV* (hereafter Potthast), 2 vols. (Berlin: Rudolph Decker, 1874–75), no. 11096.

3. Before their conversion to Christianity, the Lithuanians were described as "existens in perfidie tenebris." Innocent IV, *Spiritu exultante percepimus, Vetera Monumenta Poloniae et Lithuaniae,* ed. Augustin Theiner (hereafter Theiner), 4 vols. (Rome: Typis Vaticanis, 1860–64), 1: 50–51, no. 106; Berger, no. 5441; Potthast, no. 14363.

4. "In huiusmodi namque traditionibus (quae Talmud hebraice nuncupantur, et magnus liber est apud eos, excedens textum Bibliae in immensum, in quo sunt blasphemiae in Deum et Christum eius, ac Beatam

Virginem manifeste, intricabiles fabulae, abusiones erroneae, ac stultitiae inauditae) filios suos docent ac nutriunt, et a legis, et prophetarum doctrina reddunt ipsos penitus alienos....

"Et licet dilectus filius cancellarius Parisiensis, et doctores regentes Parisiis in sacra pagina, de mandato felicis recordationis G. Papae predecessoris nostri, tam praedictum abusionis librum, quam alios quosdam cum omnibus glossis suis perlectis in potestate, ac examinatos ad confusionem perfidiae iudaeorum, publice coram clero et populo, incendio concremarint." Innocent IV, *Impia iudaeorum, Bullarum, diplomatum, et privilegiorum sanctorum Romanorum pontificum*, 25 vols. (Turin: S. Franco, H. Fory and H. Dalmazzo, 1857–72), 3: 508–9; Berger, no. 682; Potthast, no. 11376; see also Synan, *The Popes and the Jews*, pp. 111–12.

5. Ibid.: "Firmiter inhibendo ne de caetero nutrices, seu servientes habeant christianos, ne filii liberae filiis famulentur ancillae." Occasionally, at least, there were also fears that Christians would convert to Judaism, Baron, *A Social and Religious History of the Jews*, pp. 23–24; Synan, *The Popes and the Jews*, pp. 105–6, 121–22.

6. Concerning Christian-Moslem relations, see Robert I. Burns, *Islam under the Crusaders: Colonial Survival in the Thirteenth-Century Kingdom of Valencia* (Princeton: Princeton University Press, 1973); "Immigrants from Islam: The Crusaders Use of Muslims as Settlers in Thirteenth Century Spain," *American Historical Review* 80 (1975): 21–42; "Christian-Islamic Confrontation in the West: The Thirteenth Century Dream of Conversion," *American Historical Review* 76 (1971): 1386–1434; see also Elena Lourie, "Free Moslems in the Balearics under Christian Rule in the Thirteenth Century," *Speculum* 45 (1970): 624–49.

7. On the career of James I, see Roger Biglow Merriman, *The Rise of the Spanish Empire in the Old World and in the New*, 4 vols. (New York: Macmillan, 1918–34; reprint ed., New York Cooper Square, 1962), 1: 281–98, 312–20, 430–36; Joseph F. O'Callaghan, *A History of Medieval Spain* (Ithaca, N.Y.: Cornell University Press, 1975), pp. 334–35, 345–49, 361–77, 437–50; Robert I. Burns, "The Spiritual Life of James the Conqueror King of Arago-Catalonia, 1208–1276: Portrait and Self Portrait," *Catholic Historical Review* 62 (1976): 1–35.

8. O'Callaghan, *A History of Medieval Spain*, p. 465; Lourie, "Free Moslems in the Balearics," pp. 628–30. Moslem rulers occasionally had similar problems with their coreligionists over the employment of Christians. One result of this conflict between religious and political interests was that Moslem rulers placed restrictions on the public display of Christian symbols by the Christian communities that remained in North Africa.

9. Lourie, "Free Moslems in the Balearics," p. 628. The fear of Christians converting to Islam was so strong that Castilian law decreed forfeiture of all goods, and even death, for those who converted: see Alfonso X, *Las Siete Partidas*, trans. Samuel P. Scott (Chicago: Commerce Clearing House, 1931), p. 1440.

10. Burns, *Islam under the Crusaders*, pp. 327–28; O'Callaghan, *A History of Medieval Spain*, pp. 348–49.

11. Theiner, 1:49, no. 101. On the conversion of the Lithuanians, see Jonas Totoraitis, *Die litauer unter dem könig Mindowe* (Freiburg: St. Paulus-Druckerei, 1905).

12. See, for example, the criticisms that Henry of Livonia (ca. 1188–after 1259) leveled against the magistrates who administered the lands of the converts: *The Chronicle of Henry of Livonia*, ed. James A. Brundage (Madison: University of Wisconsin Press, 1961), p. 67.

13. Theiner, 1: 49, no. 101: "Quia vero gens huiusmodi olim solita lege nature vivere, divinis institutionibus et preceptis aut canonicis sanctionibus servandis non potest de facili sic plene animum applicare. . . . quod in exigendis ac percipiendis decimis circa predictum Regem ac eiusdem subditos ita se habeant, ut ipsa sub onore ac iugo domini non pressure aut asperitatis tedium, sed lenitatis ac suavitatis invenisee solatium gratulantes, scandalo perturbari non valeant, nec a bono proposito revocari."

14. "Now, however, because God gave plentiful aid and victory to our duke and to the other princes, the Slavs have been everywhere crushed and driven out. A people strong and without number have come from the bounds of the ocean, and taken possession of the territory of the Slavs." Helmold, *The Chronicle of the Slavs*, ed. Francis J. Tschan, Records of Civilization, Sources and Studies, no. 21 (New York: Columbia University Press, 1935), pp. 235–36. The charters authorizing Christian settlement of various regions occasionally refer to the fact that the native population had been killed or driven off: see Herman Helbig and Lorenz Weinrich, eds., *Urkunden und Erzählende Quellen zur Deutschen Ostseidlung im Mittelalter*, 2 vols. (Darmstadt: Wissenschaftliche Buchgesellschaft, 1968–70), 1: 544–46.

15. Concerning Innocent IV's views on the just war, see Russell, *The Just War*, pp. 135, 145–46, 199–201.

16. Innocent IV called for support of Louis IX's crusade against the Moslems at the same time that he was calling for a crusade against Frederick II, a fact that caused the papacy a good deal of embarrassment: see Joseph R. Strayer, "The Political Crusades of the Thirteenth Century," in Setton, *History of the Crusades*, 2: 343–75 at 356–57.

17. Berger, no. 1375; Potthast, no. 11727; Burns, *Islam under the Crusaders*, p. 16.

18. See, for example, Berger, nos. 1758, 1832, 2960.

19. X.5.6. *Significavit* and *Quod olim*.

20. Berger, nos. 621 and 3303.

21. There were obviously some economic repercussions for Europe as well. Innocent IV granted the inhabitants of Majorca an exemption from the ban on trade with the Moslems "cum propter novitatem incolatus in multis peruriam patiuntur pro sustentatione ipsorum, et quod terra propitiante Deo comodius et plenius reddi populosa valeant, eis portandi et venendi victualia Sarracenis licentiam impendere curaremus, cum sicut asserunt non possint ad presens illorum carere commercio absque dictorum civium dispendio manifesto." Berger, no. 3303. The importance of the Majorcan trade with the Moslem world is illustrated by the treaties that James I of Aragon made with the Moslems: see *Traités de paix et de commerce et documents divers concernant les relations des Chretiens avec les Arabes de l'Afrique Septentrionale au moyen age*, ed. M. L. de Mas Latrie (hereafter Mas Latrie), 2 vols. (Paris: 1866; reprint ed., New York: Burt Franklin, n.d.), 2: 182–85, 279–80. Partial translations of two such documents can be found in Muldoon, *Expansion of Europe*, pp. 84–87.

22. Berger, no. 163; Potthast, no. 11137; Theiner, 1: 37–8, no. 77; *Epistolae saeculi XIII*, 2: 20–21, no. 24.

23. Berger, no. 4619; Potthast, no. 13039.

24. Charles W. Connell, "Western Views of the Origins of the 'Tartars': an Example of the Influence of Myth in the Second Half of the Thirteenth Century," *Journal of Medieval and Renaissance Studies* 3 (1973): 115–37, at pp. 121–22, 134–35.

25. Berger, no. 30; Potthast, no. 11096; *Epistolae saeculi XIII*, 2: 3–4, no. 2.

26. Berger, no. 1420; Potthast, no. 11827; *Epistolae saeculi XIII*, 2: 98–9, no. 131. Concerning Frederick II's relations with Hungray, see Kantorowicz, *Frederick II*, pp. 553–54.

27. Berger, no. 4088; Potthast, no. 12814; *Epistolae saeculi XIII*, 2: 241.

28. For Innocent IV's relations with Frederick II, see Strayer, "Political Crusade," pp. 354–59; Setton, *The Papacy and the Levant*, 1:64, Kantorowicz, *Frederick II*, pp. 578–82.

29. The various editions of *Cum hora undecima* that appeared during the thirteenth century have been published in the *Pontifica Commissio ad redigendum Codicem Iuris Canonici Orientalis:* Fontes, ser. 3 (Vatican City: Typis Polyglottis Vaticanis, 1943–): *Acta Honorii III (1216–1227) et Gregorii IX (1227-1241)*, ed. Aloysius L. Tăutu (1950), pp. 286–87, no. 210; *Acta Innocentii PP. IV (1243–1254)*, ed. T. T. Haluscynskyj and Meletius M. Wojnar (1962), pp. 36–42, no. 19; *Acta Alexandri P.P. IV (1254–1261)*, ed. T. T. Haluscynskyj and M. M. Wojnar (1966), p. 73, no. 38; *Acta Urbani IV, Clementis IV, Gregorii X (1261–1276)*, ed. A. L. Tăutu (1953), pp. 26–28, no. 7; *Acta Romanorum Pontificum ab Innocentio V ad Benedictum XI (1276–1304)*, ed. F. M. Delorme and A. L. Tăutu (1954), pp. 42–44, no. 79, pp. 184–85. no. 110, pp. 252–55, no. 153.

30. For the place of apocalyptic thinking in the early history of the Franciscans, see E. Randolph Daniel, *The Franciscan Concept of Mission in the High Middle Ages* (Lexington: University Press of Kentucky, 1975), pp. 76–100.

31. *Acta Honorii III*, p. 286: "Cum hora undecima sit diei hominibus, ut exeant ad opus usque ad mundi vesperam deputati et illud Apocalypsis eulogium cito credatur cum matris Ecclesiae consolatione complendum, videlicet oportere viros spiritualis vitae munditiam et intelligentiae gratiam cum Iohanne sortitos populis et gentibus, linguis regibusque multis denuo prophetare, quod non sequitur reliquiarum Israel per Isaiam prophetata salvatio, nisi iuxta Paulum Apostolum prius introeat gentium plenitudo."

32. Ibid., p. 287: "per exhortationem vestram converti ad unitatem christianae fidei cupientes . . . audire confessiones . . . excommunicatos, iuxta Ecclesiae formam, absolvere . . . reconciliare et ab anathematis vinculo, quo tenentur, absolvere valeatis."

33. *Acta Innocentii PP. IV*, p. 36: "Dilectis filiis fratribus de Ordine Fratrum Minorum in terras Saracenorum, Paganorum, Graecorum, Bulgarorum, Cumanorum, Ethyoporum, Syrorum, Iberorum, Alanorum, Gazarorum, Gothorum, Zicorum, Ruthenorum, Jacobinorum, Nubianorum, Nestorinorum, Georgianorum, Armenorum, Indorum, Mesolitorum aliorum infidelium nationum Orientis seu quarum cunque aliarumque partium proficiscentibus." The various peoples listed here are

identified in ibid., pp. 39–42. The most extensive recent discussion of the Eastern Christians is Anna-Dorothee von den Brincken, *Die "Nationes christianorum orientalium" im Verständnis der lateinischen Historiographie von der Mitte des 12. bis in die zweite Hälfte des 14. Jahrhunderts,* Kölner historische Abhandlungen, 22 (Cologne: Böhlau, 1973).

34. *Acta Innocentii PP. IV,* p. 38.

35. X.4.17,15, *Gaudemus* and 4.19.8, *Gaudemus.* For the importance of this decretal, see James Muldoon, "Missionaries and the Marriages of Infidels: The Case of the Mongol Mission," *The Jurist* 35 (1975): 125–41; Noonan, *Power to Dissolve,* p. 347.

36. Mas Latrie, 2: 8: "Hanc itaque caritatem nos et vos specialibus nobis quam ceteris gentibus debemus, qui unum Deum, licet diverso modo, credimus et confitemur, qui eum creatorem saeculorum et gubernatorem hujus mundi quotidie laudamus et veneramur." See also *Das register Gregors VII,* ed. Erich Caspar, *Monumenta Germaniaea Historica, Epistolae selectae,* 2 vols. (Berlin: Weidmannsche Buchhandlung, 1955), 1: 287–88.

37. Concerning Innocent III's interest in missionary activity, see Achille Luchaire, *Innocent III,* 6 vols. (Paris: Hachette, 1906–8), vol. 4, *La question d'Orient.*

38. Mas Latrie, 2: 8–9. For a brief history of the Trinitarian order, see "Trinitarians," *NCE,* 14: 293–95.

39. Mas Latrie, 2: 9.

40. Ibid., 2: 10; Potthast, no. 9207.

41. The Moroccan ruler's letter does not exist. The mission is known only through Gregory IX's response: see Mas Latrie, 2: 11; Potthast, no. 9901.

42. Berger, no. 1511; Potthast, no. 11904; Mas Latrie, 2: 12–13.

43. Berger, no. 2244; Potthast, no. 12327; Mas Latrie, 2: 13.

44. Concerning the extent of trade between Europe and North Africa before 1250, see S. D. Goitein, *A Mediterranean Society,* 2 vols. (Berkeley: University of California Press, 1967–71), 1: 42–47.

45. Mas Latrie, 2: 14–15: "quatenus aliqua loca munita in terra tua, in quibus, necessitatis tempore, dicti Christiani se receptare valeant." Potthast, no. 12337.

46. Ibid., 2: 16–17: "quod cum nos olim tibi direxerimus preces nostras ut Christianis illarum partium munitiones et castra sita supra ripam maris, in quibus secure habitare possent et contra impugnatores suos necessitatis tempore se tueri liberaliter largireris . . . nam cum oporteat multos ex illis frequenter ad exercitum tuam ire, vel alias pro tuis servitiis laborare, nec habeant tuta loca bi uxores, filios ac alios consanguineos relinquere valeant, Sarraceni opportunitate captata, multos ex eis interficiunt et nonnulos cogunt fidem catholicam abnegare." Berger, no. 5172; Potthast, no. 14245; Mas Latrie, 2: 16–17.

47. Mas Latrie, 2: 16–17.

48. There is an extensive literature on the Mongol mission. The basic study is Giovanni Soranzo, *Il papato, l'Europa christiana e i Tartari* (Milan: Università cattolica del Sacro Cuore, 1930). The bibliography has been brought up to date in de Rachewiltz, *Papal Envoys.* In addition, see G. Golubovich, *Biblioteca Bio-Bibliografica della terra santa e dell'oriente francescano,* 19 vols. (Florence, Quaracchi: College of St. Bonaventure, 1906–48). The basic collection of missionary reports on

the various expeditions to the East is *Sinica Franciscana,* ed. A. van den Wyngaert, 5 vols. (Quaracchi, Florence: College of St. Bonaventure, 1929–54), vol. 1, *Itinera et relationes Fratrum minorum. Saeculi XIII et XIV* (1929). English translations of many of these documents can be found in Christopher Dawson, ed., *The Mongol Mission,* (New York: Sheed and Ward, 1955).

49. *Epistolae selectae XIII,* 2: 75, no. 105: "Cum non solum homines verum etiam animalia irrationalia nec non ipsa mundialis elementa machine quadam nativi federis sint unione coniuncta." Berger, no. 1365; Potthast, no. 11572.

50. Thomas Aquinas wrote a *summa* apparently designed to provide missionaries with a body of information to win infidels to the fold by a process of rational argument: see his *On the Truth of the Catholic Faith,* ed. Anton C. Pegis, 2 vols. (Garden City, N.Y.: Doubleday, 1955–57).

51. *Epistolae selectae XIII,* 2: 72–73, no. 102: "et si putassemus, quod fructuosiores et gratiosiores vobis existerent, vel aliquos ecclesiarum prelatos ad vos aut potentes alios misissemus." Berger, no. 1364; Potthast, no. 11571.

52. Odorico Rinaldi (Raynaldus), *Annales ecclesiastici* (hereafter Raynaldus), 38 vols. (Lucca: Venturini, 1738–59), 1247: 57–68 at 64.

53. De Rachewiltz, *Papal Envoys,* pp. 116–17.

54. Dawson, *Mongol Mission,* pp. 85–86.

55. Ibid.

56. Berger, no. 4682; *Acta Innocentii PP. IV,* pp. 119–20, no. 67.

57. Le Bras, "Innocent IV, Romaniste," p. 309.

58. The degree to which the Aristotelian revival influenced the political thinkers of the thirteenth and fourteenth centuries is a matter of scholarly debate. On the one hand: "The influence of Aristotle from the second half of the thirteenth century onwards wrought a transmutation in thought that amounts to a conceptual revolution. In fact and in theory the Aristotelian avalanche in the thirteenth century marks the watershed between the Middle Ages and the modern period." Walter Ullmann, *A History of Political Thought: The Middle Ages,* rev. ed. (Harmondsworth: Penguin, 1970), p. 159. Ullmann's views on the importance of Aristotelian thought have not gone unchallenged. See Francis Oakley, "Celestial Hierarchies Revisited: Walter Ullmann's Vision of Medieval Politics," *Past & Present,* no. 60 (August 1973): 3–48.

59. *Bull. Ro.,* 3: 519–22, no. 9; see also John Moorman, *A History of the Franciscan Order from its Origins to the Year 1517* (Oxford: Oxford University Press, 1968), pp. 111–22.

60. John of Plano Carpini, "History of the Mongols," in Dawson, *Mongol Mission,* p. 7. The canonists seem to have assumed that infidels were always polygamous. In *Gaudemus,* Innocent III wrote: "Quia vero pagani circa plures insimul foeminas adfectum dividunt coniungalem." X.4.19.8.

61. Muldoon, "Missionaries and the Marriages of Infidels," p. 133.

Chapter 3

1. In general, for the late thirteenth-century papacy, see Mann, *Lives of the Popes,* vols. 15–19.

2. Setton, *The Papacy and the Levant*, 1: 83–95; Jean Longnon, "The Frankish States in Greece, 1204–1311," in Setton, *History of the Crusades*, 2: 235–74 at pp. 247–48, 253–55.

3. Steven Runciman, "The Crusader States, 1243–1291," in Setton, *History of the Crusades* 2: 557–98 at pp. 593–98.

4. Clement IV, *Bull. Ro.*, 3: 785–86, no. 24; Synan, *The Popes and the Jews*, pp. 117–19, 241 (text); Baron, *A Social and Religious History of the Jews*, 9: 57–60.

5. Gregory X, *Bull. Ro.*, 4: 24–25, no. 7; Potthast, no. 20798; Nicholas IV, *Bull. Ro.*, 4: 88, no. 2; Potthast, no. 23391.

6. Clement IV, Potthast, no. 19911; Raynaldus, 1266: 29–33.

7. Raynaldus, 1289: 29.

8. Synan, *The Popes and the Jews*, p. 117.

9. Nicholas III, *Bull. Ro.*, 4: 45–47, no. 3; Potthast, no. 21383; Synan, *The Popes and the Jews*, pp. 119–21.

10. Alexander IV extended papal protection to a group of Jewish merchants traveling in papal territory; *Epistolae saeculae XIII*, 3: 335, no. 370. Nicholas IV ordered his vicar for Rome to protect Jews from harassment by Christians: *Reg.* 4184; Potthast, no. 23541.

11. Clement IV, Potthast, no. 20081; Synan, *The Popes and the Jews*, p. 119.

12. Clement IV, Potthast, no. 19911; Raynaldus, 1266: 29.

13. Eventually, in the sixteenth century, this imagined fear became a reality: see Andrew C. Hess, "The Moriscos: An Ottoman Fifth Column in Sixteeth-Century Spain," *American Historical Review* 74 (1968): 1–25.

14. O'Callaghan, *A History of Medieval Spain*, pp. 348–49; J. N. Hillgarth, *The Spanish Kingdoms, 1250–1516*, vol. 1, *1250–1410: Precarious Balance* (Oxford: Clarendon Press, 1976), pp. 155–214; Burns, *Islam under the Crusaders*, pp. 184–219.

15. Clement IV, Potthast, no. 19911.

16. Alexander IV, Potthast, no. 15855; *Bull. Fran.*, 2: 46, no. 57.

17. Alexander IV, Potthast, no. 16112; *Bull. Fran.*, 2: 93–94, no. 134.

18. Boniface VIII, Potthast, no. 24161; Raynaldus, 1295: 37.

19. Clement IV, Potthast, no. 19156; Raynaldus, 1265: 32–34.

20. Wadding, 4: 294.

21. Clement IV, Potthast, no. 20522; *Bull. Ro.*, 4: 11–13, no. 2.

22. Nicholas III, Potthast, no. 21387.

23. Nicholas III, *Reg.* no. 4403: "Cum autem intelleximus quod inter te ac alios christianos de partibus illis, ex parte una, et soldanum Babilonie, ex altera, treugue inite fuerint, in quarum conventione specialiter est expressum quod mercatores hinc inde merces deferre libere valeant . . . non obstante constitutione predicta, quamdiu memorate treugue duraverint mercatoribus christianis deferendi de partibus Terre Sancte in Alexandriam vel alia Sarracenorum loca." In addition, see the letters authorizing trade between Italy and Egypt, *Reg.* nos. 6784–6788.

24. Nicholas IV, Potthast, no. 23180; Wadding, 5: 599–600; Mas Latrie, 2: 17–18.

25. Nicholas IV, Potthast, no. 23183; Wadding, 5: 600–601.

26. Nicholas IV, Potthast, no. 23180; Wadding, 5: 599–600; Mas Latrie, 2: 17–18.

27. Nicholas IV, *Reg.* no. 2223; Potthast, no. 22997; see also Mann, *Lives of the Popes*, 17: 132.

28. Concerning the history of the Ethiopian Church, see "Ethiopian Rite," *NCE*, 5: 586–89.

29. Boniface VIII, *Bull. Ro.*, 4: 152–55, no. 13.

30. Mas Latrie, 2: 18–19: "nos, attendentes quod tu easdem insulas eripuisti potenter, ut praedicitur, de manibus hostium crucis Christi, et laudabile propositum, quod habere te asseris, ut in insulis ipsis orthodoxa fides propagetur et vigeat, cultusque servetur inibi divinorum. . . . tuis supplicationibus inclinati . . . memoratas insulas et earum quamlibet, cum omnibus juribus et pertinentiis suis, in merum et mixtum imperium, jursdictionem plenariam temporalem videlicet in eisdem, auctoritate apostolica et de apostolica plenitudine potestatis . . . in feudum perperpetuum concedimus." Potthast, no. 24161.

31. Examples of this include: Poland (990) and Hungary (1000): G. Barraclough, *The Origins of Modern Germany*, rev. ed. (Oxford: Basil Blackwell, 1947), p. 42. Perhaps the most famous example of this policy was King John's surrender of England to Innocent III in 1213: see *A History of England*, ed. Sir Charles Oman, vol. 2, H. W. C. Davis, *England Under the Normans and Angevins*, 11th ed. (New York: G. P. Putnam's Sons, 1937), p. 368.

32. Weckmann, *Las Bulas Alejandrinas;* see also his brief summaries of his position in "The Alexandrine Bulls," *NCE*, 1: 306, and "The Alexandrine Bulls of 1493: Pseudo-Asiatic Documents," in *First Images of America: The Impact of the New World on the Old*, ed. Fredi Chiappelli, 2 vols. (Berkeley: University of California Press, 1976), 1: 201–9.

33. *Decretum*, D.96 c.14, *Constantinus*. The fundamental study of the Donation is Maffei, *La Donazione di Cosantino*. The text of the Donation can be found in Ernest Henderson, ed., *Select Historical Documents of the Middle Ages* (London: G. Bell, 1925), pp. 319–29.

34. Mas Latrie, 2: 19.

35. Russell, *The Just War*, makes no mention of the Donation as a basis for a just war.

36. For a general introduction to the work of the Teutonic Knights, see Alexander Bruce-Boswell, "The Teutonic Order," in *Cambridge Mediaeval History*, ed. H. M. Gwatkin and J. P. Whitney, vol. 7, *Decline of Empire and Papacy* (Cambridge: Cambridge University Press, 1932), pp. 248–69. In addition, see the texts in Helbig and Weinrich, *Urkunden und Erzählende Quellen zur Deutschen Ostseidlung im Mittelalter.*

37. Alexander IV, Potthast, no. 16482; Theiner, 1: 71, no. 139.

38. Alexander IV, Potthast, no. 16653.

39. Alexander IV, Potthast, no. 16944.

40. Alexander IV, Potthast, no. 15721.

41. Alexander IV, Potthast, no. 18433.

42. Urban IV, Potthast, no. 18937; Theiner, 1: 77, no. 149.

43. Urban IV, Potthast, no. 18752.

44. Clement IV, Potthast, no. 20229.

45. Boniface VIII, Potthast, no. 24842; Theiner, 1: 111–12, no. 196.

46. Jean, Sire de Joinville, "Chronicle of the Crusade of St. Lewis," in *Memoirs of the Crusades*, trans. Frank Marzials (London: J. M. Dent, 1908; reprint ed., New York: E. P. Dutton, 1958), pp. 253–59. The significance of St. Louis' contacts with the Tartars is discussed in René

Grousset, *The Empire of the Steppes*, trans. Naomi Walford (New Brunswick, N.J.: Rutgers University Press, 1970), pp. 273, 276–82. The king's representative in the East was the Franciscan friar William of Rubruck: see his report in Dawson, *The Mongol Mission*, pp. 87–220.

47. According to Joinville, the khan informed Louis: "So we admonish thee to send us, year by year, of thy gold and of thy silver, and thus keep us to be thy friend; and if thou wilt not do this, we will destroy thee and thy people, as we have done to the kings already named." The result was that the French king repented "sorely that he had ever sent envoys to the great King of the Tartars." Joinville, "Chronicle of the Crusade," pp. 258–59.

48. Alexander IV, Potthast, no. 17678; *Acta Alexandri P.P. IV*, pp. 82–88, no. 42: for the situation in Hungary, see Grousset, *Empire of the Steppes*, pp. 266–67.

49. *Acta Alexandri P.P. IV*, p. 85: "Certo nempe fidei vinculo teneri nequeunt, cum veram fidem non habeant infideles."

50. Ibid., p. 86: "Matrimonii quoque nexus nec christiano paganum nec christianum pagano coniungit: quia etiam inter ipsos paganos, etsi verum sit tamen, propter defectum fidei non est ratum et inseparabile apud eos matrimonii sacramentum." Concerning such marriages see Muldoon, "Missionaries and the Marriages of Infidels," pp. 127–31; Noonan, *Power to Dissolve*, pp. 347–48.

51. *Acta Alexandri P.P. IV*, p. 86: "Si ergo, quod absit, filium vel filiam tuam contingat gentilis conubii contagio maculari, ex hoc utique facto, quod non iuris effectum, sed solum Creatoris tui contumeliam continebit, foederi pacis aut pactionibus mediis nihil pro veniet firmitatis."

52. See Connell, "Western Views," 115–37.

53. X. 4.19.8: "Quia vero pagani circa plures insimul feminas affectum dividunt coniugalem, utrum post conversionem omnes, vel quam ex omnibus retinere valeant." See also Muldoon, "Missionaries and the Marriages of Infidels," pp. 127–30.

54. Grousset, *Empire of the Steppes*, pp. 353–67, 397–98; Setton, *The Papacy and the Levant*, 1: 115–16; de Rachewiltz, *Papal Envoys*, pp. 150–53.

55. Grousset, *Empire of the Steppes*, pp. 367–71; Setton, *The Papacy and the Levant*, 1: 106, 115–16, 120; de Rachewiltz, *Papal Envoys*, pp. 151–53. Concerning the council, see Deno J. Geanakoplos, *Emperor Michael Palaeologus and the West, 1258–1282* (Cambridge: Harvard University Press, 1959), pp. 258–304.

56. De Rachewiltz, *Papal Envoys*, pp. 153–54; Setton, *The Papacy and the Levant*, 1: 115–16.

57. Setton, *The Papacy and the Levant*, 1: 116–17.

58. Marco Polo, *The Book of Ser Marco Polo*, ed. Henry Yule, 2 vols. (London: Murray, 1926), 1: 22–23. The best introduction to Marco Polo's work is Leonardo Olschki, *Marco Polo's Asia: An Introduction to his 'Description of the World' called 'il Milione'* (Berkeley: University of California Press, 1960). Concerning the religious aspects of the Polo family's mission, see Olschki, pp. 111–19, 178–210.

59. Setton, *The Papacy and the Levant*, 1: 133; de Rachewiltz, *Papal Envoys*, p. 157.

60. Wadding, 5: 44–46: ". . . Magnificus Princeps Abagha . . . suis litteris et nuntiis intimavit, carissimus in Christo filius noster Quolibey,

Magnus Cham, Imperator, et moderator omnium Tartarorum Illustris, qui, Christianus asseritur." Part of this letter is excerpted in *Acta Ro. Pont...ad Benedictum XI*, pp. 55–57, no. 24; Potthast, no. 21292.

61. Nicholas III, Potthast, no. 21461; *Acta Ro. Pont . . . ad Benedictum XI*, pp. 59–60, no. 27.

62. Wadding, 5: 40–42: "eos cum securo conductu ad praefatum Cham, cum expensarum, et aliorum necessariorum provisione, matura deliberatione transmittens." Potthast, no. 21291.

63. Nicholas III, Potthast, no. 21293; Wadding, 5: 42–44.

64. De Rachewiltz, *Papal Envoys*, p. 157.

65. Ibid., pp. 158–61; Grousset, *Empire of the Steppes*, pp. 371–73; Setton, *The Papacy and the Levant*, 1: 146–47.

66. Grousset, *Empire of the Steppes*, pp. 373–75.

67. Rabban Sauma's career has attracted much scholarly attention. There is a useful discussion of the literature in Setton, *The Papacy and the Levant*, 1: 147–48, note 25; see also de Rachewiltz, *Papal Envoys*, pp. 157–59.

68. Nicholas IV, Potthast, nos. 22631, 22632, 23633; *Acta Ro. Pont. . . . ad Benedictum XI*, pp. 124–28, nos. 66, 67, 68.

69. Concerning the khan's interest in religion, see Marco Polo, *Book of Ser Marco Polo*, pp. 13–14. His predecessors had also shown similar interest: see William of Rubruck's observations in Dawson, *Mongol Mission*, pp. 189–94.

70. Nicholas IV, *Acta Ro. Pont. . . . ad Benedictum XI*, pp. 158–60, no. 90; Potthast, no. 23009.

71. Ibid., p. 159: "Porro, princeps egregie, sicut magnificentaie regiae per alias nostras litteras tibi per Ven. fratrem nostrum Raban Barsauma."

72. Ibid., p. 158: "Adiecit etiam dictus frater, quod sibi eiusque sociis, dum in tuis partibus morarentur Christi prosequentes obsequia, humanitatem grandem et benignitatem ex ubere Tua clementia exhibuit Magnitudo quodque degentibus in terris tuae ditioni subiectis imperio fidei cultoribus christianae."

73. Nicholas IV, Potthast, no. 23003; *Acta Ro. Pont. . . . ad Benedictum XI*, pp. 154–55, no. 87.

74. Nicholas IV, Potthast, no. 23004; Wadding, 5: 219–20.

75. Concerning the Jesuit approach to conversion, see "Chinese Rites Controversy," *NCE*, 3: 611–17; Ludwig Pastor, *The History of the Popes from the Close of the Middle Ages*, trans. F. I. Antrobus, et al., 40 vols. (London: K. Paul, 1901–53), 33: 393–484; G. H. Dunne, *Generation of Giants* (Notre Dame, Indiana: University of Notre Dame Press, 1962), pp. 282–302.

76. Nicholas IV, Pottahst, no. 23791; Wadding, 5: 285–86.

77. Nicholas IV, Potthast, no. 2379; Wadding, 5: 287–88.

78. Nicholas IV, Potthast, no. 23792; Wadding, 5: 288–89.

79. Wadding, 5: 288: "Ceterum tibi affectvose consulimus, et attentius suademus, quod in habitu seu vestibus vel in dictu, ne unde materia dissensionis aut scandali contra te forsitan in gente tua valeat suboriri, nullam mutationem facias, sed in eis consuetudinem illam serves, quam ante baptismi lavacrum observasti."

80. The missionaries had a low opinion of the Nestorians. Rubruck described them as drunkards (Dawson, *Mongol Mission*, pp. 144–45). Guyuk Khan's response to Innocent IV's invitation to become a Chris-

tian—should I "become a trembling Nestorian Christian"? (ibid., p. 85)—suggests that the Mongols did not hold a very high opinion of them either. According to Olschki, *Marco Polo's Asia*, p. 214, Marco Polo was "distinguished from the missionaries who preceded him in Asia by a lack of rancor against these heretics, schismatics, and heterodox Christians with whom he came into contact during his stay in the Orient."

81. Nicholas IV, *Reg.*, no. 194; Potthast, no. 22764.

82. On the brief pontificate of Celestine V, see Mann, *Lives of the Popes*, 17: 247–341.

83. Although Boniface VIII has often been viewed very critically, he has been treated sympathetically in T. S. R. Boase, *Boniface VIII* (London: Constable, 1933).

84. Boniface VIII, Potthast, no. 24813; *Acta Ro. Pont... ad Benedictum XI*, pp. 209–12, no. 127.

85. This was not unprecedented. Innocent III had done something similar when he authorized Greek monasteries in southern Italy to continue to use their traditional liturgy when they returned to the Latin rite.

86. The text of *Unam sanctam* is available in various collections; among the more convenient are: *Corpus iuris canonici, Extravagantes communes*, 1.8.1; *Acta Ro. Pont... ad Benedictum XI*, pp. 233–34, no. 139; Potthast, no. 25189. Translations include: Brian Tierney, *The Crisis of Church and State*, pp. 188–89. There is an extensive discussion of the bull and the conflict of which it was a crucial element in Charles T. Wood, ed., *Philip the Fair and Boniface VIII*, European Problem Studies, 2d ed. (New York: Holt, Rinehart and Winston, 1971).

87. The interpretation of *Unam sanctam* as a very traditional document was first developed by Jean Rivière, *Le problème de l'Église et de l'État au temps de Philippe le Bel* (Louvain and Paris: E. Champion, 1926). Regarding the relationship of *Unam sanctam* to the canon law tradition, see James Muldoon, "Boniface VIII's Forty Years of Experience in the Law," *The Jurist* 31 (1971): 449–77.

88. Innocent IV, *Acta Innocenti PP. IV*, pp. 43–47, no. 20; Potthast, no. 11606.

89. John XXII, *Acta Ioannis XXII*, pp. 89–93, no. 46; Mollat, no. 16093.

Chapter 4

1. The fundamental expression of this viewpoint is Archibald R. Lewis, "The Closing of the Mediaeval Frontier, 1250–1350," *Speculum* 33(1958): 475–83.

2. Friedrich Heer, *The Medieval World: Europe 1100–1350*, trans. Janet Sondheimer (London: Weidenfeld and Nicolson, 1962), p. 1.

3. This sharp distinction is reflected in the titles of various modern books dealing with overseas expansion that generally use a fifteenth-century date to designate the beginning of European overseas expansion: Parry, *Europe and a Wider World: 1415–1715;* Boxer, *The Portuguese Seaborne Empire, 1415–1815;* Penrose, *Travel and Discovery in the Renaissance, 1420–1620*.

4. The widespread popularity of travel books during the fourteenth and fifteenth centuries is discussed in: J. H. Parry, *The Age of Recon-*

naissance (Cleveland: World Publishing Co., 1963), pp. 5–9; C. Raymond Beazley, *The Dawn of Modern Geography*, 3 vols. (Oxford: John Murray, 1897–1906; reprint ed., New York: Peter Smith, 1949), 3: 319–20; Donald F. Lach, *Asia in the Making of Europe*, vol. 1, book 1, *The Century of Discovery* (Chicago: University of Chicago Press, 1965), pp. 59–65, 74–80.

5. Samuel Eliot Morison, ed., *Journals and Other Documents on the Life and Voyages of Christopher Columbus* (New York: Heritage Press, 1963), p. 384, note 5.

6. Penrose, *Travel and Discovery*, pp. 268–70.

7. It is possible, however, that the Franciscans did retain some memories of the order's contacts with China: see Samuel Eliot Morison, *The European Discovery of America*, vol. 2, *The Southern Voyages* (New York: Oxford University Press, 1974), p. 34.

8. The basic work on the crusading movement in the fourteenth century is Aziz S. Atiya, *The Crusade in the Later Middle Ages* (London: Methuen, 1938; reprint ed., New York: Kraus, 1965); see also his "The Crusade in the Fourteenth Century," in Setton, *History of the Crusades*, 3: 3–26.

9. Various historians have given different figures concerning the impact of the Black Death: see the discussion in Philip Ziegler, *The Black Death* (New York: John Day, 1969), pp. 224–31. He concludes that approximately one in three persons died, although other scholars have estimated that as many as three out of every five died.

10. The basic study on the Avignon period is G. Mollat, *The Popes at Avignon, 1305–1378*, trans. Janet Love (London: Thomas Nelson, 1963). The translation from the ninth French edition did not include the extensive bibliography found in the original: see G. Mollat, *Les papes d'Avignon*, 9th ed. (Paris: Letouzey & Ané, 1950).

11. Vatican Register (RV) 62, fol. 1*r: "Incipiunt Rubrice litterarum seu scriptuarum tangentium de negotiis Tartarorum partium ultramarinarum et infidelium ac scismaticorum tempore felicis recordationis Clementis v. Iohannis xxii. Benedicti xii. et Clementis vi. per eos missarum et receptarum."

12. Concerning the history and the organization of the papal registers, see Leonard E. Boyle, *A Survey of the Vatican Archives and of Its Medieval Holdings* (Toronto: Pontifical Institute of Mediaeval Studies, 1972), pp. 103–31.

13. Because of the sheer bulk of modern official files, the files are purged of what is judged unnecessary material before being consigned to the archives.

14. Innocent III, *Regestum Inocentii III papae super negotio Romani imperii*, ed. F. Kempf, Miscellanea Historiae Pontificiae, vol. 12 (Rome: Pontifical Gregorian University, 1947).

15. RV 62, fol. 1*r.

16. Boyle, *Survey of the Vatican Archives*, pp. 7–8.

17. It has been suggested that RV 62 was associated with Urban V's return to Rome in 1368: see Jules Gay, *Le pape Clement VI et les affaires d'Orient, 1342–1352* (Paris: Société nouvelle de libraire et d'editions, 1904), pp. 8–9; Mollat, *Popes at Avignon*, pp. 57–58 (Urban V), 62–63 (Gregory XI).

18. Oskar Halecki, *Un empereur de Byzance à Rome* (Warsaw; Nakl. Towarzystwa Naukowego Warszawskiego, 1930, reprint ed., London: Variorum 1972). Mollat, *Popes at Avignon*, p. 58; Setton, *The Papacy and the Levant*, 1: 309–14; Deno Geanakoplos, "Byzantium and the Crusades, 1354–1453," in Setton, *History of the Crusades*, 3: 69–103 at pp. 73–79.

19. The basic introduction to this register is Gay, *Le pope Clement VI*, pp. 8–10. An indication of the lack of interest in this register is the fact that it is often described a "a collection of letters relating to the Tartars" (Boyle, *Survey of the Vatican Archives*, p. 107, note 14). In fact, the letters concerning the Tartars form only a small part of the collection.

20. The most extensive discussion of RV 62 is James Muldoon, "The Avignon Papacy and the Frontiers of Christendom: The Evidence of Vatican Register 62," *Archivum Historiae Pontificae* (1979).

21. James Bryce, *The Holy Roman Empire*, rev. ed. (New York: A. L. Burt, 1886), p. 215.

22. Between 1100 and 1304, "the popes spent one hundred and twenty-two [years] away from Rome and eighty-two in Rome." L. Gayet, *Le Grande Schisme d'Occident* (Florence: n.p., 1889), p. 3, cited in Mollat, *Popes at Avignon*, p. xiv.

23. Le Bras, *L'age classique*, pp. 15, 40, 252–56; Mollat, *Popes at Avignon*, pp. 7, 17, 45. The significance of the Avignon papacy for legal development had recently been described this way: "Le temps d'Avignon avait été celui des juristes; ils sont partout à la Curie et partout ils imposent leur esprit plus encore que leurs idées." Paul Ourliac and Henri Gilles, *La périod post-classique*, p. 87.

24. Boyle, *Survey of the Vatican Archives*, p. 111.

25. Ibid., p. 105. As a result of the vast expansion of papal judicial and administrative activity, books of epistolary formulae were increasingly used to standardize the clerks' work and make it more efficient. For the development of papal administrative practice, see Ullmann, *Short History*, pp. 247–49; Peter Herde, *Beiträge zum papstlichen kanzlei- und urkundenwesen im dreizehnten Jahrhundert* (Kallmunz: M. Lassleben, 1961), pp. 101–76; for the functioning of the Curia at Avignon, see Mollat, *Popes at Avignon*, pp. 285–305.

26. "Idem Soldanus cum Tartaris qui dudum per Centum annos Armen-orum amici extiterant." John XXII, RV 62, fol. 9r; Raynaldus, ad ann. 1322, nos. 33–39 at no. 33.

27. Benedict XII, RV 62, fols. 33r, 33v; Wadding, 7: 269–70; J.-M. Vidal and G. Mollat, *Benoît XII (1334–1342). Lettres closes et patentes intéres-sant les pays autres que la France* (hereafter Vidal and Mollat), 2 vols. (Paris: Ancienne Librairie Thorin et Fils, 1913–50), no. 2853. Benedict XII tried to end conflicts between Christian nations as well as between Christians and infidels: see Helen Jenkins, *Papal Efforts for Peace under Benedict XII, 1334–1342* (Philadelphia: University of Pennsylvania Press, 1933); C. Schmitt, *Un pape réformateur et un défenseur de l'unité de l'Église. Benoît XII et l'Ordre des Frères-Mineurs 1334–1342* (Quaracchi: College of St. Bonaventure, 1959).

28. Wadding, 6: 77–83; Wyngaert, *Sinica Franciscana*, 1: 345–55; Dawson, *Mongol Mission*, pp. 224–310. See also de Rachewiltz, *Papal Envoys*, pp. 160–72; Grousset, *Empire of the Steppes*, pp. 313–14.

29. Monte Corvino's apparently casual mention of another European living in Peking suggests that he was pointing out the comparative ease of a journey for anyone who might wish to join him in his mission. He does not seem to have found it strange or unusual that a fellow European was to be found there. Dawson, *Mongol Mission*, p. 226.

30. Ibid., p. 225: "I have baptized about 6,000 persons there up to the present. . . . And if it had not been for the aforesaid slanders I might have baptized 30,000 more."

31. Raynaldus, ad ann. 1307, nos. 29–39; Wadding, 6: 76–77, 102–13.

32. John XXII, RV 62, fols. 26v–27¹v; *Acta Ioannis XXII (1317–1334)*, ed. Aloysius L. Tăutu, Pontificia commissio ad redigendum codicem iuris canonici orientalis, *Fontes*, ser. 3, vol. 7 part 2 (Vatican City: Typis Polyglottis Vaticanis, 1952), pp. 255–58, no. 138; John XXII, *Lettres communes analyseés d'après les registres dits d'Avignon et du Vatican*, ed. G. Mollat, 16 vols. in 17 (Paris: Ancienne Librairie Thorin et Fils, 1904–47), no. 63873.

33. RV 62, fol. 27¹r: "Hec est enim fides recta . . . diffundit et divulgavit usque ad terminos orbite mundialis et quam dicta Romana ecclesia mater cunctorum christifidelium et magistra docet predicat, atque credit extra quam non est penitus ulla salus." *Acta Ioannis XXII*, p. 256.

34. John XXII, RV 62, fols. 27¹v–27²r; *Bull. Fran.*, 5: 557–58, no. 1039b; Mollat, *Lettres communes*, no. 63874.

35. John XXII, RV 62, fols. 27²v–28v at fol. 28r; *Bull. Fran.*, 5: 558, no. 1039d; Mollat, *Lettres communes*, no. 63875.

36. John XXII, *Acta Ioannis XXII*, p. 266, no. 143; Mollat, *Lettres communes*, no. 63514.

37. De Rachewiltz, *Papal Envoys*, p. 187.

38. Wadding, 7: 247: "Nos mittimus Nuncium nostrum Andream Francum cum quindecim sociis ad Papam, Dominum Christianorum in Franchiam ultra septem maria, ubi sol occidit, ad aperiendum viam nunciis saepe mittendis per nos ad Papam, et per Papam ad nos."

39. Scholars are divided on the question of whether Friar Nicholas ever reached his destination. According to Wyngaert, *Jean de Monte Corvino*, cited in *Acta Ioannis XII*, p. 258, Nicholas reached Peking, where he died in 1368. Arthur C. Moule, *Christians in China before the Year 1550* (London: Society for Promoting Christian Knowledge, 1930), pp. 196–97, argued that Nicholas never reached China, an opinion accepted by Grousset, *Empire of the Steppes*, p. 319. According to Moule and de Rachewiltz, *Papal Envoys*, p. 186, Nicholas reached Almaliq, near the modern city of Kulja in Sinkiang, but did not proceed beyond there.

40. Benedict XII, RV 62, fols. 31r–31v; Wadding, 7: 251; Vidal and Mollat, no. 1866.

41. Benedict XII, RV 62, fol. 31v; Wadding, 7: 251–52; Vidal and Mollat, no. 1867.

42. Benedict XII, RV 62, fols. 31v–32r; Wadding, 7: 252; Vidal and Mollat, no. 1868.

43. Grousset, *Empire of the Steppes*, pp. 341–42.

44. Benedict XII, RV 62, fols. 30r–30v; Wadding, 7: 249–50; Vidal and Mollat, no. 1864.

45. Benedict XII, RV 62, fols. 30v–31r; Wadding, 7: 250; Vidal and Mollat, no. 1865.

46. John dé Marignolli, "Recollections of Travel in the East," in *Cathay and the Way Thither*, ed. Henry Yule, rev. by Henri Cordier, Society Publications, nos. 33, 37, 38, 41, 4 vols. (London: Hakluyt Society, 1913–16), 3: 177–269; de Rachewiltz, *Papal Envoys*, p. 196; Grousset, *Empire of the Steppes*, pp. 319, 342, 404.

47. Benedict XII, RV 62, fols. 33r–33v; Wadding, 7: 269; Vidal and Mollat, no. 2853.

48. Benedict XII, Wadding, 7: 269. This part of the letter was omitted in RV 62.

49. Benedict XII, RV 62, fol. 33v; Wadding, 7: 270–71; Vidal and Mollat, no. 2854: see also Benedict XII, RV 62, fol. 33v, Wadding, 7: 271–72; Vidal and Mollat, no. 2855. Both letters are represented in RV 62 by brief headings giving the dates of the letters and the names of the recipients. The complete texts are in Wadding.

50. Benedict XII, RV 62, fols. 33v–34r; *Acta Benedicti XII* (*1334–1342*), ed. Aloysius L. Tăutu, Pontificia commissio ad redigendum codicem iuris canonici orientalis, *Fontes*, ser. 3, vol. 8 (Typis Polyglottis Vaticanis, 1958), pp. 106–7, no. 50; Vidal and Mollat, no. 2856.

51. De Rachewiltz, *Papal Envoys*, pp. 196–97.

52. John XXII, RV 62. fols. 16v–17v: "quod quondam predecessor tuus Mindowe cum toto suo Regno fuit ad fidem Christi conversus, sed propter atroces et inimicabiles iniurias dilectorum filiorum Magistri et fratrum ordinis Theotonicorum sancte marie Ierosolimitani, a fide huiusmodi recesserunt et in errorem pristinum sunt relapsi." Theiner, 1: 193–95, no. 293; Mollat, *Lettres communes*, no. 20325.

53. Ibid.

54. Ibid.

55. Ibid.

56. Paul W. Knoll, *The Rise of the Polish Monarchy* (Chicago: University of Chicago Press, 1972), pp. 138–39.

57. John XXII, RV 62, fols. 18v–19r; Theiner, 1: 196, no. 296; Mollat, *Lettres communes*, no. 20328.

58. John XXII, RV 62, fols. 14r–16r; Theiner, 1: 190–92, no. 290; Mollat, *Lettres communes*, no. 20322.

59. John XXII, RV 62, fols. 19v–20v; Theiner, 1: 197–98, no. 298; *Acta Ioannis XXII*, p. 157, no. 76b (incomplete); Mollat, *Lettres communes*, no. 20330.

60. Ibid.

61. Knoll, *Rise of the Polish Monarchy*, pp. 136–38.

62. Clement VI, RV 62, fols. 88r–88v; Theiner, 1: 525–26, no. 691; *Clement VI. Lettres closes, patentes et curiales intéressant les pays autres que la France*, ed. É. Déprez and G. Mollat, (hereafter Déprez and Mollat) (Paris: E. de Boccard, 1900–61), no. 2498.

63. Clement VI, RV 62, fols. 88v–89r; Theiner, 1: 526, no. 692; Déprez and Mollat, no. 2067.

64. Clement VI, RV 62, fols. 89r–89v; Theiner, 1: 526–27; Déprez and Mollat, no. 2068.

65. Concerning early European attempts to colonize the Canary Islands, see Merriman, *Rise of the Spanish Empire*, 1: 142–66. Beazley, *The Dawn of Modern Geography*, 3: 428–29, Edgard Prestage, *The Portuguese Pioneers*, The Pioneer Histories (London: A. and C. Black, 1933; reprint ed., New York: Barnes & Noble, 1967), pp. 5–9.

66. Clement VI, RV 62, fol. 61r; *Lettres closes, patentes et curiales du pape Clement VI (1342–1352) se rapportant à la France,* ed. E. Déprez, J. Glenisson, G. Mollat (hereafter Déprez, Glenisson, Mollat) 4 vols. (Paris: A. Fontemoing, 1910–61), no. 1314.

67. Gay, *Le pape Clement VI,* p. 62; Setton, *The Papacy and the Levant,* 1: 195–214. Humbert of Vienne received a copy of *Cum inter cetera:* RV 62, fols. 61v–62r; Déprez, Glenisson, Mollat, no. 1348. Copies of this letter were also sent to the king and queen of France and to the king and queen of Sicily: RV 62, fol. 62r.

68. Clement VI, RV 62, fol. 61r: "quod ipse ad acquirendas fortunie ac quasdam alias Insulas in partibus affrice consistentis et eidem adiacentes ut ex illis eliminata Paganei erroris."

69. Clement VI, *Bull. Ro.,* 4: 474–78, no. 5: "tibi et haeredibus tuis, et successoribus catholicis ac legitimis, et in devotione ipsius Romanae ecclesiae persistentibus, tam maculis quam foeminis in feudum perpetuum de fratrum nostrorum consilio et assensu ac apostolicae plenitudine potestatis sub modo, forma tenore, conditionibus, et conventionibus contentis praesentibus concedimus et donamus, teque praedicto feudo per sceptum aureum praesentialiter investimus . . . ac tu et ipsi singulis successoribus nostris Rom. pont. per vos vel procuratores vestros ad hoc legitime constitutos recognitionem et homagium ligium facere, et plenum vassallagium et fidelitatis juramentum praestare tenebimini juxta formam." "Raynaldus, ad ann. 1344, no. 44.

Chapter 5

1. Concerning the Schism and its effects, see: Walter Ullmann, *The Origins of the Great Schism* (London: Burns Oates & Washbourne, 1948; reprint ed., Hamden, Conn.: Archon Books, 1967); Brian Tierney, *Foundations of the Conciliar Theory* (Cambridge: Cambridge University Press, 1965); John Holland Smith, *The Great Schism, 1378* (New York: Weybright and Talley, 1970).

2. Wadding, 8: 102; de Rachewiltz, *Papal Envoys,* p. 201.

3. De Rachewiltz, *Papal Envoys,* p. 202.

4. Urban V, *Acta Urbani PP.V (1362–1370),* ed. Aloysius L. Tăutu, Pontificia commissio ad redigendum codicem iuris canonici orientalis, *Fontes,* ser. 3, vol. 11 (Vatican City: Pontifical Gregorian University, 1964), p. 15, no. 10.

5. Ibid., pp. 112–18, nos. 70, 71.

6. Mollat, *Popes at Avignon,* p. 58.

7. Urban V, *Acta Urbani V,* p. 298, no. 174. The pope gave his reasons for reissuing this bull in another letter: ibid., p. 297, no. 173.

8. Ibid., pp. 298–99, no. 175.

9. Ibid., pp. 320–21, no. 188; John XXII, *Acta Ioannis XXII,* pp. 260–62, no. 140.

10. X.4.17.15, *Gaudemus* and X.4.19.8, *Gaudemus.* For the importance of this letter in the eastern mission, see Muldoon, "Missionaries and the Marriages of Infidels."

11. Wadding, 8: 261; Raynaldus, ad ann. 1370, no. 9; de Rachewiltz, *Papal Envoys,* p. 202; Grousset, *Empire of the Steppes,* p. 319.

12. Wadding, 8: 723–24; John XXII, *Acta Ioannis XXII*, pp. 259–60, no. 139.

13. John XXII, *Acta Ioannis XXII*, pp. 255–58, no. 138.

14. Wadding, 8: 262–64.

15. Ibid., 8: 264–65 (letter to officials); 8: 265–68 (letter to Tartar people).

16. Grousset, *Empire of the Steppes*, pp. 320–25.

17. Wadding, 8: 270; Gregory XI, Wadding, 8: 281; Gregory XI, *Acta Gregorii P.P. XI (1370–1378)*, ed. Aloysius L. Tăutu, Pontificia commissio ad redigendum codicem iuris canonici orientalis, *Fontes*, ser. 3, vol. 12 (Vatican City: Typis Polyglotitis Vaticanis, 1966), pp. 192–93, no. 101.

18. The pope gave the travelers a letter of introduction to the various Christian rulers of Europe: *Acta Urbani P.P. VI (1378–1389), Bonifacii P.P. IX (1389–1404), Innocentii P.P. VII 1404–1406), Gregorii P.P. XII (1406–1415)*, ed. Aloysius L. Tăutu, Pontificia commissio ad redigendum codicem iuris canonici orientalis, *Fontes*, ser. 3, vol. 13, part 1 (Vatican City: Pontifical Gregorian University, 1970), p. 260, n. 128. Concerning the Christians of St. Thomas, see "Malabar Rite," *NCE*, 9: 92–96; Eugene Tisserant, *Eastern Christianity in India*, trans. E. R. Hambye (Bombay: Orient Longmans, 1957); L. W. Brown, *The Indian Christians of St. Thomas* (Cambridge: Cambridge University Press, 1956).

19. Gregory XII, *Acta Urbani P.P. VI*, p. 290, no. 146.

20. Boniface IX, ibid., p. 260, no. 128: ". . . Abraham et Saliba sacerdotes, ut asserunt, in partibus Indiae, iuxta legem beati Thomae." The most famous example of a hoax concerning the plight of the eastern Church involved a letter supposedly sent by Prester John, a Christian king in Central Asia, to the West seeking support against the infidel nations surrounding him: see Vsevolod Slessarev, *Prester John: The Letter and the Legend* (Minneapolis: University of Minnesota Press, 1959).

21. Ruy Gonzalcz de Clavijo, *Narrative of the Embassy of Ruy Gonzalez de Clavijo to the Court of Timour at Samarcand A.D. 1403–6*, ed. Clements R. Markham, Hakluyt Society Publications, no. 26 (London: Hakluyt Society, 1859; reprint ed., New York: Burt Franklin, 1970). Concerning this mission see: Grousset, *Empire of the Steppes*, p. 453; Merriman, *Rise of the Spanish Empire*, 1: 158–64.

22. See Wadding, 9: 299, where the list of provinces for 1400 includes Provincia Tartariae and mentions the existence of a convent at the great khan's court, "In Canbalech in palatio magni Cani habent Fratres locum."

23. De Rachewiltz, *Papal Envoys*, p. 202, gives strong emphasis to the effect of the Black Death on missionary activity.

24. Kenneth Scott Latourette, *History of the Expansion of Christianity*, 7 vols. (New York: Harper, 1937–45), vol. 2, *The Thousand Years of Uncertainty, A.D. 500–A.D. 1500*, pp. 308–42.

25. Kenneth Scott Latourette, *History of Christian Missions in China* (New York: Macmillan, 1929), pp. 73–77.

26. Grousset, *Empire of the Steppes*, pp. 409–56.

27. Innocent VI, Theiner, 1: 551–52, no. 727.

28. Innocent VI, ibid., 1: 571–72, no. 764.

29. Innocent VI, ibid., 1: 577–78, no. 769.

30. Innocent VI, ibid., 1: 581, no. 776.

31. Innocent VI, ibid., 1: 588–89, no. 789.
32. Urban V, *Acta Urban PP. V*, pp. 47–48, no. 29a
33. Urban V, Theiner, 1: 629–30, no. 45: "ecclesia . . . Tarbatensis, in finibus christianitatis et inter infideles situata."
34. See for example: Urban V, Theiner, 1: 642–43, no. 866 and 1: 649–50, no. 877.
35. Gregory XI, *Acta Gregorii XI, pp.* 34–35, no. 14.
36. Ibid., pp. 35–37, no. 15.
37. Ibid., pp. 174–75, no. 90: "fiatque pax individua inter vos ac Fratres eosdem et alios christianos, ut quos una iunget fides, nulla possit presertim tam dira et prolixa discordia separare, sequatur optata tranquillitas, servetur mutua charitas, et utrinque dulcedo fraternae communionis accedat."
38. Gregory XI, Theiner, 1: 695–96, no. 935 and 1: 696, no. 936.
39. O. Halecki, "From the Union with Hungary to the Union with Lithuania: Jadwiga, 1374–99," in *The Cambridge History of Poland*, ed. W. F. Reddaway, et al., 2 vols. (Cambridge: Cambridge University Press, 1950–51), 1: 188–209.
40. Boniface IX, Wadding, 9: 177–81. Concerning the society, see John Moorman, *A History of the Franciscan Order from its Origins to the Year 1517* (Oxford: Clarendon Press, 1968), p. 434.
41. See, for example: Boniface IX, *Acta Urbani P.P. VI*, pp. 266–67, no. 132 (partial text); Wadding, 9: 591–97 (complete text).
42. Boniface IX, Theiner, 1: 769–71, no. 1041.
43. Ibid., 1: 771–73, no. 1042.
44. Gregory XII, *Acta Urbani P.P. VI*, pp. 302–3, no. 151.
45. John XXIII, Theiner, 2: 5–6, no. 8.
46. Wadding, 8: 195–96.
47. Ibid., 8: 718–19.
48. Ibid., 8: 717–18.
49. Concerning this campaign and its consequences, see: Setton, *The Papacy and the Levant*, pp. 258–84; Harry Luke, "The Kingdom of Cyprus, 1291–1369," in Setton, *History of the Crusades*, 3: 340–60 at 352–60.
50. Urban V, Raynaldus, ad ann. 1366, no. 13; Setton, *The Papacy and the Levant*, p. 274.
51. Gregory XI, *Acta Gregorii P. P. XI*, pp. 84–85, no. 41.
52. Gregory XI, Wadding, 8: 373–74, 374–75.
53. Gregory XI, *Acta Gregorii P.P. XI*, p. 131, no. 71.
54. Boniface IX, *Acta Urbani P.P. VI*, p. 59, no. 24.
55. Ibid., 121–23, nos. 60–62.
56. Gregory XI, Raynaldus, ad ann. 1376, nn. 21–22.
57. Urban V, *Bull. Ro.*, 4: 522–23.
58. Concerning early European contacts with these islands, see Prestage, *Portuguese Pioneers*, pp. 35–53.
59. The Portuguese Infante, Henry the Navigator (1394–1460), was a strong proponent of this view, see Gomes Eannes de Azurara, *Chronicle of the Discovery of Guinea, and Conquest* ed. C. R. Beazley and E. Prestage, 2 vols. (London: Hakluyt Society, 1896, 1899). 1: 27–30. The standard biography of Henry the Navigator remains C. Raymond Beazley, *Prince Henry the Navigator* (New York: G. P. Putnam's Sons, 1895; reprint ed., New York: Barnes & Noble, 1967).

60. Urban V, Raynaldus, ad ann. 1369, no. 14.
61. Wadding, 9: 310.

Chapter 6

1. Concerning the papal role as mediator in international conflicts, see Walter Ullmann, "The Medieval Papal Court as an International Tribunal," *Virginia Journal for International Law* 11(1971): 356–71.

2. The state of the Church in the fifteenth century has attracted a great deal of scholarly attention because of the debate about the role of ecclesiastical corruption as a cause of the Reformation: for a recent survey of the issue, see R. Aubenas, "The Papacy and the Catholic Church," *New Cambridge Modern History*, ed. G. R. Potter, vol. 1, *The Renaissance, 1493–1520*, (Cambridge: Cambridge University Press, 1957), pp. 76–94. Pastor, *History of the Popes*, vols. 1–10, presents the traditional Catholic position. The older Protestant view is presented in M. Creighton, *A History of the Papacy during the Reformation*, 5 vols. (London: Longman, Green, 1882–94).

3. The bulls that marked the development of papal involvement in exploration and expansion beyond Europe have been identified and examined in Charles-Martial de Witte, "Les bulles pontificales et l'expansion portugaise au XVe siècle," *Revue d'histoire ecclesiastique* 48 (1953): 683–718; 49 (1954): 438–61; 51 (1956): 413–53, 908–36; 53 (1958): 5–46, 443–71.

4. For a survey of the literature dealing with the role of medieval legal thought in the development of international law, see Muldoon, "The Contribution of the Medieval Canon Lawyers."

5. For the history of the conflict between the Knights and the kingdom of Poland in the fifteenth century, see: O. Halecki, "Problems of the New Monarchy: Jagello and Vitold, 1400–34," and A. Bruce Boswell, "Jagiello's Successors: The Thirteen Years' War with the Knights, 1434–66," in *The Cambridge History of Poland*, 1: 210–31 and 232–49.

6. Concerning Wyclif's theological opinions, see L. J. Daly, *The Political Theory of John Wyclif* (Chicago: Loyola University Press, 1962); Joseph Dahmus, *The Prosecution of John Wyclif* (New Haven: Yale University Press, 1952); James Muldoon, "John Wyclif and the Rights of the Indians: The *Requerimiento* Re-Examined," *The Americas*, forthcoming.

7. Concerning Donatism and Augustine's response, see Herbert A. Deane, *The Political and Social Ideas of St. Augustine* (New York: Columbia University Press, 1963), pp. 175–97.

8. The more extreme supporters of the Gregorian reform during the eleventh century have been occasionally labeled Donatists: see Christopher Dawson, *Religion and the Rise of Western Culture* (New York: Sheed & Ward, 1950; reprint ed., Garden City, N.Y.: Doubleday, 1958), p. 250. Gregory VII himself has also been charged with Donatism: Norman Cantor, *Church, Kingship, and Lay Investiture in England, 1089–1135* (Princeton: Princeton University Press, 1958), pp. 124, 244.

9. Louise R. Loomis, J. H. Mundy and K. M. Woody, trans. and eds., *The Council of Constance: The Unification of the Church* (New York: Columbia University Press, 1961), pp. 38–40.

10. Dahmus, *Prosecution of John Wyclif*, p. 153, suggests that Wyclif's works were read as part of "a more searching investigation of Wyclif's writings." Matthew Spinka, in his *John Hus: A Biography* (Princeton: Princeton University Press, 1968), pp. 250–51, argues that only the already-condemned materials were read.

11. Dahmus, *Prosecution of John Wyclif*, p. 153.

12. "Nullus est dominus civilis, nullus est prelatus, nullus est episcopus, dum est in peccato mortali," Charles-Joseph Hefele and H. Leclercq, *Histoire des conciles*, 10 vols (Paris: Letouze et Ané, 1907–36), vol. 7, part 1, p. 517; see also John Wyclif, *De Givili Dominio*, ed. R. L. Poole and J. Loserth, 4 vols. (London: Trübner, 1885–1904) 1: 21–22. What Wyclif meant by this has been disputed: Carlyle and Carlyle, *History of Mediaeval Political Theory*, 6:60; Daly, *Political Theory*, p. 769. The difficulty of understanding Wyclif was well put by Dahmus, *Prosecution of John Wyclif*, p. 18: "So carefully did Wyclif obscure the logical consequences his theories on dominion would have meant for the nobility that the duke [John of Gaunt], the notoriously immoral son of an equally immoral father, together with the vicious Percy, appeared as his champions at St. Paul's."

13. Wyclif, *De Civili Dominio*, 1: 37–38.

14. Ibid., 2: 9–10.

15. Ibid., 2: 255.

16. Ibid., 2: 244.

17. Ibid., 2: 249.

18. Peter of Mladŏnovice, "An Account of the Trial and Condemnation of Master John Hus in Constance," in *John Hus at the Council of Constance*, ed. Matthew Spinka, Records of Civilization: Sources and Studies, no. 73 (New York: Columbia University Press, 1965), pp. 87–234 at pp. 171–72.

19. Ibid., p. 171 note 25. In addition, see Spinka, *John Hus: A Biography*, pp. 248–49, where Spinka argues that Gerson's criticisms of the Church were essentially in agreement with those that Hus had expressed, but that Gerson simply accepted "the calumnies of Hus' enemies for the truth" and thus failed to see the areas of agreement he shared with the Bohemian.

20. Spinka, *John Hus at the Council of Constance*, pp. 202–3.

21. Heinrich Finke, ed., *Acta concilii Constanciensis*, 4 vols. (Münster: Regensbergschen Buchhandlung, 1886–1928), 4: 363, 365.

22. Paulus Vladimiri, "Opinio Hostiensis," in *Paulus Vladimiri and his Doctrine Concerning International Law and Politics*, ed. Stanislaus F. Belch, 2 vols. (The Hague: Mouton, 1965), 2: 864–84 at 867. Belch's work is an aggressive attempt to demonstrate the significance of Vladimiri in the development of international law. The Knight's position has been defended by Erich Weise, *Die Amtsgewalt von Papst und Kaiser und die Ostmission besonders in der 1. Hälfte des 13. Jahrhunderts*, Marburger Ostforschungen, no. 31 (Marburg/Lahn: J. G. Herder-Institut, 1971).

23. Vladimiri, "Opinio Hostiensis," 2: 864; see also "Articuli contra Cruciferos de Prussia," 2: 905–88 at 917.

24. Vladimiri, "Opinio Hostiensis," 2: 864.

25. Ibid.

26. Ibid., 2: 864–65.

27. Ibid., 2: 866–67.
28. Ibid., 2: 868.
29. Ibid., 2: 868–69.
30. Ibid., 2: 873.
31. Ibid., 2: 873–74.
32. Ibid., 2: 876.
33. Ibid., 2: 874.
34. Ibid.: "Unde in extravagenti Bonifacii Octavi, quae incipit *Unam sanctam,* in fine, concluditur quod de necessitate salutis est credere omnem humanam creaturam subesse Romano Pontifici."
35. Ibid.
36. Ibid., 2: 875.
37. Ibid., 2: 875–76.
38. *Acta Concilii Constanciensis,* 4: 403.
39. Vladimiri, "Opinio Hostiensis," 2: 878.
40. Ibid.
41. Ibid. 2: 882.
42. Ibid., 2: 884.
43. *Acta Concilii Constanciensis,* 4: 430.
44. Ibid., 4: 364.
45. Prestage, *Portuguese Pioneers,* pp. 122–24, 144–45; Merriman, *Rise of the Spanish Empire,* 2: 173.
46. Merriman, *Rise of the Spanish Empire,* 1: 144–45.
47. Concerning the Castilian-Portuguese wars, see Merriman, *Rise of the Spanish Empire,* 1: 117–25; O'Callaghan, *History of Medieval Spain,* pp. 523–24, 528–34; Hillgarth, *The Spanish Kingdoms,* 1: 385–87, 392–99.
48. Wadding, 8: 718–19.
49. De Witte, "Les bulles pontificales," 48: 718.
50. Ibid., pp. 702–3. The bull itself does not seem to have survived. See also James Muldoon, "A Fifteenth-Century Application of the Canonistic Theory of the Just War," in *Proceedings of the Fourth International Congress of Medieval Canon Law,* ed. Stephan Kuttner. (Vatican City: Biblioteca Apostolica Vaticana, 1976), pp. 467–80.
51. The text of this letter is in de Witte, "Les bulles pontificales," 48: 715–17; there is an English translation in Muldoon, *Expansion of Europe,* pp. 54–56.
52. De Witte, "Les bulles pontificales," 48: 716.
53. Ibid.
54. Ibid.
55. Ibid., 48: 717.
56. Ibid.
57. Ruy de Pina, *Chronica d'el-rei D. Duarte* (Lisbon: Escriptorio, 1901), pp. 89–92.
58. C. M. de Witte found them in the Vatican Library, Cod. Vat. lat. 1932, fols. 100r–112v, 114r–122v. A copy of the king's letter was bound in with these documents, fols. 99r–99v: see de Witte, "Les bulles pontificales," 48: 700–702; Muldoon, "A Fifteenth-Century Application," pp. 471–72.
59. Cod. Vat. lat. 1932, 100r, 114r; Muldoon, "A Fifteenth-Century Application," p. 472.
60. Ibid.
61. Ibid.

62. Ibid., fols. 104–105v; Muldoon, "A Fifteenth-Century Application," p. 473.

63. Ibid.

64. Ibid., fol. 120v: "qui fuit lumen iuris et melius ceteris intellessit iura." Muldoon, "A Fifteenth-Century Application," p. 475.

65. Cod. Vat. lat. 1932, fols. 115r–115v; Muldoon, "A Fifteenth-Century Application," p. 474.

66. Cod. Vat. lat. 1932, fols. 121r–121v; Muldoon, "A Fifteenth-Century Application," p. 476.

67. Cod. Vat. lat., 1932, fol. 119r; Muldoon, "A Fifteenth-Century Application," p. 475.

68. Ibid., fol. 121r; Muldoon, "A Fifteenth-Century Application, p. 475.

69. Ibid., fols. 121r–121v; Muldoon, "A Fifteenth-Century Application," p. 476.

70. Ibid., fol. 121v; Muldoon, "A Fifteenth-Century Application," pp. 476–77.

71. Ibid.: "Set ego non credo quod isti uerum dicunt et nimium querunt iura pape ampliare." Muldoon, "A Fifteenth-Century Application," p. 476.

72. De Witte, "Les bulles pontificales," 48: 718: "Romanus pontifex, beati Petri celestis clavigeri successor, vicarius Jhesu Christi, ex superna Dei providencia, cuius est orbis terre et plenitudo eius, in supreme dignitatis specula constitutus, ad singula mundi climata ex pastoralis officii debito aciem sue considerationis extendit."

73. In reality papal attempts to protect the natives or to ameliorate the conditions of the conquest had little effect: see D. J. Wölfel, "La Curia Romana y la Corona de España en la defensa de los aborigénes Canarios," *Anthropos* 25 (1930): 1011–83 at p. 1014.

74. There is an extensive literature on the Fourth Crusade and the role Innocent III played in the conquest of Constantinople. The most complete study of the crusade is Donald Queller, *The Fourth Crusade* (Philadelphia: University of Pennsylvania Press, 1977).

Chapter 7

1. Barraclough, *Origins of Modern Germany*, pp. 254–58.

2. Martin V appointed a Franciscan to serve as vicar general for the Moroccan Christians in 1419: see Wadding, 10: 30; Mas Latrie, 2: 20.

3. Wadding, 10: 42.

4. Ibid., 10: 249–51.

5. Ibid., 12: 166–67.

6. Ibid., 11: 11.

7. A vicar general was appointed for the Canary Islands in 1423: Wadding, 10: 419–20. The papacy was aware of a Franciscan house in the Madeira Islands by 1450: Wadding, 12: 619–20.

8. Merriman, *Rise of the Spanish Empire*, 1: 156–58; A. H. de Oliveira Marques, *History of Portugal*, 2 vols. (New York: Columbia University Press, 1972), 1: 162–63.

9. Concerning the application of the theory of the just war in the fifteenth century, see Russell, *The Just War*, pp. 302–3.

10. Nicholas V, *Bull. Ro.*, 5: 110–15, no. 8. The text of this bull, as well as the texts of several other bulls dealing with overseas expansion, can be found in *European Treaties Bearing on the History of the United States and its Dependencies to 1648*, ed. Frances G. Davenport, 4 vols. (Washington, D.C.: Carnegie Institution, 1917–37; reprint ed., Gloucester, Mass.: Peter Smith, 1967), text, 1: 13–20, at pp. 13–14; trans., 1: 20–26, at p. 21.

11. *European Treaties*, text, pp. 16–17; trans., p. 23.

12. Christians could not be enslaved. The victors could legitimately extract ransom from the vanquished: see M. H. Keen, *The Laws of War in the Late Middle Ages* (London: Routledge & Kegan Paul, 1965), pp. 156–57.

13. *European Treaties*, text, p. 18; trans., p. 24.

14. The reign of King Alfonso V of Portugal (1438–81) was an important period in the history of Portuguese expansion into West Africa: see Eannes de Azurara, *The Chronicle of the Discovery and Conquest of Guinea;* and *The Voyages of Cadamosto and Other Documents on Western Africa in the Second Half of the Fifteenth Century*, ed. G. R. Crone, Hakluyt Society Publications, series 2, no. 80 (London: Hakluyt Society, 1937); *European in West Africa, 1450–1560*, ed. John W. Blake, Hakluyt Society Publications, series 2, nos. 86, 87 (London: Hakluyt Society, 1942). The various Portuguese writers whose works are contained in these volumes all stress the religious motives that underlay Portuguese expansion.

15. Merriman, *Rise of the Spanish Empire*, 2: 172–73; O'Callaghan, *History of Medieval Spain*, pp. 576–77.

16. The best introduction to Columbus, one that emphasizes his links to both the medieval and the modern world, is Samuel Eliot Morison, *Admiral of the Ocean Sea* (Boston: Little Brown, 1942), esp. pp. 5–6.

17. Ibid.

18. These bulls are available in various editions. The most convenient is *European Treaties*, 1: 56–78. Concerning the literature about these bulls, see de Witte, "Les bulles Pontificales," (1958): 443–454; see also James Muldoon, "Papal Responsibility for the Infidel: Another Look at Alexander VI's *Inter Caetera*," *The Catholic Historical Review* 64 (1978): 168–84.

19. For example, Morison, *Admiral of the Ocean Sea*, pp. 367–68.

20. ". . .therein dwell very many peoples living in peace, and, as reported, going unclothed, and not eating flesh." Alexander VI, *European Treaties*, 1: 58–61 at p. 58; trans., 1: 61–63 at p. 62. For Columbus' description of the Indians, see "The Journal of the First Voyage of Columbus," in *The Northmen, Columbus and Cabot*, ed. J. E. Olson and E. G. Bourne, Original Narratives of Early American History (New York: Scribner's Sons, 1906; reprint ed., New York: Barnes & Noble, 1953), pp. 110–11. European views of the peoples they encountered in the sixteenth century are discussed in Margaret Hodgen, *Early Anthropology in the Sixteenth and Seventeenth Centuries* (Philadelphia: University of Pennsylvania Press, 1964); Lee Eldridge Huddleston *Origins of the American Indians: European Concepts, 1492–1729* (Austin: University of Texas Press, 1967).

21. *European Treaties*, text 1: 60; trans., 1: 63.

22. Ibid., text, 1: 86–93; trans., 1: 93–100.

23. Ibid., text, 1: 113–15; trans., 115–17.

24. Ibid., text, 1: 171–85; trans., 1: 185–98.

25. Merriman, *Rise of the Spanish Empire*, 2: 226–34.

26. The text is in *Colección de documentos ineditos relativos al descubrimiento, conquista y organización de las antiguas posesiones españolas de ultramar*, 2d series (Madrid: Est. Topográfico, 1885–), 20: 311–14. There is an English translation in Sir Arthur Helps, *The Spanish Conquest in America and its relation to the History of Slavery and to the Government of the Colonies*, 4 vols., reprint ed. (New York: AMS Press, 1966), 1:264–67.

27. Muldoon, "John Wyclif and the Rights of the Indians," in press.

28. Manuel Giménez Fernández, quoted in Juan Friede, "Las Casas and Indigenism in the Sixteenth Century," in *Bartolomé de Las Casas in History*, ed. Juan Friede and Benjamin Keen (DeKalb, Ill.: Northern Illinois University Press, 1971), pp. 127–234 at pp. 149–50.

29. The value of studies dealing with the legal theories underlying the Spanish conquest has been called into question in recent years: see Lewis Hanke, "More Heat and Some Light on the Spanish Struggle for Justice in the Conquest of America," *Hispanic American Historical Review* 44 (1964): 293–340; and "A Modest Proposal for a Moratorium on Grand Generalizations: Some Thoughts on the Black Legend," ibid. 51 (1971): 112–27. In response, see Benjamin Keen, "The Black Legend Revisited: Assumptions and Realities," ibid. 49 (1969): 703–19; and "The White Legend Revisited: A Reply to Professor Hanke's 'Modest Proposal,'" ibid. 51 (1971): 336–55. The importance of the medieval legal tradition in shaping the Spanish attitude toward non-Europeans in the sixteenth century was given its most famous expression in Frank Tannenbaum, *Slave and Citizen* (New York: Knopf, 1947); see also Herbert S. Klein, *Slavery in the Americas* (Chicago: University of Chicago Press, 1967); and E. N. van Kleffens, *Hispanic Law Until the End of the Middle Ages* (Edinburgh: Edinburgh University Press, 1969).

30. Concerning the use of the *Requerimiento*, see Hanke, *Spanish Struggle*, pp. 31–36.

31. Ibid., p. 33.

32. Bartolomé de Las Casas, *Historia de las Indias*, ed. Agustín Millares Carlo, 3 vols. (Mexico City: Fondo de cultura económica, 1951), 3: 25–28.

33. Juan Lopez de Palacios Rubios, *De las Islas del mar Océano*, ed. Silvio Zavala (Mexico City: Fondo de cultura ecónomica, 1954), pp. 41–42. In spite of this, however, the editor asserted that Palacios Rubios accepted the Hostiensian position on *dominium;* ibid., p. xc.

34. Ibid., p. 115.

35. Hanke, *Spanish Struggle*, pp. 150–52.

36. Ibid., pp. 113–32.

37. Ibid., pp. 124–26; see also Lewis Hanke, *Aristotle and the American Indian* (Austin: University of Texas Press, 1959; reprint ed., Bloomington: University of Indiana Press, 1970).

38. Franciscus de Victoria, *De Indis et de iure belli relectiones*, ed. Ernest Nys, Classics in International Law (Washington, D.C.: Carnegie Institution, 1917; reprint ed., New York: Oceana, 1964), text, p. 222; trans., p. 119. The place of Vitoria and the other Spanish writers on international law has been the subject of controversy. The literature is

surveyed in Muldoon, "The Contribution of the Medieval Canon Lawyers," pp. 488–91, 493–94; see also Robert L. Benson, "Medieval Canonistic Origins of the Debate on the Lawfulness of the Spanish Conquest," in Fredi Chiapelli, ed., *First Images of America: The Impact of the New World on the Old*, 2: 327–34.

39. Victoria, *De Indis*, text, pp. 223–24; trans., p. 120; concerning Vitoria's use of canonistic material, see James Muldoon, "A Canonistic Contribution to the Formation of International Law," *The Jurist* 28 (1968): 265–79.

40. Victoria, *De Indis*, text, p. 223; trans., p. 120.

41. Ibid., text, p. 224; trans., p. 121.

42. Ibid., text, p. 225; trans., p. 122.

43. Sext, 5.2.19, Victoria, *De Indis*, text, p. 226; trans., p. 123.

44. Victoria, *De Indis*, text, pp. 226–28; trans., pp. 123–25.

45. Ibid., text, p. 229; trans., p. 125.

46. Ibid.

47. Ibid., text, p. 234; trans., p. 130.

48. Ibid. For Dante's views, see Dante, *Monarchy and Three Political Letters*, trans. Donald Nicholl and Colin Hardie (New York: Noonday Press, 1954); see also Carlyle and Carlyle, *History of Mediaeval Political Theory*, 6: 110–23; and Thomas G. Bergin, *Dante*, Riverside Studies in Literature (Boston: Houghton Mifflin, 1965), pp. 177–94; A. P. d'Entrèves, *Dante as a Political Thinker* (Oxford: Clarendon Press, 1952).

49. Victoria, *De Indis*, text, p. 235; trans., p. 131.

50. Ibid., p. 239; trans., p. 134.

51. Ibid., p. 240; trans., p. 135. Concerning Innocent III's views on the French king's independence from imperial jurisdiction, see Brian Tierney," 'Tria Quippe Distinguit Iudicia. . . .' A Note on Innocent III's Decretal *Per venerabilem*," *Speculum* 37 (1962): 48–59.

52. Victoria, *De Indis*, text, p. 243; trans., p. 138.

53. Ibid., text, p. 252; trans., p. 146.

54. Ibid., text, pp. 265–66; trans., pp. 159–60.

55. Ibid., text, p. 254; trans., p. 148.

56. Ibid., text, p. 257; trans., p. 151.

57. Ibid., text, p. 264; trans., p. 158.

58. Ibid., text, p. 266; trans., p. 160.

59. Ibid., text, pp. 264–65; trans., p. 159.

60. Ibid., text, p. 265; trans., p. 159.

61. Ibid., text, p. 266; trans., p. 160.

62. Ibid., text, p. 267; trans., pp. 160–61.

63. Pennington, "Bartolome de Las Casas," p. 155.

64. Ibid., pp. 157–58.

65. Ibid., pp. 158–59.

66. Ibid., p. 159.

Conclusion

1. Concerning this issue, see Stephan Kuttner's introduction to the modern edition of Johanes Andreae's work, pp. xiii–xiv.

2. See Denys Hay, *Europe:The Emergence of an Idea* (Edinburgh:

Edinburgh University Press, 1957; reprint ed., New York: Harper & Row, 1966), pp. 117–18.

3. Hugo Grotius, *The Law of War and Peace*, trans. Francis W. Kelsey, The Classics of International Law (Washington, D.C.: Carnegie Endowment for International Peace, 1925), book II, ch. xx, title 40, n. 4, p. 506. Grotius' use of canonistic material has yet to be discussed at length.

BIBLIOGRAPHY

Primary Sources: Introduction

The basic sources for this book fall into two categories: papal letters and the writings of the canon lawyers. Each of these categories has some special problems that deserve mention.

The papal registers for the thirteenth and much of the fourteenth centuries are calendared and available in printed editions. The sheer volume of the later papal registers has effectively blocked the publication of full editions of the letters. As a result, analysis of papal letters from this later period must be based upon those letters published in general histories of the Church. The oldest of these, and one that has not had a modern edition, is Odorico Rinaldi (Raynaldus), *Annales ecclesiastici*, 38 vols. (Lucca: Venturini, 1738–59). Other papal letters have been published in the *Bullarum, diplomatum, et privilegiorum sanctorum Romanorum, pontificum*, 25 vols. (Turin: S. Franco, H. Fory and H. Dalmazzo, 1857–72). The Franciscan order, which was one of the major forces in the medieval missionary effort, has for several centuries been engaged in publishing the records of its activities. The most extensive work of this sort was begun in the seventeenth century with the work of Luke Wadding. His *Annales minorum*, 32 vols., 3d ed. (Quaracchi, Florence: College of St. Bonaventure, 1931–64) has been reedited, and a number of papal letters have been added to it. Other letters are scattered through various collections of materials from the Vatican Archives published in the nineteenth century by scholars such as Augustin Theiner, prefect of the Vatican Archives in the middle years of the century. For the present study, the unpublished Vatican Register 62 was the only manuscript source used. The best introduction to the Vatican Archives, the materials it contains, and the printed editions of those materials is Leonard E. Boyle, *A Survey of the Vatican Archives and of Its Medieval Holdings* (Toronto: Pontifical Institute of Mediaeval Studies, 1972).

The writings of the canon lawyers of the fourteenth and fifteenth centuries, in contrast to the papal registers, are generally available in printed editions from the sixteenth and seventeenth centuries. The best introductions to the *consilia* material, which contains legal opinions on particular problems, are: Peter N. Riesenberg, "The Consilia Literature: A Prospectus," *Manuscripta* 6 (1961): 3–22; and Guido Kisch, *Consilia. Eine Bibliographie der juristischen Konsiliensammlungen* (Basel: Helbing and Lichtenhan, 1970).

Note on Abbreviations

Publications of the Pontificia Commissio ad redigendum Codicem Iuris Canonici Orientalis, Vatican City: Typis Polyglottis Vaticanis (or Pontificiae Universitatis Gregorianae) are abbreviated "P.C.R.C.I.C.O., V.C." (or "P.U.G.").

Papal Sources

Alexander IV. *Acta Alexandri P.P. IV (1254–1261)*, ed. T. T. Haluscynskyj and M. M. Wojnar. P.C.R.C.I.C.O.: *Fontes*, ser. 3, vol. 4, part 2. V.C.: T.P.V., 1966.

Benedict XII. *Acta Benedicti XII (1334–1342)*, ed. Aloysius L. Tăutu. P.C.R.C.I.C.O.: *Fontes*, ser. 3, vol. 8. V.C.: T.P.V., 1958.

———. *Benoît XII (1334–1342). Lettres closes et patentes interéssant les pays autres que la France*, ed. J. M. Vidal and G. Mollat. 2 vols. Paris: Ancienne Librairie Thorin et Fils, 1913–50.

Clement VI. *Lettres closes, patentes et curiales interéssant les pays autres que la France*, ed. É. Déprez and G. Mollat. Paris: E. de Beccard, 1900–61.

———. *Lettres closes, patentes et curiales du pape du Clement VI (1342–1352) se rapportant à la France*, ed. É. Déprez, J. Glenisson, and G. Mollat. 4 vols. Paris: A. Fontemoing, 1910–61.

Gregory VII. *Das register Gregors VII*, ed. Erich Caspar. *Monumenta Germaniae Historia, Epistolae selectae*. 2 vols. Berlin: Weidmannsche Buchhandlung, 1955.

Honorius III. *Acta Honorii III (1216–1227) et Gregorii IX (1227–1241)*, ed. Aloysius L. Tăutu. P.C.R.C.I.C.O.: *Fontes*, ser. 3, vol. 3, V.C.: T.P.V., 1950.

Innocent III. *Regestum Innocentii III papae super negotio Romani imperii*, ed. F. Kempf. Miscellanea Historiae Pontificiae, vol. 12. Rome: Pontifical Gregorian University, 1947.

Innocent IV. *Acta Innocentii PP. IV (1243–1254)*, ed. T. T. Haluscynskyj and M. M. Wojnar. P.C.R.C.I.C.O., *Fontes*, ser. 3, vol. 4, part 1. V.C.: T.P.V., 1962.

———. *Les registres d'Innocent IV*, ed. E. Berger. 4 vols. Paris: E. Thorin, 1884–1920.

Innocent V. *Acta Romanorum Pontificum ab Innocentio V ad Benedictum XI (1276–1304)*, ed. F. M. Delorme and A. L. Tăutu P.C.R.C.I.C.O.; *Fontes*, ser. 3, vol. 5, part 2. V.C.: T.P.V.

John XXII. *Acta Ioannis XXII (1317–1334)*, ed. A. L. Tăutu P.C.R.C.I.C.O., *Fontes*, ser. 3, vol. 7 part 2. V.C.: T.P.V., 1952.

———. *Lettres communes analysées d'après les registres dits d'Avignon et du Vatican*, ed. G. Mollat. 16 vols. in 17. Paris: Ancienne Librairie Thorin et Fils, 1904–47.

Urban IV. *Acta Urbani IV, Clementis IV, Gregorii X (1261–1276)*, ed. A. L. Tăutu. P.C.R.C.I.C.O., *Fontes*, ser. 3, vol. 5, part 1. V.C.: T.P.V., 1953.

Urban V. *Acta Urbani PP. V (1362–1370)*, ed. A. L. Tăutu. P.C.R.C.I.C.O., *Fontes*, ser. 3, vol. 11. V.C.: P.U.G., 1964.

Urban VI. *Acta Urbani P.P. VI (1378–1389), Bonifacii P.P. IX (1389–*

1404), *Innocentii P.P. VII (1404–1406)*, *Gregorii P.P. XII (1406–1415)*, ed. A. L. Täutu. P.C.R.C.I.C.O., *Fontes*, ser. 3, vol. 13, part 1. V.C.: P.U.G., 1970.

Vetera Monumenta Poloniae et Lithuaniae, ed. Augustin Theiner. 4 vols. Rome: Typis Vaticanis, 1860–64.

Legal Sources

Alfonso X. *Las Siete Partidas*, trans. Samuel P. Scott. Chicago: Commerce Clearing House, 1931.

Alexandrus Tartagnus. *Consilia*. 7 vols. in 4. Venice: Apud Haeredes Alexandri Paganini, 1610.

Belch, Stanislaus F. *Paulus Vladimiri and His Doctrine Concerning International Law and Politics*. 2 vols. The Hague: Mouton, 1965.

Corpus Iuris Canonici, ed. Emil Friedberg. 2 vols. Leipzig: Bernard Tauchnitz, 1879–81.

Corpus Iuris Civilis. 2 vols. Geneva: Apud Petrum et Iacobum Chouët, 1621.

Giovanni da Legnano, *Tractatus De Bello, De Represaliis et De Duello*, ed. Thomas Erskine Holland. Classics of International Law. Oxford: Oxford University Press, 1917.

Grotius, Hugo. *The Law of War and Peace*, trans. Francis W. Kelsey. Classics of International Law. Washington, D.C.: Carnegie Endowment for International Peace, 1925.

Hostiensis (Henricus de Segusio). *Lectura quinque Decretalium*. 2 vols. Paris, 1512.

Innocent IV (Sinibaldo dei Fieschi). *Commentaria doctissima in Quinque Libros Decretalium*. Turin: Apud haeredes Nicolai Beuilaquae, 1581.

Joannes Andreae. *In quinque decretalium libros novella commentaria*. Venice: 1581; reprint ed., Turin: Bottega d'Erasmo, 1963.

Niccolò de Tudeschi. *Commentaria in tertium Decretalium Librum*. Venice: 1578.

Oldratus de Ponte. *Consilia*. Venice: Franciscus Zilettus, 1571.

Palacios Rubios, Juan Lopez de. *De las Islas del mar Océano*, ed. Silvio Zavala. Mexico City: Fondo de Cultura Economica, 1954.

Petrus de Ancharano. *Consilia sive iuris responsa*. Venice: Apud Nicolaum Bevilaquam, 1568.

Other Sources

Acta concilii Constanciensis, ed. Heinrich Finke. 4 vols. Münster: Regensbergschen Buchhandlung, 1886–1928.

Azurara, Gomes Eannes de. *The Chronicle of the Discovery and Conquest of Guinea*, ed. C. R. Beazley and E. Prestage, 2 vols. Hakluyt Society Publications, nos. 95, 100. London: Hakluyt Society, 1896, 1899.

Blake, John W., ed. *Europeans in West Africa, 1450–1560*. 2 vols.

Hakluyt Society Publications, series 2, nos. 86, 87. London: Hakluyt Society, 1942.

Calvin, John. *Institutes of the Christian Religion*, ed. John T. McNeill, trans. F. L. Battles. vols. 20, 21. Library of Christian Classics, Philadelphia: Westminster Press, 1960.

Clavijo, Ruy Gonzalez. *Narrative of the Embassy of Ruy Gonzalez de Clavijo to the Court of Timour at Samarcand* A.D. *1403–6*, ed. Clements R. Markham. Hakluyt Society Publications, no. 26. London: Hakluyt Society, 1859; reprint ed., New York: Burt Franklin, 1970.

Colección de documentos ineditos relativos al descubrimiento, conquista y organizacion de las antiguas posesiones españolas de ultramar. 2d series. Madrid: Est. Topográfico, 1885–.

Crone, G. R., ed. *Voyages of Cadamosto and Other Documents on Western Africa in the Second Half of the Fifteenth Century,* Hakluyt Society Publications, series 2, no. 80. London: Hakluyt Society, 1937.

Dante. *Monarchy and Three Political Letters*, trans. Donald Nicholl and Colin Hardie. New York: Noonday Press, 1954.

Davenport, Frances G., ed. *European Treaties Bearing on the History of the United States and Its Dependencies to 1648.* 4 vols. Washington, D.C.: Carnegie Institution, 1917–37.

Dawson, Christopher, ed. *The Mongol Mission.* New York: Sheed and Ward, 1955.

Helbig, Herbert, and Weinrich, Lorenz, eds. *Urkunden und Erzählende Quellen zur Deutschen Ostseidlung im Mittelalter.* 2 vols. Darmstadt: Wissenschaftliche Buchgesellschaft, 1968–70.

Helmold, *Chronicle of the Slavs,* ed. Francis J. Tschan. Records of Civilization, Sources and Studies, no. 21 New York: Columbia University Press, 1935.

Henderson, Ernest F., ed. *Select Historical Documents of the Middle Ages.* London: G. Bell, 1925.

Henry of Livonia. *Chronicle of Henry of Livonia,* ed. James A. Brundage. Madison: University of Wisconsin Press, 1961.

Las Casas, Bartolomé de. *Historia de las Indias,* ed. Agustín Millares Carlo. 3 vols. Mexico City: Fondo de cultura económica, 1951.

Loomis, Louise R.; Mundy, J. H.; and Woody, K. M., eds. and trans. *Council of Constance: The Unification of the Church.* New York: Columbia University Press, 1961.

Marco Polo. *The Book of Ser Marco Polo,* ed. Henry Yule. 2 vols. London: Murray, 1926.

Marzials, Frank, ed. *Memoirs of the Crusades.* London: J. M. Dent, 1908; reprint ed., New York: E. P. Dutton, 1958.

Mas Latrie, M. L. de, ed. *Traités de paix et de commerce et documents divers concernant les relations des Chretiens avec les Arabes de l'Afrique Septentrionale au moyen age.* 2 vols. Paris: 1966; reprint ed., New York: Burt Franklin, n.d.

Morison, Samuel Eliot, ed. *Journals and Other Documents on the Life and Voyages of Christopher Columbus.* New York: Heritage Press, 1963.

Olson, J. E., and Bourne, E. G., eds. *Northmen, Columbus and Cabot.* Original Narratives of Early American History. New York:

Scribner's Sons, 1906; reprint ed., New York: Barnes and Noble, 1953.

Ruy de Pina. *Chronica d'el-rei D. Duarte*. Lisbon: Escriptorio, lxxx 1901.

Thomas Aquinas, *On the Truth of the Catholic Faith*, ed., Anton C. Pegis. 2 vols. Garden City, N.Y.: Doubleday, 1955–57.

Victoria, Franciscus de. *De Indis et de iure belli relectiones,* ed. Ernest Nys. Classics in International Law. Washington, D.C.: Carnegie Institution, 1917; reprint ed., New York, Oceana, 1964.

Wyclif, John. *De Civili Dominio,* ed. R. L. Poole and J. Loserth. 4 vols. London: Trübner, 1885–1904.

Wyngaert, A. van den. *Sinica Franciscana,* 5 vols. Quaracchi, Florence: College of St. Bonaventure, 1929-54. Vol. 1. *Itinera et relationes Fratrum minorum. Saeculi XIII et XIV* (1929).

Yule, Henry, ed. *Cathay and the Way Thither,* rev. Henri Cordier. 4 vols. Hakluyt Society Publications, nos. 33, 37, 38, 41. London: Hakluyt Society, 1913-16.

Modern Works

The great interest in medieval canon law in recent years has generated an extensive scholarly literature. Much of this work has dealt with the problem of relations between the spiritual and the temporal powers in medieval Europe. The best introduction to that literature is to be found in the bibliographical articles by McCready, Tierney, and Watt listed below and in Walter Ullmann's *Law and Politics in the Middle Ages.* The annual bibliographies provided in the *Bulletin of Medieval Canon Law* (1971–) present current scholarship. Most of the work that is presently being done in medieval canon law deals with the twelfth and thirteenth centuries. Although there is a great deal of canonistic material from those centuries, there are almost no guides to it, with the exception of the works by Riesenberg and Kisch.

There are virtually no studies of individual canonists. What material is available concerning them can usually be found in the *New Catholic Encyclopedia*, 15 vols. (New York: McGraw-Hill, 1967); or *Dictionnaire de droit canonique*, ed. R. Naz., 7 vols. (Paris: Letouzey et Ané, 1935–65).

Atiya, Aziz S. *The Crusade in the Later Middle Ages*. London: Methuen, 1938; reprint ed., New York: Kraus, 1965.

Baron, Salo Wittmayer. *A Social and Religious History of the Jews.* Vol. 9. *Under Church and Empire.* 2d ed. New York: Columbia University Press, 1965.

Barraclough, G. *The Origins of Modern Germany.* rev. ed. Oxford: Basil Blackwell, 1947.

Beazley, C. Raymond. *The Dawn of Modern Geography*. 3 vols. Oxford: John Murray, 1897–1906; reprint ed., New York: Peter Smith, 1949.

———. *Prince Henry the Navigator.* New York: G. P. Putnam's Sons, 1895; reprinted ed., New York: Barnes and Noble, 1967.

Bergin, Thomas G. *Dante.* Riverside Studies in Literature. Boston: Houghton Mifflin, 1965.

Boase, T. S. R. *Boniface VIII*. London: Constable, 1933.

Boxer, C. R. *Four Centuries of Portuguese Expansion, 1415–1825*. Berkeley: University of California Press, 1961.

———. *The Portuguese Seaborne Empire, 1415–1825*. New York: Knopf, 1975.

Brincken, Anna-Dorothee von den. *Die "Nationes christianorum orientalium" im Verständnis der lateinischen Historiographie von der Mitte des 12. bis in die zweite Halfte des 14. Jahrhunderts*. Kölner historische Abhandlungen, 22. Cologne: Böhlau, 1973.

Brown, L. W. *The Indian Christians of St Thomas*. Cambridge: Cambridge University Press, 1956.

Brundage, James A. *Medieval Canon Law and the Crusader*. Madison: University of Wisconsin Press, 1969.

Bryce, James. The Holy Roman Empire. rev. ed. New York: A. L. Burt, 1886.

Burns, Robert I. "Christian-Islamic Confrontation in the West: The Thirteenth Century Dream of Conversion." *American Historical Review* 76 (1971): 1386–1434.

———. "Immigrants from Islam: The Crusaders' Use of Muslims as Settlers in Thirteenth Century Spain." *American Historical Review* 80 (1975): 21–42.

———. *Islam under the Crusaders: Colonial Survival in the Thirteenth-Century Kingdom of Valencia*. Princeton: Princeton University Press, 1973.

———. "The Spiritual Life of James the Conqueror King of Arago-Catalonia, 1208–1276: Portrait and Self Portrait." *Catholic Historical Review* 62 (1976): 1–35.

Cambridge History of Poland, ed. W. F. Reddaway, et al. 2 vols. Cambridge: Cambridge University Press, 1950–51.

Cambridge Medieval History, ed. H. M. Gwatkin and J. P. Whitney. Vol. 7. *Decline of Empire and Papacy* (Cambridge: Cambridge University Press, 1932.

Cantini, J. A. "De autonomia judicis saecularis et de Romani Pontificis plenitudine potestatis in temporalibus secundum Innocentium IV." *Salesianum* 23 (1961): 407–80.

Cantor, Norman. *Church, Kingship, and Lay Investiture in England, 1089–1135*. Princeton: Princeton University Press, 1958.

Carlyle, R. W. and A. J. *A History of Mediaeval Political Theory in the West*. 6 vols. Edinburgh and London: William Blackwood and Sons, 1903–36.

Chiapelli, Fredi, ed. *First Images of America: The Impact of the New World on the Old*. 2 vols. Berkeley: University of California Press, 1976.

Connell, Charles W. "Western Views of the Origins of the 'Tartars': an Example of the Influence of Myth in the Second Half of the Thirteenth Century." *Journal of Medieval and Renaissance Studies* 3 (1973): 115–37.

Creighton, M. *A History of the Papacy during the Reformation*. 5 vols. London: Longman, Green, 1882–94.

Dahmus, Joseph. *The Prosecution of John Wyclif*. New Haven: Yale University Press, 1952.

Daly, L. J. *The Political Theory of John Wyclif*. Chicago: Loyola University Press, 1962.

Daniel, E. Randolph. *The Franciscan Concept of Mission in the High Middle Ages.* Lexington: University Press of Kentucky, 1975.

Daniel, Norman. *Islam and the West: The Making of an Image.* Edinburgh: Edinburgh University Press, 1960.

Dannenfeldt, Karl H., ed. *Renaissance, Medieval or Modern.* Problems in European Civilization. Boston: D. C. Heath, 1959.

Davis, H. W. C. *England Under the Normans and Angevins.* Vol. 2, *History of England,* ed. Sir Charles Oman. 11th ed. New York: G. P. Putnam's Sons, 1937.

Dawson, Christopher. *Religion and the Rise of Western Culture.* New York: Sheed and Ward, 1950; reprint ed., Garden City, N.Y.: Doubleday, 1958.

Deane, Herbert A. *The Political and Social Ideas of St. Augustine.* New York: Columbia University Press, 1963.

Dolcini, Carlo. " 'Eger cui lenia' (1245/46). Innocenzo IV, Tolomeo da Lucca e Guglielmo d'Ockham." *Rivista di Storia della Chiesa in Italia* 39(1975):127–48.

Dunne, G. H. *Generation of Giants.* Notre Dame, Ind.: University of Notre Dame Press, 1962.

D'Entrèves, A. P. *Dante as a Political Thinker.* Oxford: Clarendon Press, 1952.

———. *Natural Law: An Introduction to Legal Philosophy.* London: Hutchinson, 1951.

Frend, W. H. C. *The Donatist Church.* Oxford: Clarendon Press: 1952.

Friede, Juan, and Keen, Benjamin, eds. *Bartolome de Las Casas in History.* DeKalb, Ill.: Northern Illinois University Press, 1971.

Ganshof, François L. *The Middle Ages: A History of International Relations,* trans. Rémy Inglis Hall. New York: Harper & Row, 1970.

Gay, Jules. *Le pape Clement VI et les affaires d'Orient.* Paris: Société nouvelle de libraire et d'editions, 1904.

Geanakoplos, Deno J. *Emperor Michael Palaeologus and the West, 1258–1282.* Cambridge: Harvard University Press, 1959.

Gilchrist, J. *The Church and Economic Activity in the Middle Ages.* London: Macmillan, 1969.

Goitein, S. D. *A Mediterranean Society.* 2 vols. Berkeley: University of California Press, 1967–71.

Golubovich, G. *Biblioteca Bio-Bibliografica della terra santa e dell'oriente francescano.* 19 vols. Florence, Quaracchi: College of St. Bonaventure, 1906–48.

Grousset, René. *The Empire of the Steppes,* trans. Naomi Walford. New Brunswick, N.J.: Rutgers University Press, 1970.

Halecki, Oskar. *Un empereur de Byzance à Rome.* Warsaw: Nakl. Towarzystwa Naukowego Warszawskiege, 1930; reprint ed., London: Variorum, 1972.

Hampe, Karl. *Germany under the Salian and Hohenstaufen Emperors,* trans. Ralph Bennett. Totowa, N.J.: Rowman and Littlefield, 1973.

Hanke, Lewis. *Aristotle and the American Indian.* Austin: University of Texas Press, 1959; reprint ed., Bloomington: University of Indiana Press, 1970.

———. "A Modest Proposal for a Moratorium on Grand Generalizations:

Some Thoughts on the Black Legend." *Hispanic American Historical Review* 51(1971): 112–27.

———. "More Heat and Some Light on the Spanish Struggle for Justice in the Conquest of America." *Hispanic American Historical Review* 44(1964): 293–340.

Hay, Denys. *Europe: The Emergence of an Idea.* Edinburgh: Edinburgh University Press, 1957; reprint ed., New York: Harper and Row, 1966.

———. *Renaissance Debate.* European Problem Studies. New York: Holt, Rinehart and Winston, 1965.

Helps, Sir Arthur. *The Spanish Conquest in America and its relation to the History of Slavery and to the Government of the Colonies.* 4 vols. Reprint ed. New York: AMS Press, 1966.

Heer, Friedrich. *The Medieval World: Europe 1100–1350,* trans. Janet Sondheimer. London: Weidenfeld and Nicolson, 1962.

Hefele, Charles-Joseph and H. Leclercq. *Histoire des conciles.* 10 vols. Paris: Letouzey et Ané, 1907–36.

Herde, Peter. *Beiträge zum papstlichen kanzlei- und urkundenwesen im dreizehnten Jahrhundert.* Kallmunz: M. Lassleben, 1961.

Hess, Andrew C. "The Moriscos: An Ottoman Fifth Column in Sixteenth-Century Spain." *American Historical Review* 74 (1968): 1–25.

Hillgarth, J. N. *The Spanish Kingdoms, 1250–1516.* Vol. 1, *1250–1410: Precarious Balance.* Oxford: Clarendon Press, 1976.

Hodgen, Margaret. *Early Anthropology in the Sixteenth and Seventeenth Centuries.* Philadelphia: University of Pennsylvania Press, 1964.

Huddleston, Lee Eldridge. *Origins of the American Indians: European Concepts, 1492–1729.* Austin: University of Texas Press, 1967.

Jenkins, Helen. *Papal Efforts for Peace under Benedict XII, 1334–1342.* Philadelphia: University of Pennsylvania Press, 1933.

Johnson, James T. *Ideology, Reason, and the Limitation of War: Religion and Secular Concepts, 1200–1740.* Princeton: Princeton University Press, 1975.

Kantorowicz, Ernst. *Frederick II, 1194–1250,* trans. E. O. Lorimer. London: Constantinople, 1931; reprint ed., 1957.

Keen, Benjamin. "The Black Legend Revisited: Assumptions and Realities." *Hispanic American Historical Review* 49(1969): 703–19.

———. "The White Legend Revisited: A Reply to Professor Hanke's 'Modest Proposal,'" *Hispanic American Historical Review* 51 (1971): 336–55.

Keen, M. H. *The Laws of War in the Late Middle Ages.* London: Routledge and Kegan Paul, 1965.

Kleffens, E. N. van. *Hispanic Law until the End of the Middle Ages.* Edinburgh: Edinburgh University Press, 1969.

Klein, Herbert S. *Slavery in the Americas.* Chicago: University of Chicago Press, 1967.

Knoll, Paul W. *The Rise of the Polish Monarchy.* Chicago: University of Chicago Press, 1972.

Kritzeck, James. *Peter the Venerable and Islam.* Princeton: Princeton University Press, 1964.

Kuttner, Stephan. *Proceedings of the Fourth International Congress of*

Medieval Canon Law. Vatican City: Biblioteca Apostolica Vaticana, 1976.

Kuttner, Stephan, and Ryan, J. J. *Proceedings of the Second International Congress of Medieval Canon Law.* Vatican City: Biblioteca Apostolica Vaticana, 1965.

Lach, Donald F. *Asia in the Making of Europe.* Vol. 1, book 1. *The Century of Discovery.* Chicago: University of Chicago Press, 1965.

Ladner, Gerhart B. "The Concepts of 'Ecclesia' and 'Christianitas' and their Relation to the Idea of Papal 'plenitudo potestatis' from Gregory VII to Boniface VIII." *Miscellanea Historia Pontificiae* 18 (Rome, 1954): 49–77.

Latourette, Kenneth Scott. *History of Christian Missions in China.* New York: Macmillan, 1929.

———. *History of the Expansion of Christianity*, 7 vols. New York: Harper, 1937–45. Vol. 2, *The Thousand Years of Uncertainty*, A.D. 500–A.D. 1500.

Le Bras, Gabriel. "Innocent IV Romaniste: Examen de l'Apparatus." *Studia Gratiana* 11(1967): 305–26.

Le Bras, Gabriel; Lefebvre, Ch; and Rambaud, J. *L'age classique, 1140–1378: sources et théorie du droit.* Histoire du Droit et des Institutions de l'Eglise en Occident, vol. 17. Paris: Sirey, 1965.

Lewis, Archibald R. "The Closing of the Mediaeval Frontier, 1250–1350." *Speculum* 33 (1958): 475–83.

Lewis, Ewart, *Medieval Political Ideas.* 2 vols. New York: Knopf, 1954.

Lourie, Elena. "Free Moslems in the Balearics under Christian Rule in the Thirteenth Century." *Speculum* 45 (1970): 624–49.

Luchaire, Achille. *Innocent III.* 6 vols. Paris: Hachette, 1906–8. Vol. 4. *Le question d'Orient.*

McCready, W. D. "Papal *Plenitudo Postestatis* and the Source of Temporal Authority in Late Medieval Papal Hierocratic Theory." *Speculum* 48 (1973): 654–74.

Maffei, Domenico. *La Donazione di Cosantino nei giuristi medievali.* Milan: A. Giuffrè, 1964.

Maitland, Frederic W. *The Collected Papers of Frederic William Maitland*, ed. H. A. L. Fisher. 3 vols. Cambridge: Cambridge University Press, 1911.

Mann, Horace K. *Lives of the Popes in the Early Middle Ages from 590 to 1304.* 18 vols. London: K. Paul, Trench, Trubner, 1902–32.

Mattingly, Garrett. *Renaissance Diplomacy.* Boston: Houghton Mifflin, 1955; reprint ed., Baltimore: Penguin, 1964.

Merriman, Roger Biglow. *The Rise of the Spanish Empire in the Old World and in the New.* 4 vols. New York: Macmillan, 1918–34; reprint ed., New York: Cooper Square, 1962.

Mollat, G. *Les papes d'Avignon.* 9th ed. Paris: Letouzey et Ané, 1950.

———. *The Popes at Avignon, 1305–1378*, trans. Janet Love. London: Thomas Nelson, 1963.

Moorman, John. *A History of the Franciscan Order from its Origins to the Year 1517.* Oxford: Oxford University Press, 1968.

Morison, Samuel Eliot. *Admiral of the Ocean Sea.* Boston: Little Brown, 1942.

——. *The European Discovery of America*. Vol. 2. *The Southern Voyages*. New York: Oxford University Press, 1974.

Moule, Arthur C. *Christians in China Before the Year 1550*. London: Society for the Promoting of Christian Knowledge, 1930.

Muldoon, James. "Boniface VIII's Forty Years of Experience in the Law." *The Jurist* 31(1971): 449–77.

——. "A Canonistic Contribution to the Formation of International Law." *The Jurist*, 28(1968): 265–72.

——. "The Contribution of the Medieval Canon Lawyers to the Formation of International Law." *Traditio* 28 (1972): 483–97.

——. " '*Extra ecclesiam non est imperium:*' The Canonists and the Legitimacy of Secular Power." *Studia Gratiana* 9(1966): 551–80.

——. "John Wyclif and the Rights of the Indians: The *Requirimiento* Re-Examined." *The Americas*, forthcoming.

——. "Missionaries and the Marriages of Infidels: The Case of the Mongol Mission." *The Jurist* 35(1975): 125–41

——. "Papal Responsibility for the Infidel: Another Look at Alexander VI's *Inter Caetera*." *Catholic Historical Review* 64 (1978): 168–84.

——, ed. *The Expansion of Europe: The First Phase*. Philadelphia: University of Pennsylvania Press, 1977.

New Cambridge Modern History, ed. G. R. Potter. Vol. 1, *The Renaissance 1493–1520*. Cambridge: Cambridge University Press, 1957.

Noonan, John T., Jr. *Contraception: A History of its Treatment by the Catholic Theologians and Canonists*. Cambridge: Harvard University Press, 1965.

——. *Power to Dissolve: Lawyers and Marriages in the Courts of the Roman Curia*. Cambridge: Harvard University Press, 1972.

——. *The Scholastic Analysis of Usury*. Cambridge: Harvard University Press, 1957.

Oakley, Francis. "Celestial Hierarchies Revisited: Walter Ullmann's Vision of Medieval Politics." *Past & Present*, no. 60(August 1973): 3: 48.

O'Callaghan, Joseph F. *A History of Medieval Spain*. Ithaca, N.Y.: Cornell University Press, 1975.

Oliveira Marques, A. H. de. *History of Portugal*. 2 vols. New York: Columbia University Press, 1972.

Olschki, Leonardo. *Marco Polo's Asia: An Introduction to his 'Description of the World' called 'il Milione.'* Berkeley: University of California Press, 1960.

Ourliac, Paul, and Gilles, Henri. *La période post-classique (1378–1500)*. Part 1, *La problematique de l'epoque les sources*. Histoire du Droit et des Institutions de l'Eglise en Occident, vol. 13. Paris: Éditions Cujus, 1971.

Pacaut, Marcel. "L'autorité pontificale selon Innocent IV." *Le Moyen Age* 66 (1960): 85–119.

Parry, J. H. *The Age of Reconnaissance*. Cleveland: World Publishing Co., 1963.

——. *Europe and a Wider World: 1415–1715*. London: Hutchinson University Library, 1966.

Pastor, Ludwig. *The History of the Popes from the Close of the Middle Ages*, trans. F. I. Antrobus, et al. 40 vols. London: K. Paul, 1901–53.

Pennington, Kenneth J., Jr. "Bartolome de Las Casas and the Tradition of Medieval Law." *Church History* 39(1970): 149–61.

Penrose, Boies. *Travel and Discovery in the Renaissance, 1420–1620.* Cambridge: Harvard University Press, 1955; reprint ed., New York: Atheneum, 1962.

Piergiovanni, Vito. "Sinibaldo dei Fieschi Decretalista: Ricerche sulla vita." *Studia Gratiana* 14(1967): 125–54.

Post, Gaines. "Blessed Lady Spain—Vincentius Hispanus and Spanish National Imperialism in the Thirteenth Century." *Speculum* 29 (1954): 198–209.

———. *Studies in Medieval Legal Thought: Public Law and the State, 1100–1322.* Princeton: Princeton University Press, 1964.

Potthast, A. *Regesta pontificum romanorum inde ab anno post Christum natum MCXCVIII ad annum MCCCIV,* 2 vols. Berlin: Rudolph Decker, 1874–75.

Queller, Donald. *The Fourth Crusade.* Philadelphia: University of Pennsylvania Press, 1977.

Rachewiltz, I. de. *Papal Envoys to the Great Khans.* Stanford: Stanford University Press, 1971.

Rivière, Jean. *Le problème de l'Église et de l'Etat au temps de Philippe le Bel.* Louvain and Paris: E. Champion, 1926.

Russell, Frederick, H. *The Just War in the Middle Ages.* Cambridge Studies in Medieval Life and Thought, series 3, no. 8. Cambridge: Cambridge University Press, 1975.

Schmitt, C. *Un pape réformateur et un défenseur de l'unité de l'Église. Benoît XII et l'Ordre des Frères-Mineurs 1334–1342.* Quaracchi: College of St. Bonaventure, 1959.

Setton, Kenneth M. *The Papacy and the Levant (1204–1571),* vol. 1, *The Thirteenth and Fourteenth Centuries.* Philadelphia: American Philosophical Society, 1976.

———. ed. *History of the Crusades.* vol. 2, *The Later Crusades, 1189–1311,* ed. Robert Lee Wolff and Harry W. Hazard. 2d ed. Madison: University of Wisconsin Press, 1969. Vol. 3, *The Fourteenth and Fifteenth Centuries,* ed. Harry W. Hazard. Madison: University of Wisconsin Press, 1975.

Slessarev, Vsevolod. *Prester John: The Letter and the Legend.* Minneapolis: University of Minnesota Press, 1959.

Smith, John Holland. *The Great Schism, 1378.* New York: Weybright and Talley, 1970.

Soranzo, Giovanni. *Il papato, l'Europa christiana e i Tartari.* Milan: Università cattolica del Sacro Cuore. 1930.

Southern, R. W. *Western Views of Islam in the Middle Ages.* Cambridge: Harvard University Press, 1962.

Spinka, Matthew. *John Hus: A Biography.* Princeton: Princeton University Press, 1968.

Spitz, Lewis W. *The Reformation: Basic Interpretations.* Problems in European Civilization. 2d ed. Lexington, Mass.: D. C. Heath, 1972.

Stickler, A. M. "Alanus Anglicus als Verteidiger des monarchischen Papsttums," *Salesianum* 21(1959): 346–406.

Synan, Edward A. *The Popes and the Jews in the Middle Ages.* New
Tannenbaum, Frank. *Slave and Citizen.* New York: Knopf, 1947.
    York: Macmillan, 1965.

Tierney, Brian. "The Continuity of Papal Political Theory in the Thirteenth Century. Some Methodological Considerations." *Mediaeval Studies* 27 (1965): 227–45.

——. *The Crisis of Church and State, 1050–1300*. Englewood Cliffs, N. J.: Prentice Hall, 1964.

——. *Foundations of the Conciliar Theory*. Cambridge: Cambridge University Press, 1955.

——. "Some Recent Works on the Political Theories of the Medieval Canonists." *Traditio* 10(1954): 594–625.

——. " 'Tria Quippe Distinguit Iudicia . . .' A Note on Innocent III's Decretal *Per venerable*." *Speculum* 37(1962): 48–59.

Tisserant, Eugene. *Eastern Christianity in India*, trans. E. R. Hambye. Bombay: Orient Longmans, 1957.

Totoraitis, Jonas. *Die litauer unter dem könig Mindowe*. Freiburg: St. Paulus-Druckerei, 1905.

Walter Ullmann. *The Growth of Papal Government in the Middle Ages*. 3d ed. London: Methuen, 1970.

——. *A History of Political Thought: The Middle Ages*. Rev. ed. Harmondsworth: Penguin, 1970.

——. *Law and Politics in the Middle Ages: An Introduction to the Sources of Medieval Political Ideas*. The Sources of History: Studies in the Uses of Historical Evidence. Ithaca, N.Y.: Cornell University Press, 1975.

——. "The Medieval Papal Court as an International Tribunal." *Virginia Journal for International Law* 11(1971): 356–71.

——. *Medieval Papalism*. London: Methuen, 1949.

——. *The Origins of the Great Schism*. London: Burns Oates and Washbourne, 1948.

Van Cleve, Thomas Curtis. *The Emperor Frederick II of Hohenstaufen: Immutator Mundi*. Oxford: Clarendon Press, 1972.

Villey, Michel. *La Croisade: essai sur la formation d'une théorie juridique*. Paris: J. Vrin, 1942.

Walther, Helmut G. *Imperiales Königtum Konziliarismus und Volkssouveränität: Studien zu den Grenzen des Mittelalterlichen Souveränitätsgedankens*. Munich: Wilhelm Fink, 1976.

Weckmann, Luis. *Las Bulas Alejandriras de 1493 y la Teoriá Política del Papado Medieval*. Mexico City: Editorial Jus, 1949.

Weise, Erich. *Die Amtsgewalt von Papst und Kaiser und die Ostmission besonders in der 1. Hälfte des 13. Jahrhunderts*. Marburger Ostforschungen, no. 31. Marburg/Lahn: J. G. Herder-Institute, 1971.

Willis, G. *St. Augustine and the Donatist Controversy*. London: Society for the Promotion of Christian Knowledge, 1950.

Witte, Charles-Martial de. "Les bulles pontificales et l'expansion portugaise au XVe siècle," *Revue d'histoire ecclesiastique*, 48(1953): 683–718; 49(1954): 438–61; 51(1956): 413–53; 809–36; 53(1958): 5–46, 443–71.

Wölfel, D. J. "La Curia Romana y la Corona de España en la defensa de los aborigénes Canarios," *Anthropos* 25(1930): 1011–83.

Wood, Charles T. *Philip the Fair and Boniface VIII*. European Problem Studies. 2d ed. New York: Holt, Rinehart and Winston, 1971.

Ziegler, Philip. *The Black Death*. New York: John Day, 1969.

INDEX